SAMS
Teach Yourself
Today

e-Trading

SAMS
Teach Yourself
Today

e-Trading

Researching and trading stocks, bonds, and mutual funds online

Tiernan Ray

SAMS

A Division of Macmillan USA
201 West 103rd Street, Indianapolis, Indiana 46290

Sams Teach Yourself e-Trading Today

Copyright © 2000 by Sams Publishing

International Standard Book Number: 0-672-31821-0

Library of Congress Catalog Card Number: 99-067049

Printed in the United States of America

First Printing: May 2000

03   02   01   00   4   3   2   1

Trademarks

Warning and Disclaimer

Acquisitions Editor
Jeff Schultz

Development Editor
Damon Jordan

Managing Editor
Charlotte Clapp

Project Editor
Christina Smith

Copy Editor
Kim Cofer

Indexer
Sheila Schroeder

Proofreader
Matt Wynalda

Team Coordinator
Amy Patton

Interior Designer
Gary Adair

Cover Designer
Jay Corpus

Copywriter
Eric Borgert

Production
Jeannette McKay

Dedication

For my mother and father.

Table of Contents

Acknowledgments

If you think the stock market can be a wild ride, just try writing a book about it. The title you hold in your hands brings together the most important concepts anyone trading securities online should know about. Quite a few people helped me to boil down the essence of margin trading, limit orders, options, day trading, and other fiendishly complex matters into an easy-to-read and (I hope) quite helpful guide for the beginning investor. My thanks first of all to the undying efforts of the editorial staff at Macmillan, especially Christina Smith, who despite my attempts to knock things off track, kept this book rolling along in one piece. The Macmillan team handled the many complex elements of the book with aplomb while demonstrating infinite patience with the author.

Kudos to Damon Jordan, the book's development editor, who slogged undaunted through the many dense discussions in the book with a careful eye to readability and intelligibility. His efforts have truly formed one voice.

I'm very grateful to my friends and family, who saw me through the many months of writing and then rewriting with humor and love and most of all, patience. Special thanks, too, to Peter Borowsky, who was kind enough to take time from his very crowded schedule to read drafts and counsel me away from the rocks of financial misunderstanding. Finally, my deepest appreciation goes to Jeff Schultz at Macmillan, who had enough confidence to send this project my way in the first place, and who held everything together with a patient, guiding hand.

INTRODUCTION

In the time that I've been working on this book, an original investment of my own hard-earned money placed in a portfolio of stocks that I purchased entirely over the Web has appreciated more than 100%. That's a pretty good investment, these days. In fact, it beats out the 57% rise in the Nasdaq Composite Index, a measure of the performance of some of America's best fast-growing tech stocks. I've beaten the market, in other words.

But that's not the most important thing about e-trading. This is a book about how to buy and sell securities over the Web, so I want you to know that you can definitely beat the market by playing your hunches.

It's definitely true that part of the appeal of trading online is testing your own ideas and your own opinions about which companies or which stocks or which mutual funds will rise or fall. For some people, this kind of a game—for it is a game—is the whole appeal of e-trading.

But you could also enjoy a high return by not playing the market at all, and instead just putting your money in one of the various well-managed mutual funds run by professional stock and bond investors. Some of these funds have produced spectacular market-beating gains in the current bull market.

Certainly the thrill of the hunt can be a part of the online investing phenomenon for those who crave that kind of excitement. You can just imagine the rush of placing your first online trade as you watch the display on your computer tick down the changes in stock prices in real-time, like some sort of submarine warfare:

> You watch, gripped, as shares of XYZ Corp. fall below the $80 mark, first by two dollars, then five, and then all the way down to $73. But you hold out; it's not yet time to buy. Shares hang at $73, wobbling between a dollar gain and a dollar dip. You know XYZ is in for more punishment. And then it comes: another $7.50 down. It's a full-scale rout! The news from the previous evening's dismal earnings conference call has decimated those who bought the stock just a few short

days ago. Just as you'd expected. Finally the selling abates at $65.12. The volume of shares traded has rapidly dried up; the bulls, upbraided for their foolish confidence, are retreating to lick their wounds. You pile in and buy 100 shares at $65.50. By close of day, you think with glee, you and the other traders will surely be on your way to a $5 per share profit.

Yes, that kind of stuff happens, and we'll talk all about the phenomenon known as "day trading" a little later on. But the practical value of this book is not to hook you on spending your weekend afternoons glued to your computer playing stock market warfare.

No, the real reason that the phenomenon of e-investing is important is not strictly higher gains or excitement or proving you know best. The important thing is that e-trading represents the future of personal wealth, period. Without knowing about e-trading, it may be increasingly difficult for you to "get a financial life" at all.

Why? Consider that investing in securities has become the mainstream of most Americans' financial future. According to one well-respected investment research group, nearly half of all U.S. households own some equities, meaning mostly common stock in public companies, a jump of 71% since the beginning of the 1990s. And more than three-quarters of households' liquid assets are in securities of one form or another versus plain old savings accounts, CDs, and other traditional bank accounts. As recently as the late 1970s, the overwhelming majority of Americans had their assets mostly in bank accounts. Whether we're a more spendthrift society, or simply because we've redefined the basics of a decent lifestyle, Americans need to get a better return on their hard-earned income than ever before.

But investing in a diversity of financial instruments is tricky, and in the case of equities, which are arguably the riskiest of the various securities, failing to carefully manage how you invest can be disastrous. Of course, you could have a professional money manager handle those decisions regarding which securities you should buy and sell. Professional brokers can counsel you on what to do with your money, and they can take care of all the messy details of placing your orders for securities.

You could argue that the sole value of e-trading is to provide a cheap alternative for those of us who can't afford all the fees and commissions that a broker charges. That's the primary reason most people open an e-trading account with an online broker, and you'll hear more about that fact later on.

The more important reason for e-trading is that merely having professional financial advice is not enough for planning the ways you'll spend and the ways you'll save. For that, you need tools that help you see how much money you have, how much you're saving, and where you're putting your money. The Web gives you those tools. Placing an order with your broker is just the beginning. e-Trading opens up a world of software and services for tracking your financial portfolio, for thinking about how you want to allocate the money that you've saved, and for setting financial goals for yourself and your family. With the shift to securities, you can't just park your money in a bank anymore. You've got to be smart about how you manage your money, and the Web and e-trading will help you to do that.

Increasingly, this kind of aggressive individual money management will be tied deeper and deeper to how we use money. e-Trading brokers are starting to roll out new kinds of bank services, such as credit card accounts and online bill payment. Margin loans, which allow you to borrow against your stock gains, are an increasingly popular form of low-cost borrowing for large lifestyle purchases such as cars, houses, and so on. In this way, your online investments will be tied into every other use you have for money, until eventually what we think of as e-trading will simply be the way all finances work.

It's heady stuff, and it's beyond the scope of this book. What follows will give you the basic tools to understand the state-of-the-art in buying and selling securities online. After reading this book you'll be better prepared to understand that brave new frontier of electronic finance.

The book is organized into six parts. Part I includes a brief discussion of why buying and selling securities online can be useful and will help you decide if it's right for you. Although I've just told you e-trading will play an increasingly important role in everyone's personal financial planning, it's important to understand what you're getting into!

Part II explains a bit about stock brokers, how markets work, and how to place your first trade. Here you'll also find instructions for completing an online account form.

Part III contains two important chapters that you should read before you make your first trade, even though the material on placing trades is presented first in the book. Chapter 10, "Understanding Your Taxes," deals with tax implications and certain tax tips to consider while you are making your trades. Chapter 11, "Troubleshooting and Ending Your Online Trading Relationship," deals with issues that can arise when you are trading online, including problems you may encounter with an e-broker's Web site and scams and fraud perpetrated by the shadier characters in the investment world. It would behoove you to read both of these chapters before making any purchases or sales of securities on the Web. In fact, it's not a bad idea to read them before you open your new brokerage account. Doing so could save you some heartache later.

Part IV gets into some more advanced topics that you might want to explore after you've had some experience buying and selling stocks online. Bonds and mutual funds are an important component of a balanced portfolio, which, just like a balanced diet, is important to nurture! They're covered in detail in this section. So are margin borrowing and options.

Part V deals with some of the cutting-edge elements of investing, such as the movement to after-hours trading and the nascent field of electronic communications networks. These are brand-new securities markets that exist outside of the traditional stock and bond exchanges, and that give investors a kind of expanded sandbox, if you will, in which to play.

Finally, Part VI lists a number of useful Web sites you can visit.

Enjoy what follows, and good luck with those e-investments!

PART I

Before You Make That First Trade

CHAPTER 1

The Pros and Cons of Online Trading

Why do we have online stock trading systems? If the flood of news about day traders and rich Internet stocks that soar in a day has left you bereft of any clear sense as to why people even trade stocks online, you've come to the right place. If you already have a broker, you're probably starting to figure out for yourself some of the many benefits of online trading versus going to a full-service brokerage, the traditional solution for trading stocks. If you're new to investing and you currently keep all of your money under your mattress, the whole phenomenon of Web-based trading probably seems very obscure. This chapter explains a bit of how we've gotten where we are and why people want to trade stocks online.

What you'll find, on the whole, is that online trading is partly a technology story and partly a story about the sweeping changes that have transformed American society in the past two decades. One driving force, certainly, is the wealth effect. As the U.S. domestic economy at the end of the Cold War has soared, and as consumers spend on credit like never before, the latest generation is flush with cash and looking for a better return than in traditional IRAs. An aging, do-it-yourself Boomer population and a smart young workforce of Gen-X'ers, mesmerized by the enormous success of technology stocks, have been lured by retail brokerages such as Charles Schwab to go out and make their own financial futures. The World Wide Web has arrived at the eleventh hour, as it were, as the final piece necessary to decentralize the old practice of placing trades. In so doing, it has helped to create a society of self-motivated investors shopping the aisles of a new kind of virtual stock supermarket.

What You'll Learn in This Chapter:

- How we got here.
- The virtues of the independent trade.
- What it means to have your own online stock account.

How We Got Here

Before you can understand online trading, you must realize how
modern stock trading with a traditional full-service brokerage has
evolved in this century. Much of what you'll find in Web stock
trading reflects legal reforms and technological changes that have
taken place in the last 70 years.

A Century of Reform

We're a long way from the so-called "bucket shops" described in
Edwin Lefevre's famous stock trading novel, *Reminiscences of a
Stock Operator*. In that book, Lefevre's hero, Larry Livingstone,
plays the market at the turn of the century by going to seedy gambling halls across the country where a bookie would take orders
for shares of stock just like a racetrack bet. As a clerk read the
change in price of stocks off of a ticker-tape machine, Livingstone would slap down a few dollars "on margin," a way to gamble on the next move in the price up or down without buying
stock. It was a popular form of stock speculation in the day, and it
regularly lured suckers by the dozens who were fleeced by the
market-rigging schemes of the bucket shop owners.

Lefevre's novel is a great reminder of how far the securities busi-
ness, and the modern brokerage industry, has come in 60 years.
The bucket shops, along with many other unsavory practices of
the securities business, were swept away in the aftermath of the
Great Depression by the New Deal administration of Franklin
Roosevelt.

Among the abuses addressed was the power stockbrokers com-
manded to charge their clients virtually any amount they wanted
in fees to buy or sell stocks on their behalf. The New Deal put in
place many of the modern features of the traditional brokerage,
which include the following:

- **Published fees and commissions**   The modern broker is
  supposed to make clear to his clients what fees the brokerage
  house charges to process an order to buy or sell stocks, bonds,
  options contracts, and so on. There should be no hidden fees
  assigned by the broker on an arbitrary basis, and the total
  amount of commission charged must be disclosed following
  each trade.

- **Responsibility to advise on suitability of investments** The modern brokerage is in business to serve the customer. That means the broker's chief role is to help the client evaluate his or her investment goals, and to make sure that each order to buy and sell securities fits with the financial goals the client has. A brokerage shouldn't be spending clients' money arbitrarily on securities that don't reflect those goals or buying and selling stocks without the clients' consent.

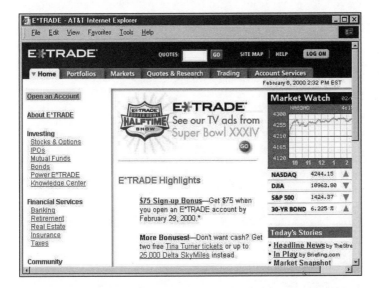

*Modern broker-ages such as E*Trade are more customer focused than the brokers of yesteryear.*

- **Responsibility of brokers to process trades for their customers before processing their own orders** The essence of a modern brokerage house is to get the best deal for its clients in the market. A broker must not try to outbid or outsell his clients, scooping up the best stock deals to enrich the brokerage house itself.

- **The broker must confirm each transaction** Another service the broker performs is to give his customer confirmation by phone or in writing that the requested order to buy or sell has or hasn't been processed and at what prices, commission, and so on.

- **Regular reporting**   A customer shouldn't have to keep his accounts in his head, like Lefevre's protagonist. A modern brokerage house sends out statements much like savings account statements, which keep the client informed of the ongoing state of his brokerage account.

A Police Force for Brokers

The Nasdaq stock market is itself the product of modern regulation. Before the Maloney Act of 1938, there was little regulation of what's known as the "over the counter" or OTC market. The OTC market is where brokers trade securities not listed on an exchange. The Maloney Act established the National Association of Securities Dealers, or NASD, as a self-regulating industry body where member firms adopt certain rules of conduct in trading OTC stocks. The NASD is composed of over 5,500 securities firms. The most profound accomplishment of the NASD may be the formulation of the NASD Automated Quotation system, or Nasdaq, the first electronic marketplace for securities trading. The Nasdaq gave a level of organization, disclosure, and discipline to the obscure world of OTC stocks comparable to the respected exchanges such as the NYSE and the AMEX. Although the NASD polices the Nasdaq market and the rest of the OTC universe, the SEC will from time to time step into disputes or issues of fraud to directly discipline member firms.

The NASD, a regulatory body, is a product of 70 years of securities reform.

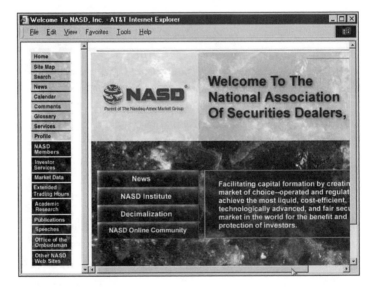

The Market Goes Digital

The transition from the traditional stockbroker to the world of online trading is all about how technology has overtaken the securities business. You're reading this book, presumably, because you want to trade stocks and bonds with nothing more than a PC and a modem. But before the e-trading craze (prior to the Internet explosion, even), the brokerage world was dramatically transformed by the evolution of electronic trading systems. At the turn of the century, orders to buy or sell stock on the New York Stock Exchange would be communicated from a broker to a "floor broker" by passing slips of paper or entering orders into ledgers. The American Stock Exchange started with traders shouting and employing hand gestures literally on the curb of the streets of New York.

Over time, that primitive system was replaced with trading terminals—basically computer displays—installed on the floor of the New York Stock Exchange and other exchanges that flash the price of new securities to brokers on the floor. Brokers carrying wireless terminals that flash prices and orders have replaced hand gestures.

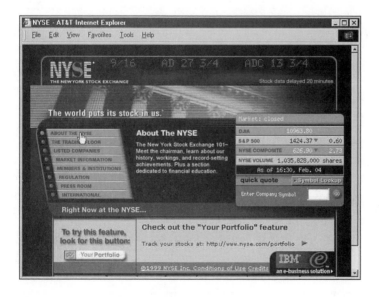

The New York Stock Exchange has come a long way from the curbsides of downtown New York.

The Nasdaq National Market, seat of most trading in dynamic high-tech stocks, originated in this century as a loose association of brokers who communicated buy and sell orders by phone.

That system was replaced in 1971 by the introduction of an actual electronic network of trading computers that communicate offers for stock instantaneously between brokerages across the country. In many cases, transactions of stock will take place solely as a negotiation of computer programs on the network, sometimes beating the human traders at their own game.

The Nasdaq National Market, the model of a modern electronic exchange.

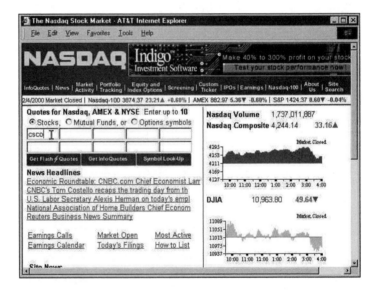

The rise of such electronic networks increased the rate of stock trading by enabling so-called "after-hours" trading, which takes place when the Nasdaq, the New York Stock Exchange, and other markets are closed. (Although the Nasdaq and the NYSE and other exchanges have started to roll out after-hours trading as well.)

The Nasdaq's electronic market also did away with much of the regionalism of stock trading. With a nationwide "virtual" network of computers, stocks traded on local exchanges such as the Cincinnati exchange or the Chicago exchange can be traded in New York and Hong Kong. At the same time, smaller, regional stock exchanges can establish competing trades for the same stocks that were once traded only at the physical headquarters of the New York Stock Exchange in New York City.

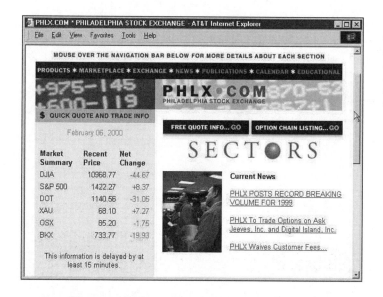

Regional exchanges like the Philadelphia Stock Exchange are both threatened and enhanced by electronic trading.

The World of Exchanges

New exchanges continue to pop up all over the world. The International Finance Corporation (IFC), a branch of the World Bank in Washington, D.C., says that at last count, there were approximately 155 securities exchanges worldwide. The actual number of securities exchanges is larger, though, because that number may represent multiple exchanges in some countries, as for example, in the U.S., where there are numerous exchanges. The IFC's emerging markets database contains listings of many new securities exchanges that have popped up in recent years. For example, in the past 10 years new exchanges have been formed in the 15 states of the former Soviet Russia.

At the cutting edge are the new Electronic Communications Networks, or ECNs, systems of incredibly sophisticated computer networks that submit bids to all the old markets simultaneously to get even more competitive prices for investors. The venerable Instinet, which has been around for decades, is an early precursor to ECNs. More modern examples with lots of financial backing and fancy computer software, such as Island ECN, are popping up all the time.

*Island ECN is
among the new
breed of Elec-
tronic Communi-
cations Networks.*

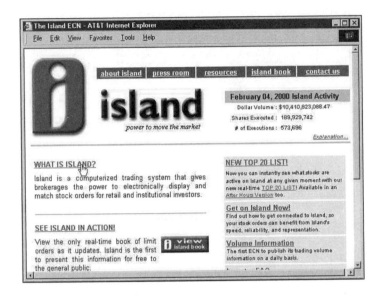

With electronic networks behind the scenes, the stage was set in
the 1990s for the arrival of the World Wide Web, which really just
puts a computer interface on top of these electronic transactions.
At the same time that trading was being moved onto electronic
networks, discount brokerages such as Schwab arose to supply a
cheaper form of stock trading. The discount brokers provided little if any advice on securities, allowing them to do away with the
expensive commissions on trades. The Web is the final piece in
cutting those costs. By filling out forms in a Web browser over
the Internet, orders can go directly into a brokerage house's order
computer, thereby obviating the need for a broker to fill out
paperwork in order to place a customer's buy or sell order.

Taking It to the Web

Trading on the Web, despite all the fanfare in the papers and on TV
news, is still in its infancy. Studies conducted by the Securities Industry
Association (SIA), a trade group, show that of all purchases of stock in
1998, only 11% were made over the Internet. The data also shows, however, that the average Internet investor makes more trades, on average,
than non-Web-based investors, by a ratio of 10 to 1. The most immediate reason is likely the reduced fees for transacting over the Web.
What's more, online accounts doubled in 1999 and are projected to
quadruple by 2003, according to the SIA.

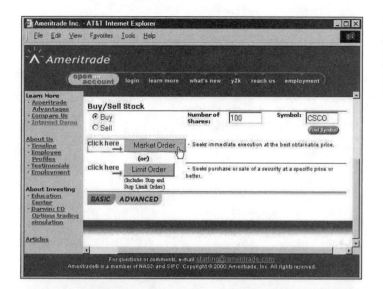

The Web puts a pleasing front end on top of the securities process, for placing trades...

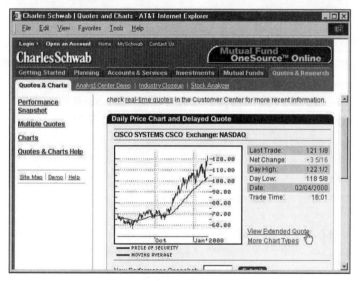

...or getting information about securities.

*SIA research
shows continued
growth for online,
e-trading accounts.*

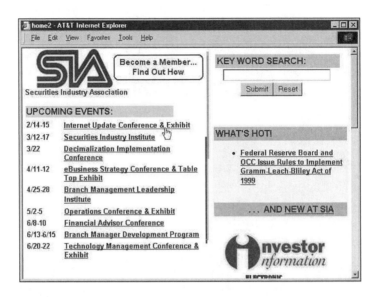

Benefits and Drawbacks of the Independent Trade

With the combination of increasingly diverse electronic markets and an easy-to-learn Web interface, the retail brokerage business has become a powerful tool for individuals to make their own decisions about securities and to manage the day-to-day—or even hour-by-hour—details of their personal finances. There are both benefits and drawbacks of this development that you should consider before jumping into e-trading.

Benefits

Two primary factors account for the appeal of online trading. The information revolution is what the Web is all about, and so of course access to information is important. Trading online means you'll have more information at the click of a mouse about the status of your stock or bond or mutual fund holdings. However, the primary reason for trading online is without a doubt reduced fees.

- **Lower fees overall**   Brokers make the bulk of their money as a percentage of the commission revenue they bring to their firm. For that reason, there is a perception, not entirely inaccurate, that most established brokerage houses don't care about the small investor who generates meager commission revenues. Discount brokerages can cut the cost of commissions for the customer by more than 50% compared to traditional brokerages by not providing the advice and handholding that's customary.

The Web is the next step. By letting Web users fill out all the paperwork for trades online and replacing the bulk of the brokers with computers processing those online orders, trading houses eliminate commissions entirely. There are still fees for inputting the transaction, but they are a fraction of the total cost charged by a full-service brokerage.

- **Ability to know precisely the fees charged for any transaction**   Even though securities regulations specify fixed transaction fees and commissions for full-service brokers, in many cases investors don't really know what they're paying in fees for each stock trade. Commissions vary by the total amount of a transaction, and that means investors have to do a lot of mental arithmetic to keep track of what they're paying. With online trading, a broker's Web site will have clearly published fee structures that vary by the amount of shares traded. Investors can refer to this information each time they make a trade to know what they'll be paying in total.

- **Ability to see the current price at any moment in time** When buying or selling stocks with a full-service broker, many customers probably have a relatively good idea of what a stock's been trading at. They may, however, leave it to the discretion of their broker to bid for them in that price range. With the Web, investors can see prices displayed for securities in real-time, giving them a sharper sense of what they are about to spend on stocks. This is not important for the large investor with wads of cash, perhaps, but for a small investor even a few percentage points can be important.

The Web gives the average investor tons of information, such as real-time quotes.

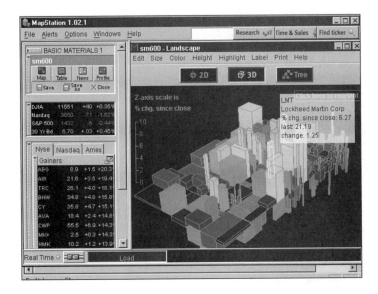

- **Ability to know the duration of an outstanding buy or sell order**   Certain types of buy or sell orders that can be requested have a limited lifespan; after a certain amount of time—hours, days, weeks—they will be cancelled if not successfully executed. Although a full-service broker can inform his clients of the lifespan of a trade, the chances clients will still remember a day later whether their limit order is still in effect are probably slim. A broker can remind them, but with the Web it becomes simpler for an individual to bring up the status of outstanding orders in his or her Web browser.

The Web gives you greater ability to monitor trades of long duration, such as limit orders.

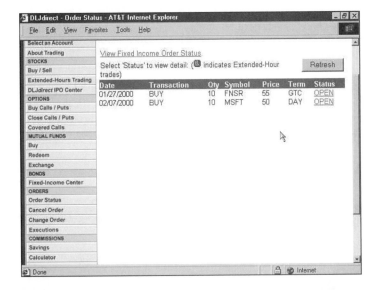

- **Ability to trade odd lots economically**   Many customers of
  traditional brokerages don't trade odd lots, meaning the buying and selling of stock in amounts less than 100 shares. That's
  because the fees and commissions make it uneconomical to
  place orders for such small amounts of stock. However, for
  investors who are cautiously trying out new stocks, or who
  want to start investing slowly, the ability to buy just one, two,
  or ten shares of stock is important. With the low fees of most
  online brokers, buying small amounts of stock is feasible.

- **Instantaneous confirmation of stock trades**   Brokerages
  are required to confirm that trades have been processed, but
  they may wait to do this until the next morning. For investors
  who want to know right away that their trades have or haven't
  gone through, the Web browser is a boon. You can surf to
  your broker's site and see a detailed update onscreen confirming your trade. (Note, you should still receive written
  notification by mail subsequently.)

- **Instantaneous access to information at any time of the
  day or night**   Not only do you want to know about whether
  or not your trade has gone through, but you may want to
  return to that information frequently during the week, when
  you're planning new investments or taking stock of your
  assets. With the Web, information about your stock holdings
  is always right there in your Web browser. That's a lot easier
  than sorting through paper receipts from your broker or having to call your broker to check up on the status of your
  account.

- **Greater control over how cash balances are reinvested**
  Typically when you buy and sell stocks, there's money left in
  your cash account that's unspent from your initial deposit.
  Brokerages will customarily reinvest this money in a money
  market fund while you're not using it. However, the Web
  allows you more freedom to research multiple financial products offered by brokers and to make choices about where you
  would like your cash balance invested.

- **Ability to integrate portfolio information with other personal financial data**   Programs such as Quicken and Microsoft Money have become important ways for individuals to track their household financial situation. These programs allow you to download data from the Web concerning your portfolio and to integrate this with the rest of your financial information. You could use the Web to do this even as a full-service customer, of course, but investing online means you're probably more likely to be vigilant about tracking your accounts with such snazzy software.

The Web lets individuals manage not just investments, but all personal finances.

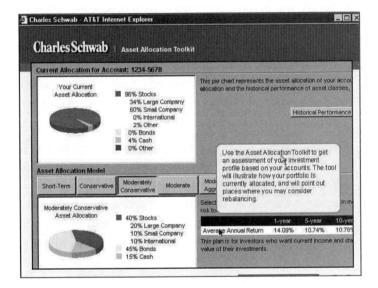

Drawbacks

The main problem with trading on the Internet is that you are giving up the professional advice that comes with a full-service brokerage. You may also be giving up some benefits that come with a discount broker.

- **No advice on financial goals or investment strategy**   If investing is about preparing for your financial future, it's especially important to define your investment profile, meaning how much risk you can afford and what your financial goals are. This is the primary goal of a traditional broker, and it is the most important thing you give up by using either a discount broker or by going on the Web.

- **No advice on the advisability of particular trades**   There are all sorts of things that can happen when you start plugging trades into a Web browser. One of the worst things that can happen is if you place an order at an inopportune time that a broker would normally warn you against. For example, if you place an order to buy stock in the evening, after the stock market is closed, you run the risk that the stock will open at a price far above where it closed. If the stock does jump in price this way, you could lose a bundle. A full-service broker will advise you against such moves.

- **You need to track individual companies on your own**   The biggest drawback about trading stocks on the Web is that, as with a discount broker, you're basically on your own as far as picking the right stocks to reach your financial goals. You have no professional advice about the suitability of stocks, and, perhaps more important, you've no one but yourself to blame if you end up speculating on highly risky stocks when your initial intention was to maintain a portfolio of conservative investments.

- **You need to gauge the shape of your portfolio on your own**   In addition to helping you decide financial goals at the outset, a good full-service broker will keep an eye on your basket of investments and alert you when it may be time to move some money into different types of securities to make sure you meet your objectives. As an online trader, it's your responsibility to monitor your portfolio and to decide if you're working toward your goals or if you need to change your investment strategy.

- **Risk of trading in an immature medium**   Everyone's heard stories: The Web doesn't always work. It's a computer network that has more people on it than it can presently support. As such, the World Wide Web is in a permanent state of "under construction." Sometimes, the Internet doesn't work as expected and, unfortunately, it can be right in the middle of when you're trading stocks. Over time, the response of the Web will improve, but there is the distinct possibility that while entering trades, the network will go down or simply have a hiccup. If that happens, your trade may be processed late or not at all, which may result in your paying too much or missing an important trade. Brokers may in some cases make good on such snafus, but it's still a risk that you run by taking your finances online.

Finally, it may sound silly, but there's always the addiction factor. Like all things on the World Wide Web, placing buy and sell orders for stocks and bonds can be addictive. Once you get the hang of it, it's just as easy to trade securities as it is to shop at your favorite online mall. The problem is, it's your financial well-being that you're playing with. Without the restraint of a broker talking your trades through with you, you may start to buy and sell quite frequently and with little restraint. If you're making good bets, great. If you're a so-so stock trader and you become addicted to plugging in orders, you could be on the fast path to blowing your savings.

What You've Learned

The online trading craze is more than investing. To some it's a status symbol or a fashion statement. To some, a hobby. Hopefully, though, you have some sense at this point that online trading is a complex development in the long history of buying and selling securities. Used well, it can help you to take control of your financial future. But you must be ready for the extra responsibility that comes with the control Web trading brings.

By now, hopefully you understand

- How Web trading has emerged as an evolution of traditional stock trading.

- The various benefits of taking control of your investment portfolio through online trading.

- The consequences of giving up the advice and counsel that come with traditional full-service brokerage operations.

CHAPTER 2

Is Online Trading Right for You?

If the information about online trading in the last chapter has left your head spinning, you've come to the right place to straighten things out. Deciding whether or not to trade stocks online is all about getting in touch with your personal investment profile. This chapter helps you to decide what your goals are and whether you're ready to use the Web to invest.

What you'll find is that investing online is for most people simply a good way to organize personal finances and to take charge of the direction of personal savings. e-Trading doesn't have to be a gambling hall indulgence or an absorbing passion. Don't be surprised, though, if the adrenaline rush of seeing your investments rise and fall on a daily basis makes you a more passionate devotee of the market!

Myths of Online Trading

If the idea of taking your financial future into your own hands fills you with dread, you've probably been watching too many television news programs about day traders. Indeed, there are many misconceptions about the type of person who uses Web-based trading. The common conception is that if you trade online you are

- A retired computer engineer who loves to spend all day long playing the market

- A college student who buys and sells stocks between classes

- Someone with tons of disposable income to waste on risky propositions

- A stock geek who loves to spend hours surfing the World Wide Web for obscure information and tips about hot companies

What You'll Learn in This Chapter:

- ▶ The myths about online trading.

- ▶ How to figure out your investment goals.

- ▶ How to discover what's waiting for you on the Web.

- ▶ How to find yourself: getting in touch with your personal investing style.

The fact is, investing online is for normal people who want a quick and easy way to start getting organized about personal finances. As explained in the previous chapter, online trading offers lower fees for trades and the ability to assert some control over how your assets are allocated. None of this has to do with being a zealot or a computer geek or a day trader running on pure adrenaline. Nor does it mean that you must invest frequently or haphazardly. With online trading you can invest as little or as much as you like. It's an arrangement that works as well for the conservative, infrequent investor as for the stock market enthusiast.

Incidentally, a nonprofit group, the Investing Online Resource Center, organized by the Washington State Department of Financial Institutions, points out some additional misconceptions about online investing. You can check out the discussion at the Center's Web site, *http://www.investingonline.org/lvl2_blue.html.*

The Investing Online Resource Center gives straight talk about the myths of e-trading.

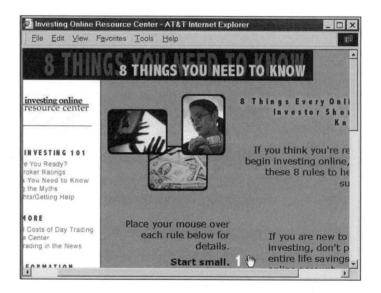

Myths of online investing are

- Thinking online investing will lead to quick, above-average returns. In fact, your returns in the stock market can be just as good or just as bad as with a normal broker when you trade online.

- Thinking that you can get into initial public offerings and make a mint. In recent years, stock of newly public companies, dubbed IPOs, have become wildly popular. We'll talk a bit about the IPO in Chapter 12, "Getting Into IPOs Online." In truth, though, you are no more likely to catch the IPO wave online than offline.

- Thinking investing online means your trades get processed faster. In fact, as we'll discuss in Chapter 11, "Troubleshooting and Ending Your Online Trading Relationship," there are serious delays and questions of performance that can impede your investing experience when you go onto the World Wide Web.

- And finally, thinking you can trade all day and all night. In fact, there are real limits to what hours of the day you can trade. They're set by the securities exchanges on which shares of stock and other securities are listed, and by your individual e-broker. We'll talk more about this in Hour 17, "After-Hours Trading and Electronic Communications Networks."

No, e-trading has little to do with either the stereotypes about investors or the get-rich-quick myths. The appeal of e-trading for most people is much simpler.

Some of the real qualities of an online investor are

- Taking seriously the need to provide a better cushion for yourself than a typical savings account.

- The willingness to do a little extra work researching stocks and bonds if it will save you substantial amounts of money on trades.

- Trusting your own instincts, both to learn how to improve at stock trading and to avoid colossal blunders like putting all your money into risky securities.

- Testing your hunches and getting to know more about how companies work and how the market functions.

- Needing a better way than calling a broker to keep on top of how your assets are performing.

- Last, but not least, you're either new to investing in general and want to ease into the process before committing large sums of capital, or else you've already tried a full-service brokerage and found the experience to be less than rewarding.

These simple truths about e-trading may not be incendiary, but they are the real reasons why most investors may be ready to try investing online.

Getting Out of the Savings Rut

The main factor driving investors to e-trading may be the same thing that's been driving them to retail and traditional full-service brokerages in past years, namely a higher rate of return. A massive shift has been going on among consumers, away from traditional savings accounts and toward investments of other kinds. The Securities Industry Association (SIA), a trade group, says that three quarters of individual investors maintain their liquid assets in equities, as opposed to savings accounts, IRAs, and other non-securities holdings. That's an amazing amount of securities investment on the part of the average investor, and a definite sign that standard interest-bearing accounts offering 2% or more a year no longer cut the mustard.

Figuring Out Your Personal Investing Style

Let's go a little further than the preceding points. One of the things a full-service broker will help you to understand is what type of investor you are. If you're thinking of going the Web-trading way, you'll have to learn to figure this out on your own. There are some formal principles to observe when evaluating your investment profile.

The Distinctions

For years, experts have recognized that there are at least two major kinds of investors: the wealth preservers and the wealth builders.

Wealth preservers are people who've already built a substantial pile of savings and assets and are focused on making sure they can protect those assets. The term tends to be applied to people in their later years, although it can also apply to young people who may have amassed a substantial savings or who may have inherited money. The point is, wealth preservers are focused not on making money but on not losing any of the money they already have.

The other class of investor, the wealth builder, is someone saving for retirement, or perhaps for the expenses of starting a family. The wealth builder has fewer savings than the wealth preserver and so is more concerned with finding an investment that will help him or her do better than a standard IRA or savings account. The wealth builder is working on the nest egg or maybe even the personal fortune. As such, he or she is less conservative than the wealth preserver, more ready to try new types of investing if it may help him or her to get an edge in setting aside funds.

Obviously, the latter category is more the type to go for online investing. A wealth preserver can sock his or her money away in some municipal bonds and probably not have to worry about inflation eating away at his or her savings. The wealth builder sees the opportunity in online trading to make above-average returns.

Even the Wealthy Must Appreciate

Though aggressive investing may seem more the province of wealth builders, there can be equal or greater pressure on wealth preservers to seek out a better-than-average investment. The more money that lies around in savings accounts earning no more than two-and-a-quarter percent is considered by investment advisers as "money left on the table." Those funds could instead be rolled into high-yield bonds, at least, or something even more promising.

The wealthy, unlike the typical online investor, already have means to grow even wealthier. Take Bill Gates, whose personal fortune at last count was north of $100 billion. Gates has his own team of investment advisors who find places to put the multibillionaire's personal stash. As detailed in a *Fortune* Magazine article in 1999, the team, known as Bill Gates Investments, is responsible for investing the cash portion of Gates's wealth, which amounts to more than $11 billion—as much as some large mutual funds.

The Bill Gates Personal Wealth Clock is an unofficial sketch of the investment problems faced by the world's richest man: where to invest it all!?!

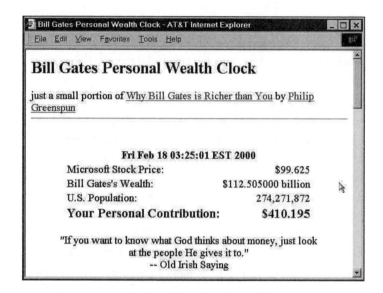

It doesn't end there. Within the wealth builder category there are usually some other shades of gray. They include

- **Speculative investor versus risk-averse investor**   Investors are defined by how much risk they are willing to take on when deciding whether or not to invest in unproven companies or bonds for debt-riddled operations—so-called high-yield "junk" grade bonds.

- **Aggressive versus conservative investor**   This point pertains more to what you hope to get out of an investment. An aggressive investor is one who pursues a return on investment above what most of the market affords, whereas a conservative investor is happy simply to make more than might be obtained from a savings account. The typical aggressive investor might invest in so-called "high-growth" stocks, those representing young companies whose earnings growth is on a tear. Conservative investors would be more inclined to look for stable, reliable companies that can be expected to provide a consistently high return over several years even if the stocks of these companies will underperform other high-flyers in the market.

- **Active investor versus casual investor**   Whether you're
  looking to improve on your return on IRAs or you're into
  finding individual stocks that can beat the market, the fact is
  you may have more or less time than the next investor to
  spend looking at public data about companies and thinking
  about the composition of your portfolio. An important differ-
  entiating factor for investors is simply how much time and
  effort they are willing to put into the task of picking and
  choosing investments.

How Aggressive Is Aggressive?

It's important to note that the meanings of many terms for different
types of investing have changed quite a bit in the last century. For most
of the last 100 years, debt securities—meaning, essentially, bonds—have
dominated. In the early decades of the twentieth century, just choosing
to invest in stocks was considered an aggressive, perhaps even speculative move. As recently as 1983, 81% of all U.S. households owned no
equity securities at all, according to the Securities Industry Association, a
trade group. As of 1999, the number of U.S. households owning some
equities had risen to almost 50%, signaling a strong general shift toward
equities. Nowadays, even a conservative investment strategy usually
includes some mix of both stocks and bonds because relying simply on
one or the other is considered poor investment strategy.

As more and more investors move into stock investing, the terms *speculative* and *aggressive* have shifted in meaning to the point where they
now refer more to the quality of stocks invested in. Investors who go for
young, hot technology companies with little earnings are speculative,
whereas those who look for a high level of revenue or profit growth may
be merely aggressive. Investors who simply want to do better than the
average of a representative sampling of stocks are deemed conservative.

Figuring Out Your Investment Goals

The terms discussed in the preceding section should give you some
sense of the various approaches you can take toward the market.
But labels are less meaningful than thinking about why you want
to get into investing in the first place. This is where the goals are
defined.

Let's try working through a few short questionnaires. There are no
right answers to these questions because there is no single profile
for an online investor. But if you are able to answer yes to a majority of these questions, you are probably in the market for being an
online trader.

Try It Yourself ▼
First, assess your present financial needs and objectives:

1. Are you looking to make money in the near term—say, the next year to two years—in order to make major purchases, such as a down payment on a new home, or purchase a new car?

2. Are you concerned about money for a longer-term goal, say for retirement?

3. Are you setting aside money for dependents?

▲ 4. Do you need extra annual income to augment salary?

The NASD Web site can help you start to think about financial goals.

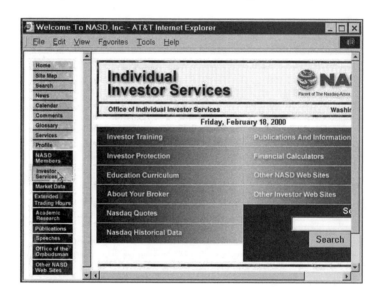

Try It Yourself ▼
Next, assess your current financial situation:

1. Do you have large sums of money in traditional interest-bearing accounts—savings, CDs—that perhaps should be invested at a higher rate elsewhere?

2. Is the level of your pension plan insufficient to meet the needs you expect to have in retirement?

3. Do you have any existing investments with mutual funds or a bond portfolio that you would like to diversify in order to limit your risk—say through adding shares of stock?

▲ 4. Do you have a certain portion of your after-tax income that you can afford to place in riskier investments?

Again, you can go to some of the popular Web sites to start thinking about the current state of your investments. For example, *Individual Investor* magazine features a discussion of "asset allocation" on its Web site, meaning the way in which your money is divided up among different classes of investments. You can check it out at *www.individualinvestor.com/investor_university/article. asp?ff_id=1404*.

You can even find tools on the Web that will help you visualize your goals. One good example is SmartMoney's asset allocation tools, which you can see at *www.smartmoney.com/si/tools/oneasset/*.

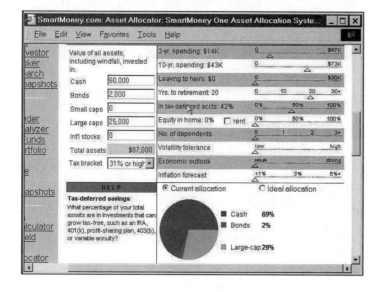

SmartMoney's allocation tools can help you evaluate your portfolio holdings.

Ask yourself a few questions about your own investment personality:

▼ **Try It Yourself**

1. Do you have time to spend reviewing and revising your financial goals?

2. Do you have time to spend thinking about the state of the stock market or bond market?

3. Do you have time to spend researching individual stocks or bonds?

4. Do you have time to spend reviewing the state of your portfolio and, possibly, revising your financial goals?

5. Do you like to make financial decisions based on your own instincts or to be in control of financial choices?

▲

Finally, you should strongly consider sitting down with a professional investment advisor and discussing all of the above questions with him. Certified financial planners (CFPs) are full-time
advisors who have passed a series of rigorous exams. The CFP
can help you decide on proper asset allocation and provide
detailed advice on what securities to hold over time. The Web site
for the North American Securities Administrators Association
describes the various types of financial advisors at *www.nasaa.org/
investoredu/informedinvestor/ii3.html*. The Web site of the CFP
Standards Board, an industry group, provides advice on how to
pick a CFP at *natasha.cfp-board.org/internet/consumer/
nd_cons_main.asp*.

*The NASAA pro-
vides guidelines as
to the different
types of financial
planners.*

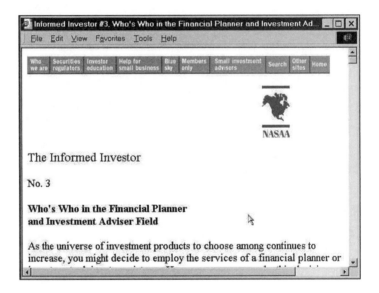

Again, it's important to remember that *this is not a test*. If you
answered no to the fourth question in the second set of questions,
"Do you have a certain portion of your after-tax income that you
can afford to place in riskier investments," this does not mean that
you can't handle trading online. Web trading doesn't have to be
high-stakes gambling. If you answered yes to a significant number
of the other questions, you are probably someone who would benefit from using the Web, albeit with a more cautious, conservative
investment strategy.

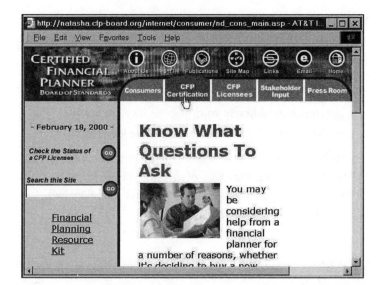

The CFP Standards Board gives you the specifics on how to pick a financial advisor.

Just for the Fun of It

Not everyone has a really good reason to be his own stockbroker. Remember the Beardstown Ladies? In 1994 they became poster girls for the do-it-yourself stock investing phenomenon when they came out with their own book describing how their investment club had netted a gain of 24.3%, far above the return of the Standard & Poor's 500 Index of leading stocks. Shortly thereafter it was revealed, much to their chagrin, that the Ladies had figured their math wrong. In fact, the investment portion of their wealth, aside from mundane instruments such as savings accounts, had grown by only 9%, far below the S&P's 14.3% average return. However, a recent article in *SmartMoney Magazine* says that the Beardstown Ladies are still investing with fervor in their investment club, and apparently having just as much fun as ever. The moral: If you enjoy picking and choosing stocks, you may have a grand old time investing online even if you're not beating the market.

What You've Learned

The overriding theme of this chapter is that there are many different kinds of investors in the market, with different goals. Fashion has changed for those seeking aggressive investments and those playing it safe, just as it will continue to change in the future. However, the benefits of online trading apply to a much more diverse set of investors than might seem apparent at first blush.

Hopefully by now you realize

- That the myths about the kinds of people who use online trading accounts are nothing more than myths.

- That on the Web or in a traditional brokerage situation, investors have different sorts of goals they are pursuing, including wealth preservation and wealth building.

- And finally, that you should only jump into Web trading after considering what kind of investor you are based on your financial goals, your current financial situation, and your personal tendencies.

CHAPTER 3

Selecting the Right Online Broker for Your Needs

By now you realize the context of traditional brokerages in which the online trading world has taken shape. Hopefully, you have also started to think about what goals you have and what strengths you may bring to online trading. You might be tempted to just go to the first Web site you hear about on TV and sign up for an account, and that's fine; after all, on a certain level, buying stocks is the same set of paperwork wherever you go. However, there are 200 online brokerage services at last count, and climbing, according to the Securities Industry Association. The competition has driven a raft of competing features. You owe it to yourself, therefore, to consider your options carefully.

Brokers' claims are flying fast and furious, of course, with major retail brokers such as Schwab and Web-only ventures such as E*Trade pouring millions of dollars into advertising campaigns to woo you. The trickiest part of all of this for you as an investor is that much of the discussion will be arcane, with obscure comparisons of prices on trades, claims about the speed with which your transactions will be processed, and boasts about the kinds of information you will enjoy as a client.

This chapter helps you understand how the services differ and what to pay attention to. In general, though, your big advantage is the fact that with online information plentiful, you can scrutinize the offerings, make notes, and see how the competition stacks up.

What You'll Learn in This Chapter:

▶ Differences between brokers.

▶ How to relate criteria to your personal investment profile.

▶ How to evaluate the offerings.

Differences Between Brokers

As you set about choosing a broker, you may find that the land-scape is utterly daunting. Among the 200 or so online operations, the kinds of offerings are all over the map. There are traditional retail brokers, such as Schwab, that have thriving online offerings. There are brand new Web-based services, such as E*Trade. Then there are the cut-rate brokerages such as Brown & Company and the boutique trading houses such as Siebert. All of these broker-ages bring something unique to the party. The task is to figure out which one is right for you.

Before we get into any concrete comparisons, it might not hurt to gather some general intelligence about how to review different brokers. There are literally dozens of sites that can help you to start thinking about the problem. They include consumer-oriented financial sites such as SmartMoney.com, which has broker ratings at *www.smartmoney.com/si/brokers/*.

SmartMoney.com's broker ratings are one way to get started choosing an e-broker.

Another source is the Securities and Exchange Commission's Web site. The SEC provides no recommendations of individual broker-ages, but rather suggestions as to what to look for in an individual broker. You'll find them at *www.sec.gov/consumer/pick.htm*.

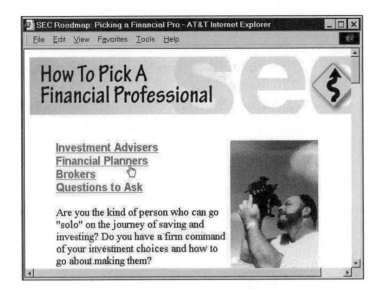

The SEC provides general guidelines on how to pick an e-broker.

Just as important as reviews are sites that will protect you against fraud or misrepresentation. The NASD features an online search form, located at *www.nasdr.com/2002.htm*, by which you can review an individual broker's felony records, if he has any, his employment history, and any criminal records for brokerage firms, as well as lots of other information.

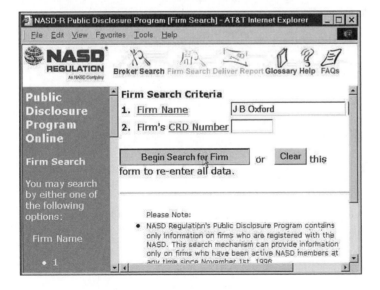

The NASD provides a searchable database of background information on brokerages and individual brokers.

The Main Criteria

Online brokerages differ along five lines: price, features, information, performance, and products. Here's a summary of the main differences within each category:

- **Price**   As mentioned in the preceding two chapters, paying less in fees and eliminating commissions on stock trades entirely is the main reason that consumers pass up traditional brokers for the Web.

- **Features**   You have to balance price with the number of different ways a broker will let you make your trade.

- **Information**   Because you've effectively chucked the high-priced advice that comes with traditional brokerages, it's important to compare what kinds of research tools brokers will provide to help you make decisions on your own.

- **Performance**   The Web is an insecure medium that's unreliable for most tasks, including stock trading; it's your broker's job to make sure he or she does the best to process your trade in a timely manner.

- **Products**   In addition to trading stocks and bonds and getting into mutual funds, online brokers are increasingly offering a dizzying array of products, including tax-free instruments.

Let's talk for a moment about each of these five criteria.

Price

You can save a lot by moving to the Web, though the difference is not always easy to quantify. Traditional full-service brokerage fees and commissions vary quite a bit, not just according to the number of shares purchased, but also according to how frequently an investor trades with his full-service broker. As an example of the disparity, a trade that could cost $50 with a full-service broker for 100 shares of stock could be had at an ultra-cheap online broker like Brown & Co., which charges no fees, for just $5 in commission. Some brokers will charge annual fees for maintaining your account under certain conditions, such as when your account drops below a certain minimum balance. Others eliminate fees altogether. The minimum initial deposit requirement falls under this category. Some e-brokers will require no money deposited up front; you can start trading as soon as you're approved and send money only to cover the cost of stock purchases plus fees. Other brokers require balances of $500 to $2,000, on average.

Brokers such as Brown & Company offer no guidance, but they slash commission rates to just a few dollars for each trade.

Merrill Lynch is one of the traditional full-service brokerages trying to transition to the e-trading world.

Running to Catch Up

What's it like to be a full-service brokerage in the time of electronic trading? Consider the plight of Merrill Lynch, one of the world's largest portfolio management firms, with $30 billion in market capitalization, $1.7 trillion in client assets under management, 950 offices around the world, and 67,200 employees. Much of Merrill's business is built on managing investments for institutions and wealthy individuals. Merrill is the paradigm of the full-service brokerage under siege. Merrill's solution? The company has rolled out an online investing site called Merrill Lynch Direct. The fees for buying shares of stock are still higher than certain online brokers, but Merrill is betting that even if customers don't want a broker's advice they will be lured by expensive research that Merrill offers on the site. For example, there are model portfolios prepared by Merrill's stock analysts that can help you decide how to assemble a group of stocks for a given investment goal.

Features

Getting the order into the broker is the heart of online trading. When you are following up on a hot stock tip and you submit an order to buy or sell stock at whatever price is current, you want to make sure you can submit a trade fast and with minimal fuss. Will the broker let you call in your buy or sell order by phone if you can't reach the Web site? Are there any live operators to answer questions on the weekends? Are confirmations sent by email as well as by regular mail, or do you have to surf to the broker's Web site to check if your trade has been processed?

Information

You could wind up paying higher fees to a broker who overloads you with information, or you could choose a bare-bones Web broker and find out you don't really have enough information to make any trading decisions. Some tools are inconsequential, such as the buckets of financial news feeds that every broker offers these days. However, some brokers, especially those that maintain full-service operations in addition to the Web, may throw in real-time quotes on stock prices and research reports that would cost a lot of money without an account. Real-time quotes means that you are given the actual price of the security quoted at that moment in time on the exchange where that security is traded. This is important because many sites on the Web offer only delayed quotes, where you see the price as of 15 minutes earlier. It's important for tax purposes to make sure you get good information about prices at which you've purchased stocks, bonds, and mutual fund shares, as you'll see in Chapter 10, "Understanding Your Taxes."

Performance

You don't want to submit an order to your broker to buy 100 shares of stock and find that you've been charged a price 20% higher than you were expecting. Yet this has happened to individuals when orders submitted over the World Wide Web were processed after a substantial delay, either because a broker's computers were down or because his connection to the Internet (or yours) was too slow to process your order in time. You can find numerous sites on the Web that will tell you about the relative performance of various brokers. One such site is Keynote Systems, whose home page has data on brokerage Web site performance (check *www.keynote.com/ measures/brokers/*). However, you also want to check out whether options such as phone orders are available as a backup if there are problems with a broker's Web site or with the Web in general. Also, you'll want to know if brokers have a standard policy for honoring trades that you placed but that may not have been successfully transacted for one reason or another.

Products

Brokers don't just want a little bit of your business, they want it all. Increasingly, Web brokers are trying to provide additional financial instruments and personal savings options to get a greater share of your wallet. Many are forming online banks that will offer you traditional checking and savings accounts linked to your stocks. Many aggressive investors want to get into the initial public offerings of young companies, meaning the first day their stock trades publicly. Brokers offer access to IPOs on different terms, including higher minimum balance requirements or additional fees. It's also important to consider whether your broker has tax-deferred or tax-free investment opportunities because you may want to convert some of your investments into these vehicles later on, for tax purposes. Individual Retirement Accounts (IRAs), which are tax-deductible, and tax-free municipal bonds are a standard part of a well-built portfolio.

Decide for Yourself

At last count there were about a zillion different articles in print and on the Web purporting to rate various online brokers, with the result that every broker seems to be at the top of someone's list. Make sure that you compare some of these different ratings to get a feel for how brokerages are being judged, and don't just go with the first broker listed as number one by a magazine or Web site.

Broker Profiles

You'll come across numerous different kinds of brokers. Let's get an idea of how a few might differ. Following are three very different brokerages to compare on features:

- Charles Schwab & Co., a traditional retail brokerage.

- E*Trade, a Web-only pioneer of electronic investing.

- MyDiscountBroker, a division of an investment bank, SouthWest Securities Group.

How do these firms compare? Let's take a look.

Founded in 1975, Charles Schwab has been around the longest. Long before the online investing craze, the company pioneered the discount brokerage phenomenon, which also challenged the full-service brokerages with cheap deals on commissions, innovative electronic trading, and an extensive retail branch network across the U.S. Today, Schwab maintains over 300 branch offices across the country.

Charles Schwab & Co. pioneered discount brokerage and has moved to the Web.

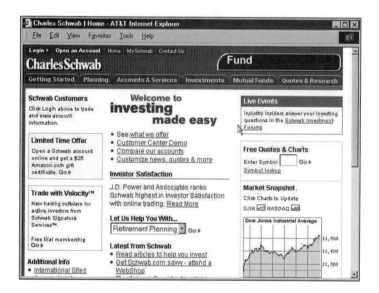

- The Schwab branch network means there are actual offices with actual people that you can visit in your town to get information or to ask for help. Schwab also boasts its ability to offer telephone support in the event that you have problems using the Web for a particular trade.

- Schwab makes a point of offering several different tiers, or levels, of account. For example, investors with the Schwab Platinum service, for those with a starting minimum balance of $1 million, really enjoy much more than simple online trading. They get special access to a small team of investment advisors to help them make investment decisions. While this may seem a little beside the point in the world of online investing, being able to trade up to such rich services within the same brokerage offers a certain superstar status that other brokers can't offer.

- Schwab offers its own trading software, called Velocity, for experienced traders who want a more sophisticated tool that offers, for example, stock charts and graphs. It also offers not just real-time quotes, but "streaming" real-time quotes, meaning you can see a display of the current prices for securities changing as they change on the exchange itself. (We'll talk more about such software in Chapter 4, "Tools of the Trade: Hardware and Software Considerations.")

E*Trade pioneered the Internet approach to investing when the company rolled out electronic trading on AOL and other online services in 1992. In the mid-1990s, E*Trade was first to introduce super-cheap trading, with $14.95 average trades. E*Trade has expanded in the past couple of years, offering initial public offerings (IPOs), mutual funds, bonds, and all the other standard fare of a retail brokerage.

Some of the company's competitive features are

- Power E*Trade, a service for heavily active traders, which discounts the cost of trades down to $4.95 for investors who make more than 75 trades every three months.

- E*Trade has an arrangement with Archipelago, a so-called Electronic Communications Network (ECN), which gives E*Trade investors a chance to place orders for securities into several different markets at once to get better prices.

- E*Trade has a major Wall Street investment bank, Goldman Sachs, as one of its backers, and the company offers research reports on stocks to its customers from professional securities analysts on Wall Street.

E*Trade is the online investing pioneer.

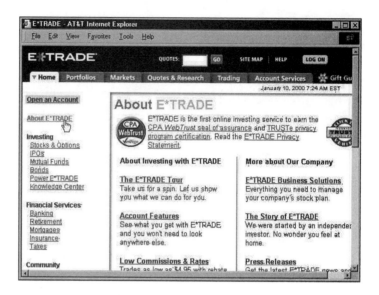

MyDiscountBroker boasts its connection to SouthWest Securities, a regional investment bank based in Dallas, Texas. The importance of the connection is that SouthWest Securities serves as a clearing firm, the entity that processes trades for other brokerages. The securities clearing involves the actual exchange of legal title for securities, as well as the electronic transfer of funds in transactions. SouthWest argues it can offer better performance than other brokerages because it has a computer system built for speed in order to handle its many clearing services clients.

MyDiscountBroker leverages its parent, SouthWest Securities, and offers no-minimum accounts.

Some features of MyDiscountBroker are

- Zero minimum investment. Unlike Schwab and E*Trade, MyDiscountBroker requires no minimum up-front investment. Once you've completed the application form and been approved for trading, you can start placing orders right away and wire funds to your account to pay for the trades.

- The firm's commission rates are lower than either of the other brokerages. MDB charges just $12 for trades of up to 5,000 shares, with incremental charges for share amounts above that.

- MDB is rolling out something called MyBankUSA, which will essentially offer all the traditional checking and savings features of a standard bank account. That's convenient for investors who want one single banking statement for their checking, savings, and securities.

Aside from these differences, you'll find brokerages talking up any number of different features:

- The number of mutual funds you can get access to, and whether they are offered with the standard fees waived.

- Whether there are extra charges for more exotic types of stock trades. In Chapter 8, "Placing Your First Trade," we'll talk about the difference between different types of securities trades you can make over the Web. Suffice it to say that some types are more complex than others, and some brokers may charge you extra to process these orders.

- Whether you can trade "after hours," meaning after the close of market. We'll talk more about this in Chapter 17, "After-Hours Trading and Electronic Communications Networks."

Relating Broker Profiles to Your Profile

Now that you understand how brokers differ, you can start to match what they offer to what you want. You hopefully have a sense of your personal financial goals by now, as well as a sense of what you want to accomplish in trading stocks and bonds. Matching those two things is a tricky business; there's no easy connect-the-dots rule to tell you what broker features match your goals. And because the five qualities mentioned in the preceding section represent tradeoffs, you can't just go with the best broker according to some survey (though you should be sure to ask friends and relatives who trade online who their favorite brokers are).

Try It Yourself ▼   Following are some questions to ask that will help you to start making connections:

1. If you're new to investing and have relatively little savings, do you want to go with a broker who offers multiple financial products so that you can immediately start to diversify your holdings? Or are your needs for savings, checking, mutual funds, and so on already taken care of?

2. Are you an aggressive trader who wants to make frequent stock trades? If so, you may consider the cheapness of the fees your main criterion.

3. Do you expect to make trades for hot stocks whose price fluctuates wildly? If so, choosing a broker with a higher reputation for reliability may be very important.

4. Do you plan to carefully track the stocks, bonds, or mutual funds you're interested in? If so, you may want to go with a broker that offers exclusive research and information.

5. Will you be both the trader and the financial planner for your household? If so, you may want a site that offers free software and online tools to track all of your finances.

6. Do you plan on getting into stock trading a little at a time or a lot? You should check very carefully which broker will give you the cheapest trades for small amounts and large amounts depending on how much you expect to invest on a regular basis.

7. Can you afford to make a large minimum payment to open an account, or do you need a cheap way to get started? If the latter, you may want to look for offers that will allow you to pay some of the minimum balance up front and the rest through monthly deposits.

8. Do you want to toy with exotic investments such as initial public offerings and options contracts? If so, you'll have to make sure your broker provides such services and that extra fees for participating are not out of your reach.

Evaluating the Offerings

If the preceding guidelines have helped you to think about what you want out of the various brokerages, it's time to try to actually pick one. One of the first things to do is to bulk up on information about how to pick a broker. You can find plenty of advice at the NASD's Web site, *www.nasdr.com/2000.htm*.

You've got a few options.

Try any or all of the following:

▼ Try It Yourself

1. Read whatever you can get your hands on about the different brokers. Sources on the Web and in print, listed in Appendix A, "Useful Web Sites for the Investor," will help get you started.

2. Spend some time watching friends or relatives make trades with their account. You'll get to see what services they enjoy with their broker and where they run into frustration.

3. Find a Web site that will allow you to set up a mock portfolio. There are literally dozens of such sites on the Web. Many will let you input data about broker fees when you place mock trades. Try this for a couple of weeks, using the information from various brokers about their transaction fees. This will give you a feel for placing trades and hopefully some sense of the charges you will incur if you go with this or that broker.

4. Lastly, you can sign up for more than one account, if you have enough cash to make the minimum balance requirements of several brokers at once. This way you can compare the process of placing orders at each broker's site. Make sure, however, that the brokers you choose will let you move accounts into and out of other brokerages. You may decide after a few weeks that you want to close an account that doesn't satisfy you and move those investments into the one or two accounts you decide to stick with.

What You've Learned

By now you should be pleasantly bewildered. Realizing the vast ocean of options available when choosing a broker is the first step in figuring out what's right for you. Hopefully, too, you realize that there are some commonalities between brokers, and that choosing one comes down to a few basic criteria you should compare with your own needs based on your own investor profile. But now you should know

- There are a handful of categories into which you can classify the differences between brokers.

- You should compare the differences in brokers with your individual needs as an investor.

- Finally, you should have some ideas about how to start evaluating individual brokers.

PART II

Getting Started— Going Online

CHAPTER 4

Tools of the Trade: Hardware and Software Considerations

How to Get Online

The essence of getting into e-trading is, of course, getting onto the World Wide Web. If you already have a connection to the Internet and are accustomed to surfing the Web for hours and hours, you should check your setup against the following list to make sure you've got a comfortable system for browsing the Web.

To get online, you'll need the following:

- **A PC or Macintosh computer** If you're using a PC, even the cheaper, so-called "sub-$1,000" computers are usually fast enough for inputting basic trades. However, Web browser software has become increasingly bulky as features have been tacked on. If you want to use special software packages provided by your brokerage (and there's good reason to consider such software, as you'll see), you'll be putting even more stress on your machine. For that reason, you should consider going for a PC with at least a Pentium II processor. Macintosh computers last a good long time, but if you're considering running some of the more ambitious software, you should consider upgrading to a Power Macintosh or an iMac. With both PCs and Macs, 32 megabytes of memory is the absolute minimum amount of RAM to ensure a comfortable surfing experience, but 64 megabytes is even better. Stock trading shouldn't take up too much disk space, so the standard disk drive that ships with most PCs should be good enough.

What You'll Learn in This Chapter:

- ▶ Basic software and hardware requirements.
- ▶ What brokerage software is, and what it can do for you.
- ▶ How to use portfolio management tools effectively.

- **An external or built-in modem**   These days, most computers, both PCs and Macs, come with built-in modems of the
  56 kilobit per second (kbps) variety. Speed is important when
  you're dealing with financial transactions, so if your modem
  is slower than 56 kilobits per second, you might consider
  upgrading.

- **A connection to the Internet**   Of course, you will need to
  have a subscription to an Internet service provider (ISP),
  which will get you hooked up to the Internet. Most likely you
  will use your 56kbps modem, but phone companies and cable
  companies are increasingly offering very fast cable modems
  or so-called digital subscriber line (DSL) connections to the
  Internet running at anywhere from 256 kilobits per second to
  7 million bits per second. These high-speed lines will cost
  you between $40 and a couple hundred dollars—plus the cost
  of the modem itself and the installation—and the connections
  may take several weeks to obtain from your local service
  provider. But if speed is an issue in getting your trade to market with utmost haste, you might want to consider a cable
  modem or DSL.

Superfast DSL or cable modem connections from your phone or cable company could give you a trading edge.

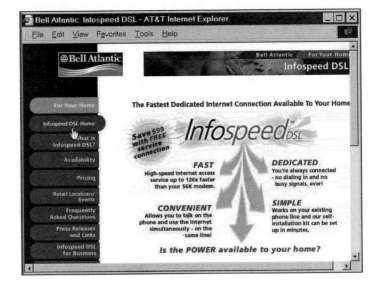

- **Web browser software** It's best to make sure you have either Internet Explorer 5 or Netscape Navigator 4.5 because these are the most recent versions of the two most popular browsers as of this writing. Internet Explorer 4.5 is the latest version of Microsoft's browser for the Macintosh.

The nice thing about the World Wide Web is that some of the best software you'll find is available online, free of charge. First and foremost, you can find plenty of small programs on various investor Web sites that will let you calculate the yield on a bond or figure out how you should be spreading out your investments. These sorts of tools are constantly being updated, and new kinds of tools are coming out all the time. They range from rather primitive programs, such as the calculator on the SEC Web site that helps you determine the cost of investing in a mutual fund (at *www.sec.gov/mfcc/mfcc-int.htm*) to slightly more sophisticated graphic programs, such as Island ECN's real-time "book" of streaming stock quotes (at *www.island.com/BookViewer/index.html*).

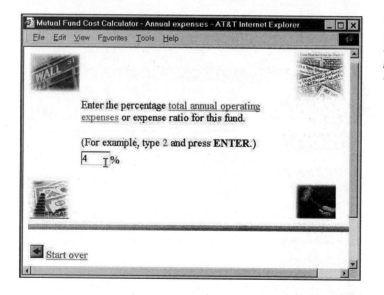

And then there are much more sophisticated programs, such as SmartMoney.com's Map of the Market, which will chart the overall change in different sectors of the stock market in a pleasing 2D representation.

AOL Is Not an Island

If you're connecting to the Internet through AOL, never fear. As long as you can use AOL to surf the Web, everything else about an e-broker's Web site should work just fine. There are a couple of instances where particular software packages or programs running on a Web site—such as the programs highlighted in Chapter 9, "Managing Your Portfolio"—may run into problems with AOL. You should check the fine print when working with these programs to see if there are any problems.

The SEC mutual fund calculator is a simple HTML program that can be quite useful.

Island ECN's real-time quote "book."

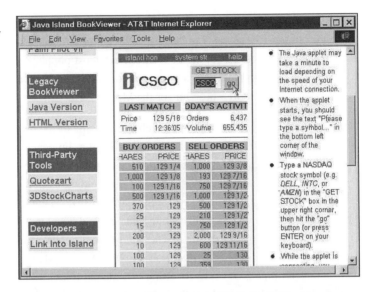

SmartMoney's Map of the Market is an example of some of the most sophisticated Web-based software around.

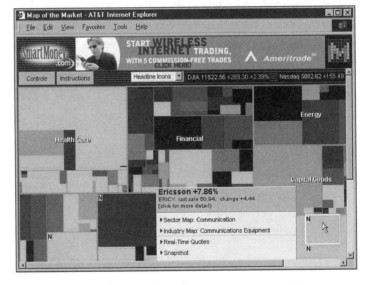

Again, almost all of these Web-based programs can be used free of charge—or, at most, with some kind of subscription.

Brokerage Tools

The Web-based tools are mostly informational; they won't really help you accomplish the task of placing trades and tracking useful market data as it is streaming from the securities exchange. For that you will want to check out some dedicated programs from various brokers and from some third-party sources.

Most brokerage sites will let you view your holdings and your transaction history in a summary format in a Web page, but you'll probably outgrow those rather primitive portfolio tools fairly quickly. To encourage you to upgrade to more expensive accounts (and place more trades!), many brokerages have started to offer fancy stock-tracking programs you can download to your computer. These tools let you work with information from the Web, and also check your stocks and mutual funds when you're not connected. The software usually comes free with a brokerage account.

Some of the brokerage software packages available for use are

- **DLJ Direct MarketSpeed for Windows 95, 98, and NT**
  MarketSpeed is a free software program for all account holders. The program places a toolbar on the Windows desktop from which a series of pop-up windows will allow you to quickly enter a trade on impulse. By paying an extra fee of $24.95 a month, the program will stream price quotes to your desktop, meaning that new quotes are updated in real-time to reflect the actual prices at any moment.

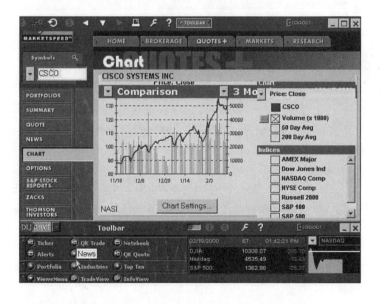

MarketSpeed brings streaming stock price quotations and snazzy graphics.

- **Charles Schwab Velocity for Windows 95 and 98**
  Velocity is hefty order-placement and portfolio-tracking software. The main advantage of Velocity is the ability to set up

multiple buy or sell orders in a single screen on your computer and then place them with Schwab's service with the single click of a button (saving you loads of time versus entering trades via the Web page). Another advantage is that you can set up trades even if you're not connected to the Web and then transmit the orders when you next connect to the Web. Schwab reserves its Velocity software for investors with a minimum balance of $100,000 or a certain level of trades per year, but you can try out the software for 30 days with a basic Schwab One account.

Charles Schwab & Co. reserves Velocity for its premium clients.

• **Powerstreet Pro for Windows 95, 98, and NT** Powerstreet Pro is for clients of the Powerstreet brokerage operation of mutual fund giant Fidelity Investments. Pro is a special program that provides advanced portfolio display and charting within your browser. You must use it with Microsoft Internet Explorer—Netscape Navigator and Communicator will not work. The program integrates stock information and news from a number of Web-based content sources and uses stock-screening software from CBS Marketwatch, the online venture of CBS, Inc. This will let you search a large group of stocks to find just those that match your criteria. As with Velocity and MarketSpeed, you can place multiple trades right from within the Powerstreet program, without the need to go to the Fidelity Web site. Fidelity reserves the software for what it calls "active traders," meaning those who make 36 or more trades per year.

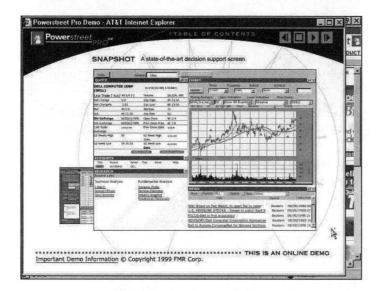

Powerstreet lets Fidelity brokerage customers enter multiple complex orders from one screen at the same time.

- **Streamer for Windows 95 and 98** Streamer is for customers of Datek Online. Streamer runs outside of the browser and is mainly meant to deliver real-time quotes in a continuous fashion. However, there is a trading screen where you can enter buy and sell orders directly. Streamer comes with a Datek account, but you can download a free copy just for registering on the site if you're not ready to open a Datek account.

You can download
Streamer software
to experiment
with, even if you're
not a Datek Online
customer.

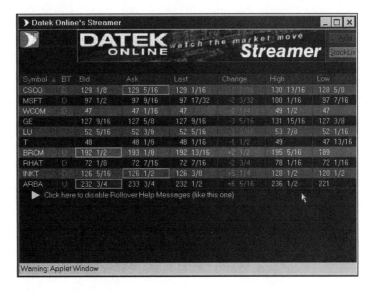

Day Trading Software

In addition to brokerage software, there are also certain programs
that are oriented toward really aggressive investors who want the
latest high-tech gear. Mostly this software is put in the basket of
day trading programs. We'll talk about day trading in Chapter 16,
"Day Trading Online," but it's worth considering the kinds of
software packages that go into this category for a moment.

These programs all provide a number of similar features. Like the
brokerage programs, they serve up a constant stream of real-time
quotes, along with breaking news stories about various securities,
pulled from the wire services. They usually allow you to enter
trades as well, provided your broker is one of the brokerages sup-
ported by the software. Alternatively, some of the software packages come with their own offers for trading accounts that you can
open once you've installed the software.

In addition, these tools may have much more complex charting or
graphing functions than brokerage software. That is because the
individuals who use such software often rely on what's called
technical analysis.

Technical analysis is the use of data about the change in price of a
security as the sole guideline for trading in that security. Technical analysts, as some devotees call themselves, believe that

through careful study of stock charts, they can make accurate assumptions about future price movements without worrying about other macroeconomic or microeconomic factors. Technical analysis is often contrasted to fundamental analysis, in which the health of the entity underlying a security is assessed in order to anticipate how that security may trade.

There are dozens if not hundreds of these software packages. Some representative examples are

- **CyberTrader from Cybercorp** CyberTrader is one of the more prominent day trading software packages. If you go to brokerage houses frequented by day traders, you may well see this software being used on speedy workstation computers to perform lightening fast trades. Like many day trading packages, CyberTrader lets you see a display of not just the prices for a given stock, but also who is buying and who is selling the security from moment to moment. Because day traders are often racing against time to get an order to market, CyberTrader includes an ability to automate stock trades, which you won't find in other packages. You could, for example, set a certain price at which the computer will automatically forward a "buy" order to your broker.

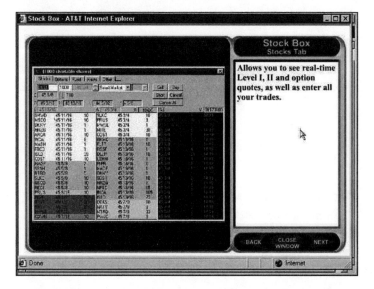

CyberTrader automates trade placement for day traders.

- **eSignal from Data Broadcasting Corp**   Another feature-rich day trading package that offers several different versions with increasingly complex features. You can get live stock charts that change from moment to moment as stock prices stream into the program from over the Web. Like CyberTrader, eSignal features something called Nasdaq Level II, which lets you see who's actually placing orders to buy and sell a given security. You won't normally see this in standard brokerage packages.

eSignal is a day trading program that displays information about who's buying and selling securities.

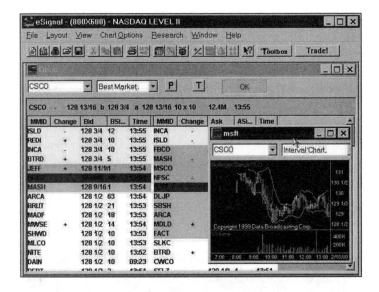

Get Ready to Keep Paying

Unlike brokerage programs, which are free, and most commercial software, which you purchase once, many of the day trading programs are priced on a subscription basis. Moreover, prices may be established on an a la carte basis, with lots of extra goodies—mainly additional information—that all costs extra. You can quickly find yourself adding on extras and facing a monthly bill of a couple hundred dollars or more.

Be aware that the day trading software, unlike most of the brokerage software, will require that you complete an online agreement when you purchase the software. That's basically your way of shaking hands with the securities exchanges that are providing the real-time price quotes and the advanced information, such as Nasdaq Level II data.

Macintosh Software

It's a sorry fact that all of the brokerage software churned out by the investment houses themselves runs only on Windows PCs. That just means that, as in all cases, the Macintosh software is a cottage industry in this field. There are a couple of good programs you should consider if you are a Macintosh user. They include

- **MacChart and Personal Analyst, both from Trendsetter Software**   These programs offer the kinds of detailed technical analysis tools that day traders crave.

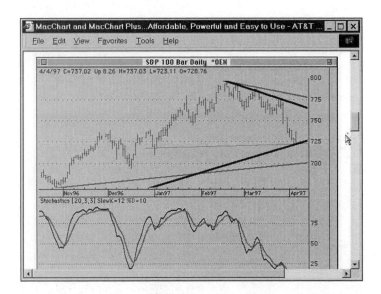

MacChart offers advanced technical analysis tools for Macintosh.

- **ProTA by Beesoft**   Features charts and analysis of not just stocks but also mutual funds and options contracts. The software will also analyze a portfolio of holdings.

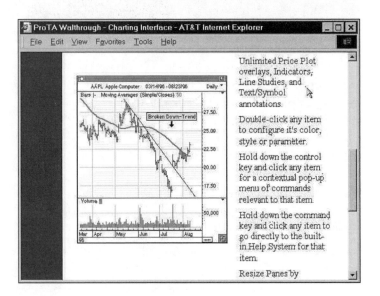

ProTA is a charting and portfolio analysis tool for the Macintosh.

Some of these Macintosh tools will let you download data from your brokerage account, which means you don't have to be left out of the fun of tracking your portfolio throughout the week.

Exotic Software

In addition to software that helps you input trades and track market prices, there are a few programs for more sophisticated traders that let you perform analysis on exotic securities of one kind or another. One example is Limit Up!, which lets you track trades in more esoteric types of securities such as "futures" and "derivatives."

Limit Up! is designed for more exotic types of securities trading, such as derivatives.

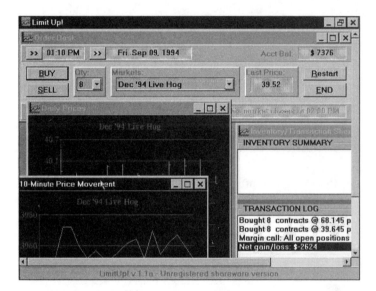

A Web of Trading Software

Many Web sites have compiled lists of the kinds of programs we're discussing. If you perform a search for "day trading software macintosh" on a major search engine, you should be able to find your way to a page of links.

Does Anyone Use This Stuff?

The day trading software, the Macintosh programs, and the more exotic commodities software are all made by small software companies. For that reason, you may want to check with other investors and professional traders to see if they have tried or can recommend any of these programs.

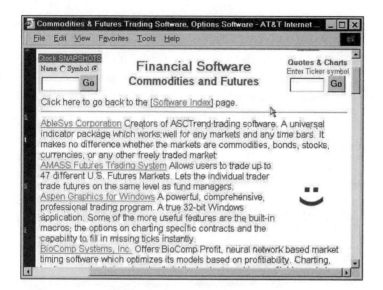

Sites such as InvestorLinks feature whole lists of obscure trading software for Macintosh and PC.

Portfolio Management Tools

In addition to surfing and analyzing your portfolio, you'll probably want to use your computer to keep track of your assets and to integrate your stock holdings with the rest of your personal finances. There are several tools of this sort, but two of the best are Quicken from Intuit and Microsoft Money, as described in the following list:

- **Quicken by Intuit** The latest version of Quicken, Quicken Deluxe 2000 for Windows and for Macintosh, will let you download information from your brokerage account directly into the software, along with the latest stock prices. (You'll have to check first to see if your brokerage supports the software for the operating system you're using.) Quicken will also let you chart and graph your investments and compare rates of return on your stocks in a number of ways. Quicken also tracks 401K funds and it can help you with tax planning.

- **Microsoft Money** Although less mature than Quicken in some ways, Money also features powerful tools for tracking profits and assets. Money started out as a program to plan mortgage payments and insurance and to pay bills online.

Don't Throw Away Your Browser!

Remember that portfolio software such as Quicken and Money is strictly for tracking or planning sales of stock and bonds. These software programs will not actually allow you to enter trades to your broker. You must still use the Web and your browser—or your brokerage software—to enter trades.

The program now connects to Microsoft's MoneyCentral Web site, so you can sort through the many online investing articles from inside the program. The latest version of Money, Deluxe 2000, contains support for more sophisticated types of stock transactions, such as long and short options. There is no Macintosh version of this software.

Aside from software you download, you should also consider some of the better financial Web sites, which have their own tools for tracking investments. You'll find a list of these in Appendix A.

You Can Take It with You

One of the most exciting innovations in online trading technology is the advent of wireless trading. If you own a cell phone, a pager, or one of several mobile handheld computers, such as the PalmPilot from 3Com, you can get software that will allow you to see stock quotes and news and even place trades from such devices. Pagers have been used for years by business professionals to receive alerts of price targets, but typically at a very high price.

Among those offering wireless software are E*Trade, Dreyfus Brokerage Services, DLJ Direct, Fidelity Powerstreet, Morgan Stanley Dean Witter Online, and Ameritrade. The features in these packages vary quite a bit. E*Trade provides a piece of software for the Palm VII that will let you check delayed pricing information for a small number of "portfolio" stocks, though these stocks will not automatically reflect your actual E*Trade portfolio.

DLJ, on the other hand, has produced software for pagers, cell phones, and Palm VII computers that not only downloads your current account status, but also allows you to send buy and sell orders for stocks and options right from these devices.

Your Results May Vary

Bear in mind that with a wireless device such as a cell phone or a palm-top computer, you take extra risks that your trade may not go through as expected. Most wireless technologies will usually be slower than the connection you enjoy at home. And they will likely make connections that are inherently less reliable simply because of the nature of wireless technology. Although these gadgets are great for impulse trading, you should not bet your most important trades on them. You should be extra careful to check your account after each trade to make sure your buy or sell order has been properly transacted.

What You've Learned

This chapter has given you all the basic tools you need to communicate with an online broker and to place trades and track
them. The essentials to keep in mind are

- To buy and sell stocks and bonds you must have at least a PC
  or Macintosh with a modem and a Web browser.

- Some brokerages will provide you more versatile software
  that can replace a Web browser, but these are often tied to
  special types of premium accounts.

- You should seek out portfolio management software, such as
  Quicken and MS Money, that will help you to integrate your
  stock purchases with the rest of your household finances.

CHAPTER 5

Researching Stocks, Bonds, and Mutual Funds Online

Stock trading may be the ultimate expression of a do-it-yourself age: If you want to survive trading stocks and bonds without the help of a full-service broker, you've got to learn to gather your own resources in order to make your own decisions. For that reason, the ability to research companies you are interested in is an essential skill to develop.

Fortunately, there is more information publicly available today than at any time in the stock market's history, all thanks to the vast filing cabinet that is the Internet. Before you begin to make any trades with an online broker, and throughout your investing lifetime, you'll learn to use the Web as a rich trove of information. This chapter gives you tips on how best to navigate the online resources.

What You'll Be Looking For

Before you set out on the sea of debate and advice on the Web, it's important to decide what exactly you hope to accomplish. Different sites on the Web will be either more or less relevant to your needs.

If you're an experienced investor who's just discovering the Web, you may very well have your own ideas about what you want to invest in. If that's the case, you'll find plenty of information to use as tools in making your trading decisions. We'll discuss these in a moment.

What You'll Learn in This Chapter:

▶ The first step: Knowing what to look for.

▶ How to navigate and use online financial Web sites.

▶ How to find, read, and take advantage of public documents.

▶ Getting geeky: Message boards and chat sites.

If, however, the Web is your introduction to buying and selling securities, the first step is to figure out what securities you're interested in. If you've decided stocks are your main interest, you'll probably want to chase down information about individual companies—what their field is, how long they've been around, and so on. The first challenge is to find some companies you're interested in. As a start, you should check out some of the various investment magazines that write about stocks and the companies they represent on an ongoing basis. Magazines such as *Money*, *SmartMoney*, *Individual Investor*, *Fortune*, and others all maintain their own Web sites, packed with stories about companies and stocks. Many of these sites can help you to learn about individual companies and stocks, or about whole industries that may interest you, such as utilities, retailers, or technology companies. Often, these magazines will offer a tool called a "screen." A stock screen compares several stocks—perhaps hundreds or thousands—to find stocks and companies that match criteria, such as high earnings growth. Use these features of financial Web sites to start thinking about companies.

You will find stock screens at financial Web sites that will help you to start identifying companies.

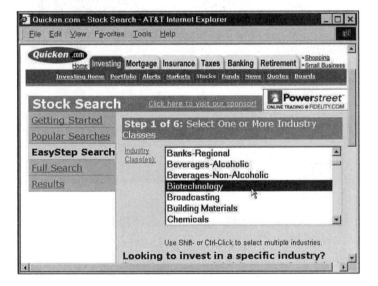

If you already know which sectors you are interested in, you may want to check out Web sites that track those sectors to see which companies they mention. In addition, a number of different organizations create formal indices, or lists, of stocks within an industry in order to observe the performance of that industry. This is another source of names of stocks you can mine. Dow Jones, for example, compiles an index of utilities (comprising companies such as Enron & Consolidated Edison), which you can view on the company's Web site at *http://interactive.wsj.com/edition/ resources/documents/charts.htm* (though you will need a subscription to *The Wall Street Journal* to view the page). Another popular one is the S&P 500 index, prepared by Standard & Poor's, Inc. The S&P 500 contains, as its name implies, 500 companies, and you can use these names to start thinking about stocks you might be interested in. The index companies can be seen at *www.spglobal.com/mktval.html*.

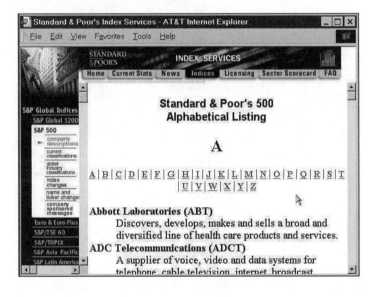

The Standard & Poor's 500 is one list that can help you to start picking some stocks.

If bonds are your game, you'll want to find materials about bond yields as well as general economic trends. Just as there are many different sectors of the economy in which to discover stocks, there are lots of different types of bonds. There are municipal bonds, issued by government offices in order to fuel civic development. These are appealing because the income they bring you is usually tax-free. There are also corporate bonds, which can be an alternative to stock if you want to invest in companies. A good place to start looking at these is at the Web site called InvestinginBonds.com, which is sponsored by the Bond Market Association, a trade group. It's at *www.investinginbonds.com.*

InvestinginBonds. com is one place to start looking for what bonds are available.

Lastly, if you're interested in mutual funds, you will, again, have to select which kind of fund you are looking for. Funds invest money in a variety of different securities. Some will place your money in risky small-capitalization stocks. Others will place it in bonds. Still a third type of mutual fund, the index mutual fund, may place your money in stocks of companies in the various indices mentioned above, such as the Dow Jones Utilities index, so that your money will grow as these overall indices appreciate. One good place to start looking for funds is at Morningstar, Inc.'s Web site, *http://screen.morningstar.com/fundsearch/fundinterim. html,* where you'll find tools for screening funds, just like the stock screening mentioned above.

Morningstar.com is one place to start looking for mutual funds.

Researching Companies and Their Stock

Okay, so you've decided you don't want to hear about anything but stocks. In case you haven't yet realized it, stocks themselves are merely paper representing ownership in a company. Therefore, if you want to trade stock, you want to know things about how that stock has traded and about the underlying company. In other words, you want to research the following:

- What is the company's main line of business?

- How long has the company been around?

- Who are the individuals running the company?

At the same time, you want to know about how the stock itself, the paper ownership, has performed in public trading. Has it appreciated? How rich is the value that the stock price represents vis-à-vis the company's underlying assets?

The following are some points about stock performance to research:

- Has the stock depreciated or declined since it was first issued, and how is it performing relative to various measures such as stock indices?

- What are the particulars of the stock's valuation, such as the price-to-earnings ratio?

- What are the technical details about the stock, such as how much is owned by institutional investors?

You could find most of this information by sifting through various documents provided by companies on their Web sites. However, the beauty of the Web is that a lot of basic research work is done for you by finance-oriented Web sites. Yahoo! Finance, run by the folks who started the Yahoo! search engine, is one such place to find data on stock price appreciation, to research a company's main line of business, or to find out who owns a certain stock. There are many other such sites, of course.

Yahoo! stock information.

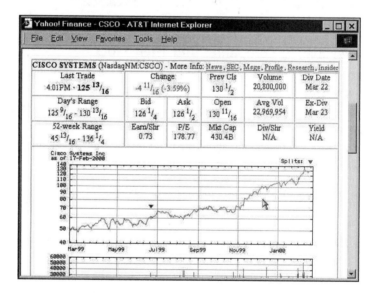

Researching Bonds

Remember that a bond is basically debt or a loan to an institution. You basically want to know about the debt level of the institution or organization issuing the bonds and what its track record is of paying back debts.

The two main things you will be looking for when researching bonds are

- A Moody's or Standard & Poor's debt rating. Because bonds are debt, you want to make sure that the institution issuing the debt is likely to pay back its obligations. Moody's and Standard & Poor's issue ratings on the credit-worthiness of debt issuers, with several different grades ranging from bad, essentially junk, to reliable.

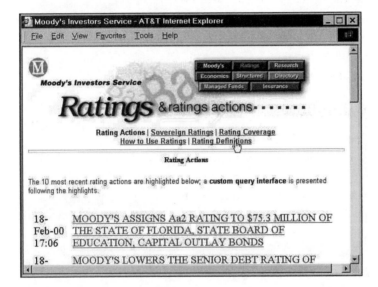

A Moody's or Standard & Poor's rating on debt is the key indicator of a bond's trustworthiness.

- The yield on the bond. If you plan to hold the bond to maturity, you want to know what sort of return the bond will pay out when it matures. We'll talk more about the concepts of yield and maturity when we talk about bond and mutual fund investing in Chapter 15, "Trading Bonds and Mutual Funds Online." Suffice it to say that yield is your payoff for putting your money in a bond, just like 2.5% annual interest may be the payoff for putting money in a savings account. With a few pieces of information in hand that are publicly available for any bond offering, namely the bond's "coupon" and the price of the bond, it is possible to use widely available "bond calculators" to figure the yield of a bond.

A bond calculator will help you to figure the yield on a bond.

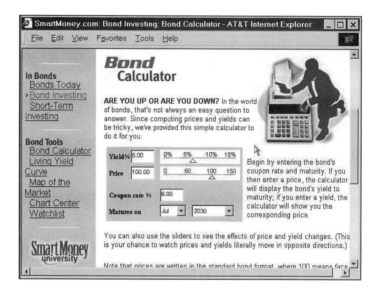

Researching Mutual Funds

As mentioned earlier, a fund is a way to pool your money with others in the hands of a professional stock picker. You want to know that the person taking your money is going to pursue the kinds of investment goals that match your own financial goals.

Mutual funds such as Vanguard pool the money of many investors to achieve a greater return on investment.

A few points to consider include

- Does the fund invest in aggressive growth stocks or simply in a stock index in order to track the market? You should be able to find information about such holdings either on the firm's Web site or on third-party financial Web sites.

Mutual fund Web sites should tell you about their holdings...

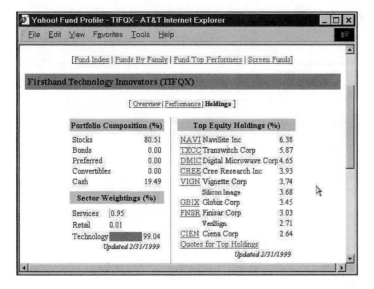

...but you can also find information about top holdings on sites such as Yahoo! Finance.

- Does the person running the fund have a track record of generating high returns? Again, a fund family's Web site should inform you of who's running the show.

Look for profiles on who's running a mutual fund at the fund's Web site.

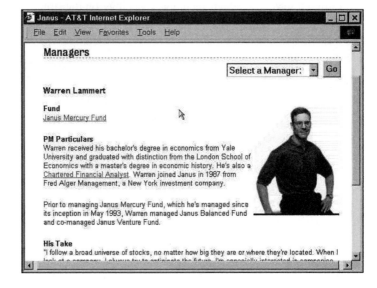

- Does the fund itself yield a high return, and over how many consecutive years? This information can be obtained from the Web sites of mutual fund rating companies such as Morningstar, Inc., which is located at *www.morningstar.com*.

The Morningstar Web site can tell you how a fund is performing.

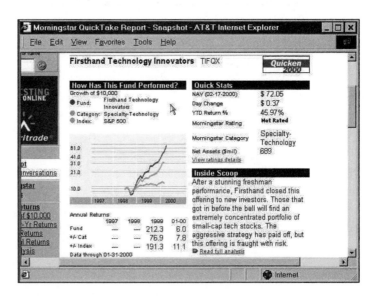

- What sorts of fees will be charged, including load? This type of information should be listed in the fund's prospectus, a document explaining the basic approach of the fund to investing and the expenses and fees of the fund. Just a few years ago you would have had to ask the fund to mail you a prospectus. Today you can find the prospectus on the company's Web site.

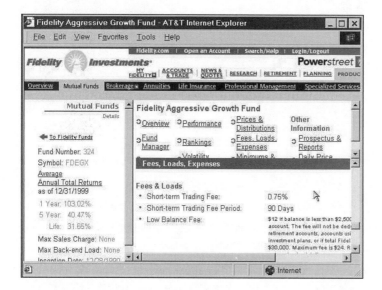

You can find a fund's prospectus on the fund's Web site.

Using Financial Web Sites

You could confine your stock research to reading the daily newspapers for interesting bits about your favorite stocks. You could consult the stock tables to see what's been up and down.

However, the Web affords a brilliant array of financial investing sites that provide not only news and stock prices, but also definitions of terms and databases chock full of historical data on stocks and mutual funds.

Appendix A, "Useful Web Sites for the Investor," lists several useful Web sites you should be sure to visit. You will also find several lists of sites on the Web. They include financial magazines.

Magazines such as SmartMoney provide links to useful Web sites.

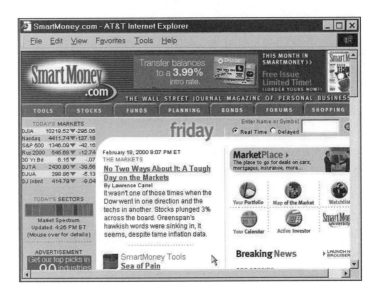

Try It Yourself ▼

Here are some steps to making best use of these sites:

1. There's a lot on some of these sites, so the first step is simply to compare different sites and see which kinds of resources they offer, which sites are best for tracking stocks, which for mutual funds, and so on.

2. Make a folder in the Bookmarks section of your Web browser, and place a bookmark there for each useful Web page you find that you'll want to visit frequently.

3. Take notes. Many of the sites offer helpful tips on how to think about company earnings or how to discern between different funds. You should keep a short list of the most useful rules of thumb these sites provide, so that you can refer back to them in the course of making your investments.

▲

(Almost) Full Service Brokerage

Remember that many online brokers offer tools and information of their own, in an attempt to provide some of the resources commonly associated with a traditional full-service brokerage. Before you get drawn into a brokerage by promises of free investing information, take a look at what you can find in other places on the Web. This will help you to determine if a broker is really providing exclusive information, or if it's simply more of the same.

Several basic tools will pop up at major sites that you should become familiar with. They include

- **Analyst ratings on stocks** These are tables that tell you how many stock analysts are rating a given stock a buy, a hold, and so on. They may also tell you how a company is expected to perform in terms of earnings and revenue growth.

Check the rest of the Web before you get sold on any broker's offering of research.

- **Valuation metrics** Stock information should tell you the price-to-earnings ratio of a given company. Price-to-earnings, or PE, as it's called, is an important measure of how expensive a stock is. Price-to-earnings is the current price per share of a stock divided by the earnings per share of the company that stock represents. Basically, it is a measure of what sort of multiple of earnings you are paying for with any given stock. Different companies will have an average PE at which they trade, and so the PE ratio can be an important indicator of whether a stock is expensive relative to its average price.

- **Important dates for stock announcements** Most sites will have some sort of calendar or timetable listing dates on which companies announce earnings or when they will split their stock. These dates are important because they can have an impact on how a stock trades in a given week or on a given day.

*Most financial
Web sites will tell
you what kind of
ratings, or grades,
analysts are giving
a stock...*

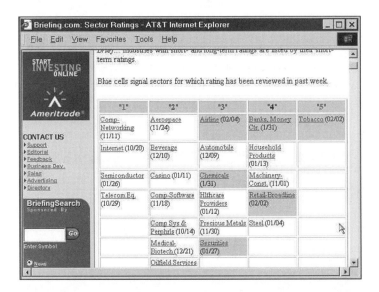

*...as well as what
you can expect
from a company
in the way of
earnings and
revenue.*

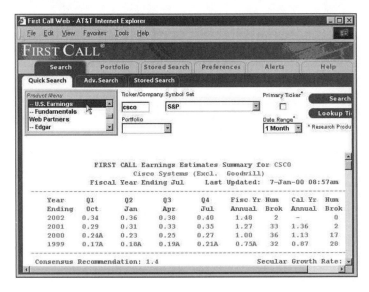

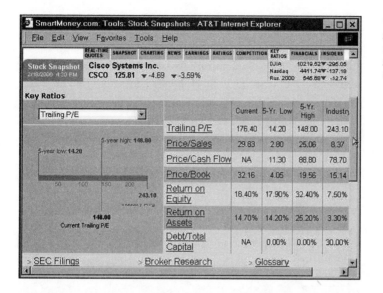

Valuation metrics, such as price-to-earnings, are a standard feature of stock profiles.

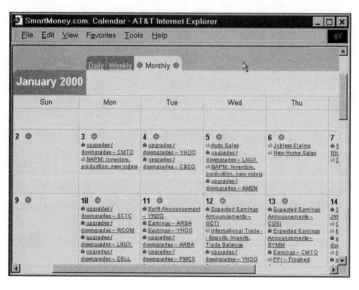

Get yourself a personalized economic calendar to keep track of important dates, such as earnings announcements for companies.

Using Public Documents

Just think how lucky you are. Five years ago, if you wanted to see the annual report that a company mailed to its shareholders, you would have had to write to the company's investor relations staff and request that a copy be sent to you. These days, you can surf to an online copy of the quarterly or annual report in just seconds by going on the World Wide Web. Most company Web sites host copies of their financial statements that you can browse online. In addition, you should check out the following:

Most companies host copies of their financial reports, such as annual and quarterly reports, on their Web sites.

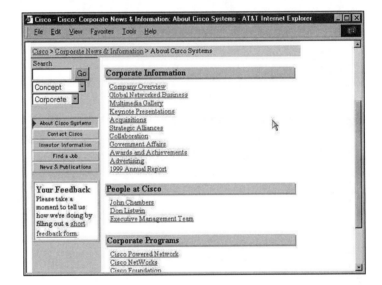

- **SEC corporate filings** The Securities and Exchange Commission, an oversight agency, has a Web site where you can find not just annual reports, but also documents filed by shareholders that may tell you who owns stock in a company or who plans to sell.

- **Press releases** All companies send out bulletins of new product announcements. You can find copies on company Web sites or on news sites. Don't put too much faith in a company's self-promotion, but keep an eye on the news just in case something significant shows up.

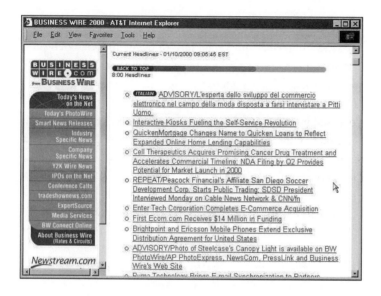

Sites such as PR Newswire and Businesswire gather lots of announcements from companies.

- **Mutual fund filings**   All mutual funds are required to file annual or semi-annual funds. These filings will tell you how much money a fund is managing and how much each share of a fund is worth at the time the report was filed with the Securities and Exchange Commission.

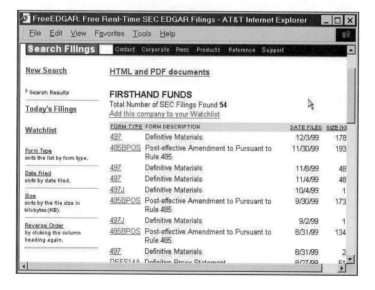

Mutual fund filings will tell you how much money a fund is managing for its investors and how much each share is worth at the date of the filing.

Message Boards and Chat Sites

In contrast to the self-important tone of many financial Web sites, an informal kind of investing advice takes place in clubs on the Web known as *message boards* or *chat rooms*.

Chat rooms are a no-holds-barred discussion of individual stocks.

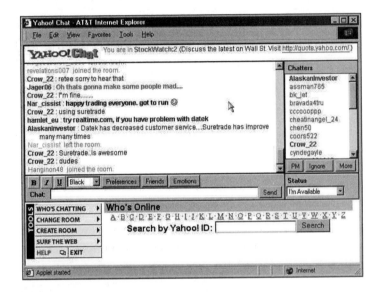

These are Web pages where you can read postings left by fellow investors and even leave your own messages about questions you have about a particular stock or an opinion you'd like to share about a particular company. Whereas message boards resemble a public bulletin board, chat rooms actually take the form of a live public discussion, where you will see your comments and those of others posted in a constant fashion on the Web page.

Some things to note about message boards and chat rooms include

- You will find message boards for stock talk on pretty much every major financial Web site.

- When you find a message board you like, you can often browse the postings for free, but you will need to sign up with the Web site (and possibly pay a subscription fee) in order to post your own messages.

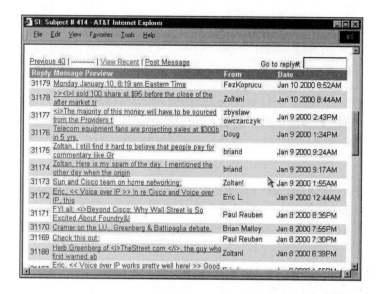

Message boards will often require that you register or subscribe in order to post messages of your own to the group.

• Chat sessions will often take place at particular times of the day on particular days of the week. You should work out a schedule that will allow you to participate in these chats.

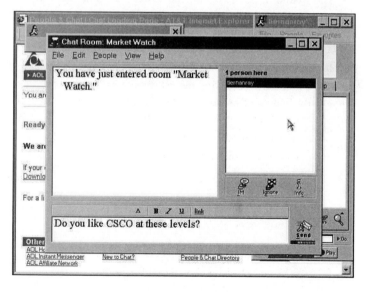

Look for special, scheduled chat sessions on particular investing topics.

Don't Believe Everything You Hear

The message boards and chat rooms are free-form, come-as-you-are discussions. Most are not moderated in any way. Although that makes the conversation particularly lively, it also means there is no one validating or checking the information provided by those who comment. Often wild rumors will swirl about a particular company, stock, or mutual fund without the least amount of substantial evidence. You should be careful to check out what you hear in newsgroup discussions before making any rash investing decisions.

What You've Learned

Hopefully, you're now starting to think about what information you need to understand the securities you will be investing in. You should have a grasp of

- What kinds of questions you need to ask about stocks, bonds, and mutual funds.

- What kinds of resources you will find on various Web sites, message boards, and chat rooms.

- The wealth of public documents available online that can provide basic research about companies.

Between bookmarking sites and keeping notes of important pieces of information, you will gradually become familiar with places you can go on the Web to find the answers to most questions that occur in the course of investing.

The next chapter covers how to complete a broker application online.

CHAPTER 6

Understanding the Basics of Stock Trading

Before you even begin to think about selecting your online broker, it's important you understand what you're buying and selling when you talk about pieces of paper called stock certificates or mutual fund receipts. This chapter guides you through the essential language and concepts of the stock and bond markets. If you already know something about the markets, you might want to skim these pages as a refresher course.

What You'll Learn in This Chapter:

▶ What is a stock, what is a bond?

▶ What are capital markets?

▶ How brokerages function.

▶ What are mutual funds?

Stocks Versus Bonds

What does it mean to buy or sell stock? *Stock*, often referred to more specifically as a "share" of stock, is nothing more than a receipt for ownership in a company. Stockholding was a crucial innovation during the days of European exploration and conquest that led to the discovery of the Americas. It was through stock ownership that investors could limit their risk in new, unproven overseas ventures to no more than the face value of a share of stock. Without this form of limited risk, many of the voyages of discovery that took place during the colonial age might not have set sail.

Bonds, on the other hand, are loans given by the bondholder to a corporation or another institution—for example, a government, in the case of state or municipal bonds. Whereas stock prices normally appreciate or depreciate in value in an uncertain manner, bonds have a specified fixed return in the form of interest at the time the bondholder first purchases them. Bonds are paid back by the borrower within a fixed time frame that is known as the "life" of the bond. When the life of the bond is up, and it's time to pay back the bondholder, the bond is said to have "matured." The U.S. government is the largest issuer of bonds in the U.S., with government bonds outstripping corporate bonds by 3 to 1.

Sites such as SmartMoney University can help you understand the basics of stock ownership.

Sites such as Invest-FAQ.com will give you a thorough introduction to bonds.

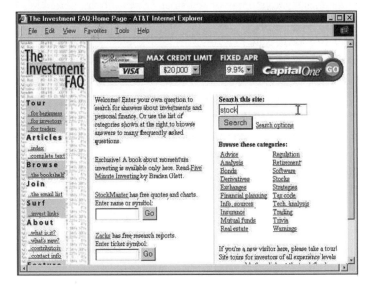

Bonding with the Web

Bonds often take a back seat to stock investing online. Although the backing of the U.S. government gives bonds the appeal of security, most individuals do not buy and sell bonds directly. This is more the practice of large institutional investors, who look for security first when moving large amounts of money. Most individuals will instead look to either bond mutual funds or mutual funds that contain some bond holdings along with stocks or other kinds of instruments. Nonetheless, some online brokers are starting to offer direct bond purchases from their Web sites. One notable example is E*Trade. Also, the U.S. government maintains a Web site where you can purchase Treasuries and other bonds directly without broker fees. (See Appendix A, "Useful Web Sites for the Investor.")

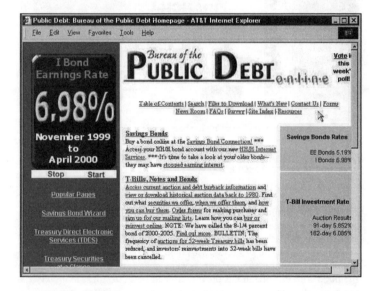

The U.S. Treasury department will let you buy government bonds online.

Debt and Equity

The most common distinction made between stocks and bonds is that stocks represent equity, meaning ownership or certain assets of a corporation, whereas bonds represent debt. In any case, both stocks and bonds represent a form of capitalization for a company or institution. Capitalization just means long-term financing. When a company or a government issues shares of stock or bonds, it is providing itself with a means of being capitalized or financed by investors. This is a very basic idea. In the early days of the American republic, the young revolutionary government was desperately poor following the War of Independence. The issuance of

$80 million in government bonds—essentially a loan—provided the Founding Fathers the funds they needed (the capitalization) to keep the country solvent.

The Museum of American Financial History is an excellent introduction to the role of debt and equity in the nation's history.

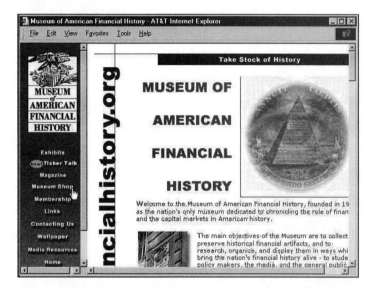

Investment Versus Speculation

Aside from the purely technical difference between the terms stock and bond, some stock market analysts have at times portrayed bonds as a vehicle of investment, whereas stocks have been portrayed purely as a means of speculation. The two terms are meant to suggest that whereas stock ownership is in some sense purely a gamble that prices of shares will go up, the buying of bonds, with their fixed return, represents the promise of a definite appreciation in value over time of money paid for the bond. This distinction has proven difficult because stocks themselves can be divided into purchases with an expected appreciation in value, meaning investments, and purchases that are just gambling on price increases.

The great dean of individual investing, Ben Graham, argued that investing, either through stocks or through bonds, was defined as any financial operation that would "guarantee safety of principal and a satisfactory return." Technicalities aside, it's true that bonds, unlike stocks, represent a guaranteed return.

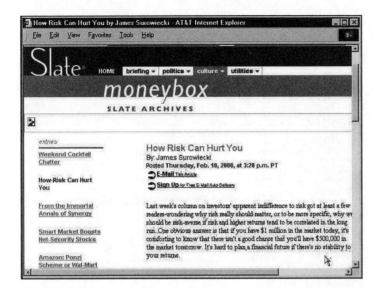

Online magazines such as Slate.com feature discussions on speculation and risk.

Principal and Return

Whether debt or equity, investors must keep in mind the two parts of an investment: the principal and the return. These are essential terms for keeping score as you establish your portfolio.

Principal is that amount of any investment that is initially put forward by the investor. Principal is what you put into a stock or bond of your own money. With a stock, principal is the purchase price of a single share of stock or the total amount paid for several shares. In the case of bonds, buyers receive a coupon stating a "par value," meaning the value of the bond at the time it is issued.

Return is the appreciation of principal in value in the course of time. You can think of it as the profit made on an initial investment. In the case of a stock, the return is represented by the increase or decrease in stock price in time over the price initially paid for the stock. A stock price depreciation is, you guessed it, a negative return, meaning a loss. (Some stocks also provide a return through an annual interest payment known as a dividend, but this form of stock income is increasingly rare.)

Bonds return in the form of interest accrued at a fixed rate on the par value of the bond. This is known as the "yield" of a bond—how much over and above the par value is paid to the bondholder at the time the bond matures. Keep in mind that bonds can be

resold for more than the par value at which they were issued. That
means bondholders may see a return simply by selling their
holdings at a profit, rather than waiting to collect the yield.

*A good way to
understand princi-
pal and return is
an investment cal-
culator like the
kind provided at
The Dismal
Scientist Web site.*

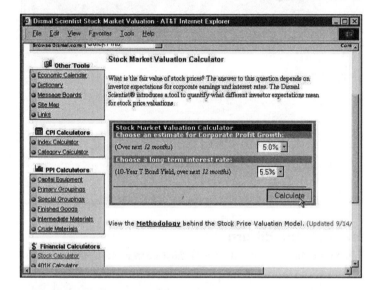

Understanding the Market

Bonds and stocks might be possible without a marketplace, but
they certainly wouldn't change hands as efficiently—or as frequently! The earliest markets grew out of informal buying and
selling relationships between a few market makers. For instance,
in the early days of Wall Street, auctioneers would spontaneously
hold bidding sessions for commodities such as tobacco, as well as
sales of shares of stock. The premise of markets back then, and
today, has always been to ensure liquidity for investors.

Liquidity is the ability for investors to cash out of their investments.
For example, if you own shares of stock in a company, you want
to be able to turn those shares into cash at some point in order to
realize your return or profit. A market for stocks ensures there
will be enough potential buyers or sellers to guarantee the ability
to cash out in this way.

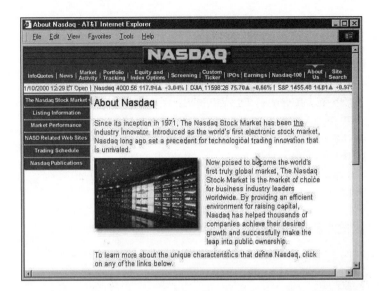

Markets such as the Nasdaq assure the liquidity that lets buyers and sellers make money.

How Brokerages Function

As exciting as the World Wide Web might be, it is really just a way of interacting with some fairly sophisticated trading systems behind the scenes. The machinery of trading has been developed over many decades by the professionals charged with trading stocks and bonds on behalf of clients, namely the brokerage firms. Every time you place an online trade, you are still connecting to the computers of a major brokerage house.

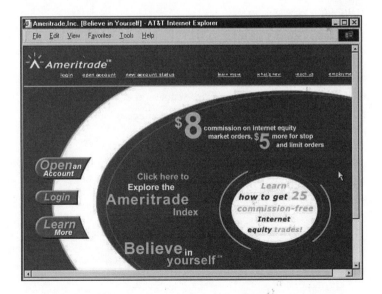

A major brokerage firm is at the heart of all e-trading.

Nature and Function of the Brokerage

Before you can understand the online broker system, you need to understand what a regular broker is. In a sense, a brokerage account is just like any other bank account, except that in the case of stocks, because of the change in stock prices, there is an element of risk. The broker's traditional role is to help individuals opening a securities account to decide what their appropriate level of risk is. This involves counseling the investor on personal financial goals, such as those discussed in Chapter 2, "Is Online Trading Right for You?"

The traditional role of the broker is to advise his clients on investment decisions.

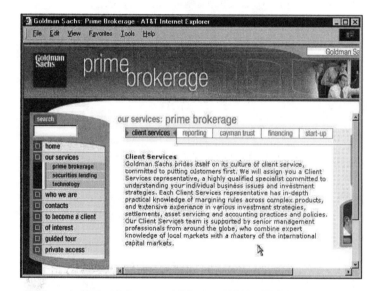

The broker, of course, also has the responsibility of placing buy and sell orders for stocks and bonds into the market on behalf of the investor. Brokerages purchase seats on the stock exchanges, allowing their individual brokers the privilege of submitting orders for consideration.

Electronic Trading Networks Mean the Ability to Trade More Shares Faster

Since the 1970s, the quaint atmosphere of the live trading floor familiar to investors from the New York Stock Exchange (NYSE) or the American Stock Exchange (AMEX) has given way somewhat to electronic trading networks. In these networks, a vast number of buy and sell orders—many more than the volume of the traditional exchanges—can be matched with one another. These exchanges often have longer trading hours—perhaps all day long in some cases, as with the Instinet system, inaugurated in 1969. The Nasdaq market is an electronic trading system where brokers' orders can be submitted in rapid fashion into a global computer system and compared for matches between bid and ask prices. This allows the average number of shares traded on the Nasdaq to greatly exceed the number of shares traded on the NYSE or AMEX. For example, in 1998 the average number of shares traded on a daily basis was more than 802 million, compared with 673 million for the NYSE.

The *bid price* is the price at which your broker submits an order into the market on your behalf to buy shares of stock.

The *ask price* is the price at which your broker submits an order into the market on your behalf to sell stock.

Paying for Stock Through a Broker

It used to be that markets functioned by brokers actually exchanging cash between one another on behalf of their customers in order to settle trades of stocks or bonds. Over the last 100 years, however, the securities industry has developed a modern system of settlements, or clearance, among brokers.

Clearance is the process by which funds are transferred between parties buying a given issue of stock or bonds and those holding the stock or bonds.

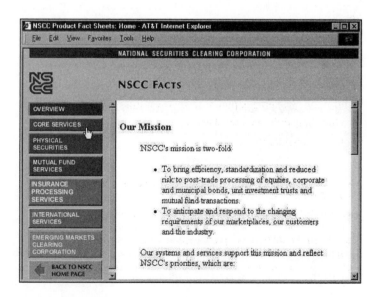

Private companies such as National Securities Clearing Corporation help to settle trades.

When you open an online trading account, just as with a traditional brokerage account you will have the option of essentially two types of accounts, each of which has different implications for how your trades are "cleared." It's important to understand these two types of accounts:

- **Cash account** Most investors will trade stock through a cash account. This means that the broker expects funds to be paid into the account to cover the cost of shares of stock or bonds purchased within a certain amount of time after the order is placed by a broker. Federal rules mandate the funds must be transmitted by the customer to a broker within three days of the initial order being submitted.

- **Margin account** A margin account, on the other hand, is used when a buyer cannot produce the funds to cover the purchase of stock. If the customer has sufficient funds in his or her account already, the brokerage will basically extend a loan to the customer to purchase the stock. Margin debt can also be used to avoid the tax consequences of withdrawing stock to purchase homes, cars, or other goods. Instead of cashing out holdings, the customer takes a bank loan based on his or her stock holdings. We'll look at margin trading in Chapter 13, "Trading on Margin and Trading Options."

Just Testing the Waters

Because of the three-day lag between when buy orders are submitted and when cash is due in a stock account, it is theoretically possible to undo the consequences of a stock trade if you have a change of heart. If you purchase stock and then see the next day that the price has dropped substantially below what you paid, you can simply fail to transmit the funds to your brokerage account, which will result in the purchase order lapsing. You might think this is a great way to gamble on a stock with an escape hatch. Don't do it: If you fail to transmit funds to cover your purchases, you will violate your agreement with your broker. At the very least, your trading privileges will be suspended for a period. If you repeatedly break the rules, your account could be dropped by your broker.

Mutual Funds

Mutual funds have been around since 1923, when the first one, the Massachusetts Investor Fund, was formed in Boston. The purpose of the mutual fund is to pool money from several investors in order to achieve leverage when buying and selling stocks or bonds or a combination of both. A mutual fund is essentially a managed portfolio of stocks or bonds. Shares of the fund are issued to investors in return for cash they put into the fund. When individuals take their money out of the fund, they sell shares back to the fund, which is known as a "redemption."

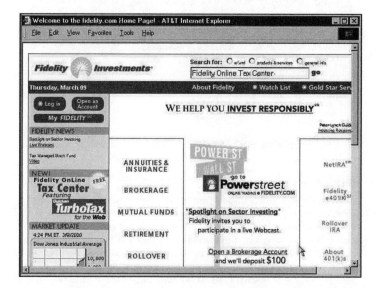

Pooling the investment money of individuals has made mutual funds like Fidelity a multi-billion dollar business.

When browsing for mutual funds, you'll be looking at two kinds:

- A *load* fund is one that charges a fee to the customer based on a percentage of the money the customer is investing in the fund. The legal maximum load that can be charged is 8.5% of the total amount invested.

- A *no-load* fund is one that does not charge any up-front fee in the form of a percentage of funds invested. However, no-load funds may still charge other fees to the customer, such as management fees.

*Sites like the
Motley Fool can
explain the intri-
cacies of mutual
fund fees.*

Go Prospecting

All mutual funds will provide a prospectus upon request, which is a document detailing the fund's fees and performance, among other things.
The prospectus will tell you what sorts of fees are charged, including the
load (if there is any), but also management fees and fees paid when you
cash out of the fund. In addition to the prospectus, you can find out
which funds are load or no-load by looking in the daily paper's financial
section. A table of mutual fund listings will contain the initials "NL" for
no-load funds.

What You've Learned

At this point you're well on your way to understanding what the
actual financial instruments are into which you'll be placing your
money. You should have a basic grasp of

- What stocks and bonds are.

- The function of a brokerage and what a mutual fund is.

- The nature of financial markets.

Next, it's time to take a look at how you research to find out
about the different brokers, funds, and stocks and bonds available.

CHAPTER 7

Signing Up with an Online Broker

By now you've figured out your financial profile, you've learned a little bit about stocks and bonds, and you're probably raring to move large amounts of your retirement money into the stock market. Okay, but wait a minute. You need an account with an online brokerage before you can start betting on your favorite Internet stocks, and the most complicated part of trading online (really!) is signing up with a broker. Hopefully the discussion in Chapter 3, "Selecting the Right Online Broker for Your Needs," and the materials in Chapter 5, "Researching Stocks, Bonds, and Mutual Funds Online," has helped you decide which broker you want to try. Perhaps you've decided to try a couple, as this book suggests. This chapter will help you set up those accounts.

An Outline of the Process

The application process essentially involves three steps:

1. You answer a series of questions about yourself and your investing goals, either directly on the Web site of your brokerage of choice or on a paper form that you print from your computer. Some brokers will let you apply by phone.

2. You print and mail a copy of the online questionnaire or the paper questionnaire you have already printed, along with a check for any funds necessary to set up the minimum balance for your account. (In some cases, your broker may not require a minimum deposit to start trading.)

3. You are approved for an account, your check is deposited to your account, and you are sent a password and ID to access your account. Or, you are informed that you have been turned down for an account and why.

What You'll Learn in This Chapter:

▶ An outline of the process.

▶ Preparing to fill out the form.

▶ Finding the right part of an e-broker's site.

▶ Completing the online form.

▼ **Try It Yourself**

Itchy Trading Finger?

Step number two may sound a bit confusing. Basically, you have a choice of whether to complete the form in writing on the paper form, by phone with a salesperson, or online by typing and clicking the mouse. But whichever option you choose, you will have to mail in a paper form to your broker's offices. The main point to realize is that in most cases, your broker must receive the forms from you in the mail before you can start trading. That means there will be a delay of a few days between the time you complete the application and the time your account is set up. A few brokerages (DLJ Direct, for example) will let you start trading as soon as you've completed the online form. However, in most cases you should not expect to start trading the same day.

Preparing to Fill Out the Form

Before you start the application process, here are a few good ways to prepare yourself:

- You'll need to have a couple of pieces of information handy to complete any investment decisions. Social Security numbers and birth dates for all members of the account are a minimum requirement. Expect to have to enter phone numbers for mailing and home addresses (if different from mailing address), as well as address and phone for your employer.

- Some brokers will also request certain financial information. They may, for example, ask that you pick your tax bracket from a list of options. Some will also ask about your salary and net worth. Whether you want to disclose this much information is up to you. However, bear in mind that the standard role of a broker, as mentioned in Chapter 6, "Understanding the Basics of Stock Trading," is to validate that you have sufficient personal wealth to engage in a pursuit that may end up costing you money. Making sure that you are solvent is actually part of the broker's fiduciary duty to protect you from taking actions that might bankrupt you.

The Company They Keep

If you've been walking around with the assumption that opening a brokerage account is all about finding the lowest fees, the requirements section of some brokerages will be your wake-up call. That's because, as mentioned in Chapter 3, some online brokers will actually deny you an application if you do not meet their criteria. One broker actually requires proof of prior trading experience simply to complete an application! Filling out the application is where you'll find out exactly which brokerages want your business and which will tell you to come back when you've got more money or more experience.

- You'll need your checkbook in order to make out payment for the minimum balance that must be sent along with your application, if a minimum balance is required.

- Finally, you should have a piece of paper and a pencil handy to write down certain information you'll receive that you will need later. For example, you'll want to record the ID name that will be assigned to you, as well as the password you receive, if in fact you receive these pieces of information during the application session. (In some cases, you will have to wait until after your application has been approved to receive this information.) Also, if you will be signing up for certain additional services, such as real-time quotes, it's good to make a note of this to make sure you get what you expected when your account is processed by the brokerage.

Find the Right Part of an e-Broker's Site

Filling out the forms for a new account is pretty simple. The drill is basically as follows:

▼ **Try It Yourself**

1. Surf to the Web address of your chosen brokerage.

2. Find the link to the section where you open a new account, usually listed as something obvious such as "Open an account."

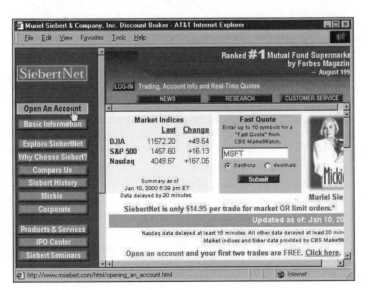

Surf to the "new accounts" section of your broker's Web site.

3. Choose which of several account types you want to complete—basic, premium, and so on.

4. Choose whether you want to complete an online form, fill out a paper form, or call your brokerage.

Choose the section for online applications.

Completing the Online Form

We'll assume you're completing the online form. If you're filling out the paper form or talking with your broker, the questions will be the same.

Try It Yourself ▼   Here's how to complete the form:

1. Decide if you will be opening an individual account or a joint account. The latter will obviously require you to enter additional data for additional account holders.

2. Decide if you will be setting up a cash account, a margin account, or some combination of the two. You may also be asked whether you would like the ability to trade options as well.

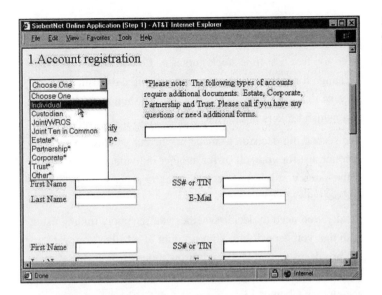

Decide which
account you want:
individual, joint,
IRA, and so on.

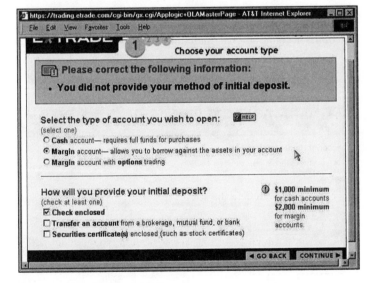

Decide if you
want a cash
account or margin
privileges with
options trading.

Accounting for Accounts

One of the most puzzling parts of applying for the online account
is the sudden requirement that you choose an account type. You
have essentially three decisions to make. The first is whether you
want an individual retirement account, which works the same as
an IRA you might obtain through your employer, but which does
not allow you to trade actively, or whether you would like a full

Of Marginal Interest

As we'll discuss in Chapter 13, "Trading on Margin and Trading Options," you must complete separate agreements to trade on margin and to trade options contracts. For that reason, you may want to skip both at this time and establish a basic account; you can always apply for these extra privileges later.

trading account for stock trading and so on, and what level of privileges you'd like. For instance, some trading accounts will offer you free real-time stock quotes and premium research in exchange for making a larger minimum initial deposit. Terms vary, so this is where you'll really want to shop around and compare which brokers offer what.

The second big decision to make is whether you are opening an account just for yourself or for another individual, say, a spouse. If the latter, you'll have to complete extra paperwork for the second account holder.

Finally, you need to decide whether you're simply trading using cash that you deposit into your account or whether you want margin privileges so that you can borrow money from your broker with which to trade. Again, we'll discuss the details of margin accounts in Chapter 13.

Try It Yourself ▼

1. Complete the personal information for yourself and any additional account holders, including name, address, Social Security number, level of investing experience, and so on. This may take several screens full of questions to complete.

Complete several screens of information about yourself.

2. You will need to declare if you are a company insider or a broker/dealer when you open your account. Be sure to mark the appropriate box.

Insiders Beware

Among other personal data, you will be asked whether you are a registered broker dealer, an employee of a securities firm, an owner or director of a public company, or a 10% or greater shareholder in a public company.

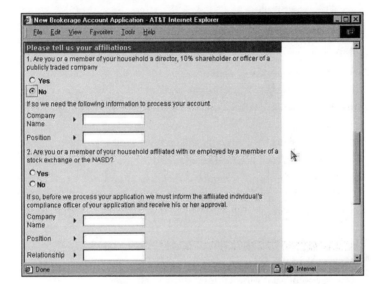

Answer whether you are a company insider or a broker dealer.

3. If you have chosen a cash account, you may be asked whether you want to place your cash balance in some kind of interest-bearing account.

Saving the Spoils

At any point in time, the part of your initial cash balance that has not been spent on buying stocks can be placed by your brokerage into an interest-bearing account, such as a money market fund. The options vary, and brokerages will give you a menu of different kinds of funds you can choose from. In most cases, this step will result in a prospectus being sent to you by mail, and so you can decide which funds you want to subscribe to at a later date.

You may be asked if you want your account balance maintained in a money market fund or another interest-bearing account.

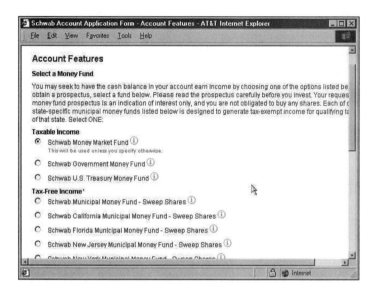

4. Some brokers will ask you to specify which method you prefer for receiving notification that trades have been processed—for example, through email or through a plain old snail mail letter. Some brokerages will automatically generate both kinds of confirmation.

5. If a broker is offering real-time stock and options quotes as a service in the account, you may need to complete separate agreements with the various stock exchanges.

6. Sign the "account agreement." After filling out the questionnaire, you'll be required to click on a form that represents your consent to certain terms established by the brokerage.

You're On Your Own Now

This is basically a way for your broker to limit his or her liability in the event your portfolio goes up in flames. In the traditional world of the full-service brokerage, a broker is trained on what stocks to recommend to you based on your level of investing experience, the amount of money you can afford to lose, and so on. In the online world, there is no broker to advise you, and so there is the possibility that you will commit certain trades that will lose you money—possibly more money than you can afford to lose. The account agreement basically says that you understand you are under your own supervision and that the brokerage cannot be held responsible if you blow your life savings. This should be your final warning that, as mentioned way back in Chapter 2, "Is Online Trading Right for You?" you've entered a world of "self-service"!

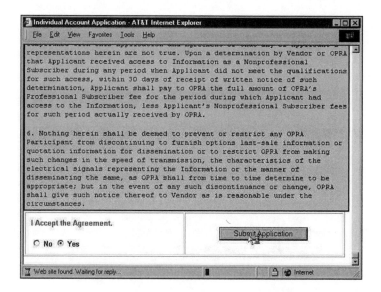

You'll be asked to read and sign (onscreen) the customer agreement.

7. You'll next be asked to assign yourself a username and a password. These can generally be any handle you want to give yourself, and any combination of letters you will remember that others can't figure out.

A Little Bit of Randomness

You should strive to make your password one that cannot be guessed simply by going through a dictionary of the English language; believe it or not, computer hackers can actually use computers to perform just such a search for simple passwords with amazing speed! If you're going to use the name of your cat, your dog, your goldfish, or your spouse, try and work some numbers or some random letters into your password to make it less obvious. Also, you should absolutely write down on a separate piece of paper the final username and password you decide on, in case you forget later.

8. The last step is to send in the printed application form. In some cases, you will have to print the form from your computer, sign it, and mail it to the brokerage. In other instances, the information will be gathered by your brokerage and a form will be sent to you in the mail to review and sign.

Assign yourself a username and a password.

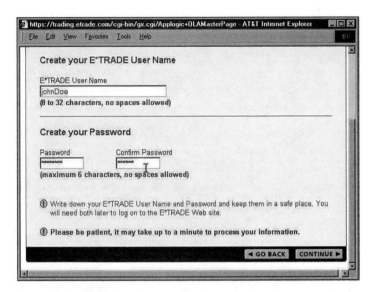

The last step is to print out the online form and mail it to your broker, along with your check for the initial deposit, if any.

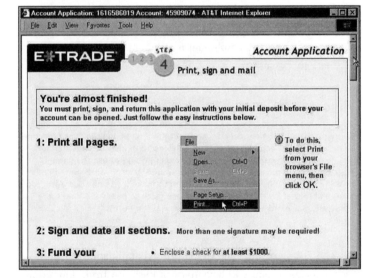

Signing the Dotted Line in the Electronic Age

Whether you choose to print out the online form or wait for a form to be sent to you in the mail, there will be a period of a few hours to a few days before you know if you've been approved to trade. Once you have been approved, you will still have to sign and return the application for your account to become active. In some cases, you can start trading as soon as you receive an email noting that you've been approved. However, if you do not mail in the signed form, your account privileges may be suspended by your brokerage until the form is received.

Be sure to keep a copy of the printed application for your records before you return it to your brokerage. Also, you may want to bookmark any Web pages that come up at the end of the application process if they contain receipts. For example, pages that are dynamically generated for you to print and sign can sometimes be bookmarked, which is good if you need to generate an extra copy of the form later.

Once you have been approved for online trading, you should receive both a letter in the mail and, probably sooner, a confirmation via email. Either or both of these documents should confirm your username and your password, or else assign you a new one of each if you were not asked to come up with one yourself in step 8. Read the confirmation letters carefully—they contain important information about trading rules, such as how much you can invest in your account, and any guidelines specific to your broker, such as handling of initial deposits and settlement of trades.

What You've Learned

Hopefully you have the patience to stomach the preceding instructions. Assuming you've made it through this chapter

- You've figured out how to find the application on an online brokerage site.

- You've figured out what materials and information you need to have ready before filling out the application.

- You're familiar with the basic steps of completing the online application.

If you've followed the steps and completed the application process, you will want to pause now, pat yourself on the back, and wait a couple of days to (hopefully) be approved. Good. Now it's on to making your first trade!

CHAPTER 8

Placing Your First Trade

This is it, the moment you've been waiting for. You're finally ready to place your first stock trade online. At this point, if you're really prepared, you've familiarized yourself with the basics of stock ownership, you understand why online brokers may be preferable to traditional trades through a full-service brokerage, and you're clear about what you are trying to achieve online.

Becoming Familiar with the Trade Screen

Once you've signed up with a broker and received clearance for a dollar amount to trade, you can use the ID and password given to you by your broker to access your account and start entering buy and sell orders.

What You'll Learn in This Chapter:

▶ The trading screen.

▶ Types of trades.

▶ Specifying the duration and price of an order.

▶ Canceling an order.

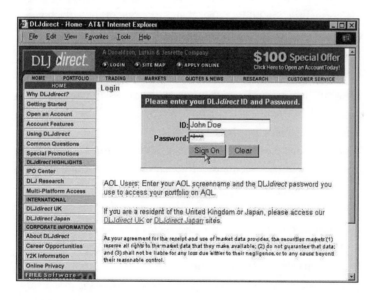

The first step is to log in to your account.

With most online brokers, it is possible to enter trades in a variety of fashions, including over the Web, using the phone, and, increasingly, through special handheld wireless devices (see Chapter 4, "Tools of the Trade: Hardware and Software Considerations"). Note that as of this writing, no online broker will accept trades through email. Don't send an email to any address at your broker's Web site and expect you've bought or sold stock!

We'll assume for the moment that you are buying through the Web. Unless you're using the special software discussed in Chapter 1, "The Pros and Cons of Online Trading," you will be entering your orders from a particular part of the broker's Web site. You will find that page usually under a section titled, simply enough, Trading or Placing Orders or Buy/Sell, which you should find after logging in to the Web site.

We'll assume for this initial stock trade that you are trading equities, meaning stock of publicly listed companies in major stock markets or on the over-the-counter market. Trading in bonds or options on underlying equities have their own idiosyncrasies, which will be covered later. Ditto for trades conducted "on margin." We'll assume too, for the moment, that you are trading during normal trading hours rather than using one of the after-hours or 24-hour exchanges. (See rules about Electronic Communications Networks in Chapter 17, "After-Hours Trading and Electronic Communications Networks.")

Most standard buy/sell order forms on the Web will have a few predictable elements. They include a field in which to type the name of the company whose stock you want to buy or sell and a button you can press to retrieve the stock ticker for that company. You can also retrieve a quote for the current price for that stock.

If you have signed arrangements in your initial application to receive real-time stock quotes, you'll automatically receive real-time quotes at this stage. If not, the quotes you get will be delayed by 15 minutes. Unless you are placing a limit order (see "Limit Orders" later in the chapter), the online broker does not guarantee that the price you end up paying will match any of the prices you see quoted, even those obtained through the broker's site. It's especially important, then, to pay attention to whether you are seeing real-time quotes or quotes that are delayed!

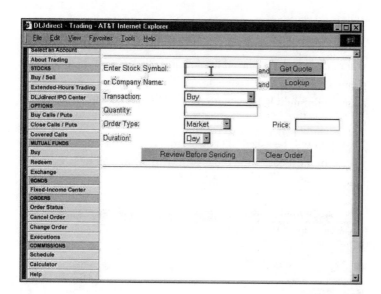

The standard trade order form.

Next, you'll be asked to choose whether you are buying shares, selling shares, or selling shares in stock that are not in your present account. Buying shares is simple enough. Selling shares will automatically allow you to select shares of stock that are in the portfolio for the present account.

If you choose the third option, to sell shares that are not in your account, it means that you have physical stock certificates that you can transfer to the broker by mail once the sale has been conducted. The brokerages are fairly strict that you must physically possess these stock certificates. In a few rare cases, you will be able to transfer shares (electronically) from another account at another broker.

Let's assume first that you are buying shares. The form will ask you to specify a quantity of shares you want to purchase. As mentioned earlier in this book, you are not confined to buying a set block of shares as with most full-service brokers. You can purchase as little as one share of stock, with the only upper limit on quantity being your dollar trading limit.

Remember, though, the commission you pay to the broker will depend upon the volume of stock you are buying, and the exact terms will vary slightly depending on the kind of account you have with the broker. For example, the broker may tell you that the entire trade will cost between $7.95 and $29.95 up to a certain amount of shares—say, the first 1,000 shares. Above 1,000 shares, you must factor in some additional amount for each share (usually pennies per share). Accounts for preferred customers maintaining a large minimum balance with the broker will usually get better rates.

Next, you will be asked to choose from a few possible kinds of trades. In most cases, the order form will allow you to select these kinds of trades from a drop-down list.

Specify the various order options.

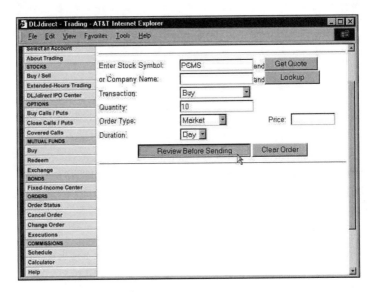

The order types you can choose from are as follows:

- A *market order* is the most common type of order. With a market order, you'll buy or sell shares at the best price the broker can obtain on the market at the time that your order is committed.

- A *limit order* is a way to control what you pay or what you make on buys and sells. The limit order lets you specify a maximum price above which you are not willing to buy, or a minimum price below which you're not willing to sell shares. If the broker can obtain a price that is more favorable than the limit you've specified, the broker will complete the transaction at that price.

- The third most common type of order is called a stop order. The *stop order* is basically a way of triggering a buy or sell market order when certain thresholds are reached. You decide to buy a stock before it goes too high above the current market price, or to sell a stock before it goes too low below the current market price.

The Different Trades Examined

Let's consider each of the three main order types in turn.

Market Orders

With the market order, bear in mind that you're not specifying a price, so you'll end up paying (or receiving, if you're selling) whatever the market is paying for that security at the time the order is actually processed on the exchange. In a certain sense you're going in blind because prices can change between when you place the order and when it is committed electronically with the market makers.

However, a market order gives you a guarantee that your requested buy or sell order will be carried out before the end of the trading day. In contrast, limit and stop orders, because they carry more stringent conditions, cannot always be filled by your broker. If for some reason the order does not go through, your broker will have to make it up to you in whatever way he has specified he will make good on failed trades—usually through a refund or some other kind of recompense.

Limit Orders

It's important to keep straight how limit orders work in the case of buying or selling stock. If you don't, you could end up either blowing a lot of money or missing an opportunity to purchase securities.

If you are trying to buy a security with a limit, you will set a maximum price—the limit price—above which you won't buy it. That price may be more than the current market price. For example, if the current price is $110, you might set a limit of $120, indicating that you're willing to pay *as much as* $10 more than the going rate, but no more. Your broker will strive to get the lowest possible price for you, and you can rest assured the price paid will not be higher than the upper limit you have set.

A limit order to sell securities from your account, on the other hand, means you're setting a price below which you will not sell the securities in question. If the price of the security suddenly drops below your minimum, your order to sell won't be completed. Again, your broker will strive to get you the highest bid for your shares of stock, but you can be sure you won't walk away with less than your limit.

From Floor to Ceiling

Keep straight the difference between a buy limit and a sell limit. You can think of a buy limit as a "ceiling." Above this ceiling, the security is too rich, and you won't buy. And think of your sell limit price as a "floor." If the market price of the security falls through this floor, you won't sell.

Limit orders can be especially useful in situations where a stock can be expected to be really volatile. For example, if you're buying a stock on the first day that it trades, you can expect that if it's a hot stock, its shares will jump up and down. If you know the price a stock is officially listed at, you may want to specify a buy order that is within a certain range of that listed price to avoid paying too much when the stock jumps at its open.

Likewise, if you're selling stock and you're afraid that a stock may drop while you're selling, you can use a limit order to make sure that if the stock drops too much, you will not sell.

We can generalize, then, the principles of using limit orders:

- Use a limit order when purchasing securities to avoid paying too much.

- Use limit orders when selling securities to make sure you make at least a specified minimum amount on your sale.

In the end, limit orders have an important drawback: they may not be processed. It's important to remember that the limit order sets certain conditions that must be met. Market conditions may not match your limit conditions, and for that reason, unlike with a market order, *your broker may not be able to complete your order.* If you absolutely must own the security, use a market order, which is guaranteed to be filled by your broker.

There's a Limit to Limits

The biggest mistake you can make with a limit order is to set a buy price that's below the current price or a sell price that's above the current price. If you do this, you may not be able to buy or sell securities at all.

Why? Let's take an example. Say a security you want to buy is trading at $110. You might set a limit order for $85. If you really want to own the security, you may be sabotaging yourself. You've set up conditions that are not likely to be met in the market. With an $85 target, you won't be able to buy the security unless by some chance it drops $25 dollars. *This is not what the limit order is for.* What you really want to do is set a limit price above the current price, but not higher than you're willing to pay. If your price is $115, for example, you have a chance, at least, to buy shares at the current market price, but you know you won't have to pay more than $115.

Similarly, don't set a sell limit far above current prices. Let's say you own a security that you purchased for $100. You see it's trading at $110, and you decide to make a profit. If you set a limit price *above* $110—say, $125—you won't be able to sell your securities at all unless the price in the market suddenly jumps by $15.

We can make the following general rules:

- Set a limit price to buy that is above the current price.
- Set a limit price to sell that is below the current price.

The Stop Order

A stop order can be thought of as the mirror image of a limit order. A stop order to sell sets a price at or below which you want to sell securities you own. If the price of the security hits your stop price, a market order will be initiated to sell the security at whatever the market price is. For that reason, a stop order can also be thought of as a conditional, or delayed, market order: Once triggered, a stop order just becomes a market order.

The point of the sell stop order is to make sure you sell securities if they start to drop precipitously. A stop order can be used to trigger a sale of your portfolio holdings when continuing to hold the securities might erode the profit you've made on them to date.

Suppose, for example, that you own 100 shares of Microsoft stock at a cost of $100. If the current price in the market is $120, and you see the price is starting to drop, you might set a stop order at $115. That means that if the price drops by five points, you want to dump the shares so that you can still get out at a profit.

A *stop order to sell* specifies a floor that, if broken, triggers a sale in the form of a normal market order.

In contrast, a stop order to buy specifies a price that, if reached, will prompt you to buy the securities. For example, let's suppose shares of Microsoft stock are trading at $100. Suddenly, the price starts to climb rapidly. Sensing that Microsoft is on a tear, you want to get in before the stock gets so expensive that you can't afford it. You set a stop order to buy if the price reaches $110, meaning that you're willing to buy at $110 or any price above or below that.

A *stop order to buy* specifies a ceiling that, if broken, triggers a buy market order.

The following table summarizes the two types of stop orders.

Stop Orders to Buy and Sell

The Security's Price...	You Initiate a Stop Order to...	In Order to...
Starts to drop sharply	Sell the stock if it should fall below a certain level	Drop the stock before you lose too much money
Starts to climb sharply	Buy the stock if it goes above a certain price	Pick up the stock before it gets out of your buying range

Stop and Think Before You Stop

It's extremely important to understand the implications of stop orders because you could lose a lot of money if you don't. We say that a stop order is in some senses a mirror of a limit order because when it triggers a purchase or a sale, the stop price sets no limit on how much you'd be willing to pay in the case of a purchase, or on how little you'd be willing to accept in the case of a sale. Because the stop order actually leads to a market order being executed, you will wind up not with a set price, but rather whatever the best price is in the market at the time the stop order is triggered. If you're lucky, the market order will be close to the stop price you specified, but there's no guarantee of that.

To return to the preceding example, if you set the stop order to sell when the price drops to $115, it's possible the price could continue to drop once it breaks $115. Between the time your stop order is triggered and when the actual sale is processed, the price in the market might drop to $95, or even lower. If that's the best price in the market at the time of execution, you'll get $95 dollars, losing $5 on the shares you hold at $100. If the price continues to drop, you could end up getting even less—or losing even more, put another way.

In contrast, if you set a stop order to buy Microsoft shares at $110 and the price keeps climbing between when your stop order is triggered and when your purchase is actually transacted, the price could keep climbing to $125. That might be fine if you're willing to pay that much, but it could be a big mistake if it's more than you wanted to pay. As a rule, then:

- Stop orders to sell are dangerous because they set no limit on how little you might end up making on a sale.

- Stop orders to buy are dangerous because they set no limit on how much you might pay once the order to buy is triggered.

To limit these deleterious effects of stop orders, securities traders sometimes use what are known as "stop-limit" orders. We'll discuss these next.

Stop-Limit Orders

Sometimes the solution to the problems of stop orders is to combine them with limit orders. If you set a stop order to buy a certain security once a certain price is reached, you might want to set a simultaneous limit order that sets a maximum on how much you're willing to pay, or a minimum on how little you'll accept in the case of a sell stop order. This combination of a stop order and a simultaneous limit order is called a *stop-limit* order.

For example, if you set a stop order to buy shares of Microsoft once they reach $115, you might set a simultaneous limit order at $120. That would tell your broker that you're willing to purchase Microsoft if it hits $115, but that you don't want to have to pay

Know When to Stop, When to Limit

Be especially careful not to confuse the uses of limit and stop orders. If a security is trading at $115 and you want to purchase it only on the condition that the price drops to $95 (or below), then you want to set a *limit order* to buy at $95, *not* a stop order to buy at $95. If you did the latter, you broker would buy the security for you at any price above $94. The result is that you would probably end up paying $115, the going rate, or even more, which is exactly what you were trying to avoid.

A good e-broker site will warn you if you are mistakenly placing a stop order.

more than $120 for it. If Microsoft stock should hit $115, a limit order will be triggered and you'll pay the best price in the market, but not more than $120.

Similarly, if you've set a stop order to sell your securities should the price drop below $115, you might want to also set a limit order at $100, meaning that you won't sell the security if the price you can get in the market is less than what you originally paid for it, namely $100. This would protect you from potentially limitless loss when you go to sell securities.

Stop Me Before I Stop Again

Because stop orders have such potential for loss if not used properly, a good e-broker will alert you when you are mistakenly placing a stop order like the kind just discussed. For example, if you try to set a stop order to buy that is below the current price, your e-broker's site should warn you—through a pop-up dialog box or an HTML page—that you are placing a stop order that is too low, and that will cause an instant market order at the current price. You may want to check out whether your e-broker provides such warnings by trying out a couple of dummy trades, which you can always cancel before confirming.

Bear in mind that not all online brokerages allow you to place a stop-limit order over the Web, but rather require you to phone in such an order because of the increased complexity of a stop-limit order. Also, some securities cannot be bought or sold with a stop-limit order. Generally, these are stocks trading on the over-the-counter bulletin board, or stock trading for under $1.

Price and Duration

OK, so you've finally chosen the type of order you want. Once you've made your selection, you'll be asked to set the price if the order is a stop or limit order. Furthermore, if your order is a stop or limit order, you will also be asked to choose the duration that the order is good for. Brokers may offer different duration options from a pull-down list. The likely options will be *same day* and *good 'til canceled*.

Same day means limit orders expire at the end of the trading day. *Good 'til canceled* means your limit order or stop order will remain until you have explicitly issued a cancel order, or until the order naturally expires within a standard time frame (usually 90 days), whichever comes first.

Once you have filled in the required fields of the order form, you'll have a chance to review the order and make any changes. Note that the total amount for the trade should be listed, including the commission for the trade. If anything doesn't look right about the total listed for the order, don't submit it! Call the customer support line for your broker to see if there may be a miscalculation in the broker commission.

Remember It 'Til It's Canceled

If you enter a good 'til canceled order, bear in mind that the order will sit in your account waiting to be executed should the market conditions change to meet the specifications of your limit order. You don't want to be blind-sided if an order comes through and you've forgotten you're on the hook to pay for it. For that reason, you should check your portfolio now and then to remind yourself of the orders you have outstanding.

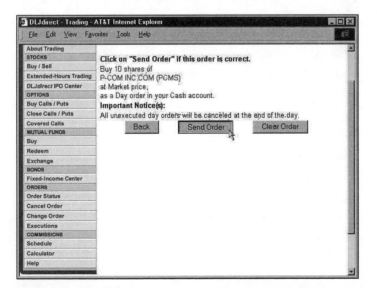

Make sure your order is correct before submitting it.

If everything looks good with the order, push the button to submit it. You've made the trade!

Confirmation

You'll receive confirmation of your order in a couple of ways. You should get an instantaneous confirmation in your browser that your order has been placed. *This doesn't mean you've bought any stock yet*. It simply means your request has been sent to your broker.

Your browser should show if your order has been received.

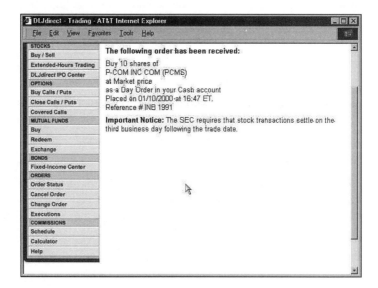

The other way to confirm the status of your order is to check the Portfolio section of the site, which is a standard feature of any online brokerage account. In the portfolio you will find a list of the stocks you currently own, including the price paid for the stock and the quantity held. You should also see a section for order status.

The Order Status screen.

Clicking on this section will give you a list of orders placed, with a status line. For example, if you placed a limit order to buy shares at a certain price and specified that the order is good 'til canceled, you may see the term "accepted" in the Status column and a note "good 'til canceled" under the column for Duration, which just means that your order is known by the system. The following are the types of order status messages you should see:

- *Pending* means your broker has not yet consented to execute the order with an exchange. Reasons an order can be pending include delays encountered while the computer system verifies your account privileges to make sure you are currently permitted to trade. During high traffic times, there's more likelihood your order will be delayed and you'll see the pending notice.

- *Accepted* means your order has been OK'd by your broker and is waiting to be completed.

- *Open* refers to a good 'til canceled limit order that is waiting to be executed. You will see this status until the order naturally expires or until it is successfully executed, whichever comes first.

- *Executed* means that your order has been sent to the exchange and has been successfully transacted. If it was a buy order, you have successfully purchased the securities. If it was a sell order, you have successfully sold the securities when you see the Executed status.

- *Partially Executed* means that a limit order was successfully transacted, but only for a portion of the shares specified in your order. If you placed an order to purchase 500 shares of a certain stock at a limit price of $150, but only 200 shares could be obtained at that price, those 200 shares will be purchased and the order will be considered partially executed. Partial orders will usually be completed only if round lots can be found that satisfy the terms. In other words, three shares at $150 would not be purchased in our example because anything less than 100 shares constitutes an odd lot, as mentioned in Chapter 1.

- *Mixed* orders are partially executed orders where the unfilled portion of the order has been canceled. This usually results, obviously, when you execute an order that has already been partially filled.

- *Canceled* is what you'll see after submitting a cancel order for a specific trade.

Once your order has been received and approved, your broker will fill the order by making a buy or sell transaction in the market for you. This will happen at the market price if it's a market order. If the order is a limit order, it will remain open until the conditions are such that it can be filled.

Once the order has been filled, the following confirmations take place:

- The order status changes to Executed (or Partially Executed).

- You receive a confirmation by email that your order has been filled.

- The Balances and History sections of your portfolio will reflect the changes in the securities held in your account, and the change in your cash position (that is, an increase for a sale, or a decrease for a buy).

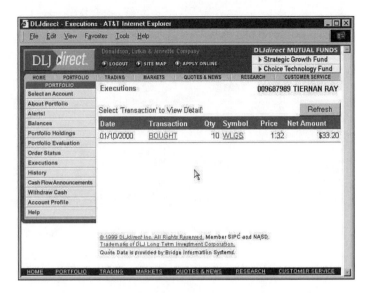

The Balances and History sections of your account will show you what you've purchased.

- Finally, you'll receive a confirmation by ordinary mail anywhere from several days later to perhaps a week later.

Changing Your Order

As long as an order has not yet been accepted you can make changes to it, including modifying the requested number of shares, changing the duration of your order, or changing from a market order to another type of order. Bear in mind that you can only change an open, a mixed, or a partially executed order. You can change the type of the order (market, limit, day, good 'til canceled, and so on), the price (if the order is a stop or limit order), and you can reduce or increase the number of shares requested.

Canceling Your Order

Before you move on to more sophisticated trading—in fact, before you make any trades at all—you should know how to cancel orders. A broker's site may give you the option to cancel an order right from the status screen, or there may be a separate section you must click in order to cancel the order.

The Final Verdict

The final confirmation will come when you receive your periodic statement of holdings. This mailing, usually sent to you once a month, should show all of your account activity up until the time the statement was printed, including the buy or sell orders completed, under what terms they were filled, and your new account balances.

The Cancel Order
screen.

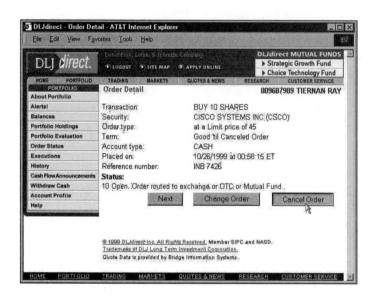

In either case, the cancel procedure should be as simple as selecting the order and pressing the Cancel button. You will be asked to
review the cancel order after pushing the Cancel button.

You will be asked
to review the can-
cel order after
submitting it.

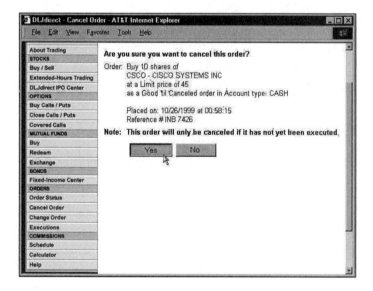

There are a few caveats here:

- First, you cannot cancel an order that has already been completed. Only pending or open orders can be canceled, or

orders that have only been partially completed in the case of limit or stop orders that may have multiple parts. If you feel a completed order was an error on your broker's part, you must pursue a grievance, not file a cancel. We'll talk more about this in Chapter 11, "Troubleshooting and Ending Your Online Trading Relationship."

- Second, any change in a limit order once it has been accepted by the system is really a cancel of that limit order. Because limit orders must wait in your broker's queue behind normal market orders, if you change a limit order (thereby initiating a new limit order), you may get bumped down the line a few places, thereby narrowing the chances of your limit order being processed at all. If timing is of the essence in placing your order, you may want to refrain from changing a limit order unless the change is really important.

- Also bear in mind that if you cancel an order that was a change to an earlier order, the earlier order will be reinstated. It's important that you understand the consequences of canceling a change of an earlier order. For example, say you place an order to purchase 100 shares of a stock and then change that order to 50 shares. If you then cancel the second order, you will end up with the first order you submitted—an order to purchase 100 shares.

What You've Learned

This chapter has given you the basic elements you need to conduct a simple stock trade. The points you should understand are

- The essential steps to completing the buy or sell order onscreen.

- The main variations in the kinds of orders you can enter and what they mean.

- How to confirm, change, or cancel your order.

PART III

Managing Your Accounts

CHAPTER 9

Managing Your Portfolio

Whether you're putting your entire life savings into online stock trading or just putting a toe in the water, there are at least a few good reasons to keep a tally of how your investment portfolio is doing. They include

- Watching yourself get rich by the minute/hour/day

- Moving money into and out of your trading account

- Preparing yourself for tax time

- Making sure you keep your stocks, bonds, and mutual funds integrated with your household finances

This chapter will give you some ideas about how you can start to actively track and manage your growing portfolio of investments.

Portfolio Tasks

What does it mean to manage your portfolio? Basically, it's the care and feeding of your investments. Keeping up with how much you're making is just part of it. You may also want to borrow against your stock portfolio. You may want to compare how your portfolio is doing to the performance of the rest of the market. You'll definitely have to deposit funds to your account now and then to maintain a balance from which to trade.

In sum, the following are things you can do online and offline to maintain your portfolio:

- See a precise history of every purchase or sale of a security you've made through your broker, as well as deposits or withdrawals of cash from your account.

What You'll Learn in This Chapter:

▶ What the portfolio tasks are.

▶ Information you can get online.

▶ How to read your portfolio online.

▶ How to manage cash in your account.

▶ Other things you can do online.

▶ More advanced portfolio management.

- Obtain a detailed listing of how your stocks, bonds, or mutual funds have increased in value.

- Construct model portfolios that allow you to plan where to put your money.

- See prices for your securities listed in decimal format or in fractions.

- View orders that have yet to be executed. For example, if you entered a trade as a limit order, meaning you want your brokerage to wait to buy only when certain conditions are met, that order can live on for weeks until the price is right. An online portfolio can tell you if you're still committed to spending money for such trades.

- See how much profit or loss you've incurred in your investments.

- Withdraw cash from your cash account.

- Set "alerts," little warnings that will be sent to you via email, or perhaps to a pager or cell phone, telling you that a stock has reached a price that you expressed interest in knowing about. You can also be notified of news stories concerning your stock.

- Take out a loan, if you have a margin account with your broker.

- Deposit funds through check or wire transfer to maintain your trading balance.

- Send stock certificates to your broker to cover short-selling transactions. (We'll talk about this in Chapter 13, "Trading on Margin and Trading Options.")

Kinds of Information You'll Find in an Online Portfolio Tool

It sounds simple, but it's not. You need to keep track of how much you've actually paid for a share of stock, an interest in a mutual fund, or a bond. Every month you'll receive a paper form from your broker telling you how much your shares of stock, mutual funds, or bonds are worth. However, these forms won't necessarily list how much you've actually spent in the first place to purchase those assets. Nor will they tell you how much the value of the assets has increased or decreased, percentage-wise, from what you originally spent. The paper receipt tells you only the current value (at the time the paper form was mailed) of your holdings.

There are certain minimum pieces of information you will want to see in your portfolio display:

- Current value of your stocks, bonds, or mutual fund ownership.

- Cost. This is basically how much you originally paid for shares of stock, bonds, or mutual fund ownership. This figure will change over time as, for example, stocks split, generating additional shares.

  The cost, which can include not just the price of the shares but also the fees paid to your e-broker for the transaction, is often referred to as your *basis* in a stock.

- Realized or unrealized gains. This basically means any money you have collected in profit or loss on your assets—that is, by cashing them in—or gains you have yet to realize. This figure basically equals "current value minus cost."

- Order history. This will be an accounting of the buy and sell orders you've submitted for stocks, bonds, and mutual funds, usually with time of day and price at which the order is expected to be executed.

How to Read Your Portfolio Online

Even if you grasp the basic information that should be mentioned in your portfolio statement, you still may feel like you're looking at ancient Greek when you go online and try to decipher how much your assets are worth. Following is a quick rundown of how to look at your broker's statement of your holdings. Bear in mind that your particular broker may list things slightly differently in his or her portfolio tracking system.

Managing this information may or may not be automatic. If your online broker provides a full suite of portfolio management tools, you should see all of these figures automatically displayed in a series of rows and columns in your Web browser. Usually, you will find the information on a section of the Web site called My Portfolio or simply Portfolio.

The Current Value Display

The current value display will tell you what your assets are worth, based on the last closing price. For example, if you're looking at stocks, you'll be looking at the closing price from the New York Stock Exchange, Nasdaq, and so on.

Try It Yourself ▼

1. You should see the ticker symbol and the name of the stock or mutual fund (or, alternatively, the CUSIP symbols and names of your bonds) in the left-hand column.

2. The number of shares of stock or mutual funds will follow; bonds will be listed as the number of bonds held.

3. You'll see a figure for "price," which really means the latest price at which the stock or mutual fund traded (or the latest par value, for a bond), *not* the price at which you originally purchased the security.

4. You'll see the change in the security on that day, either in points or in percentage terms.

5. You'll see the total current value of the holdings. Each line will be totaled by multiplying the stock or mutual fund's current price (or the bond's par value) by the number of shares (or bonds) held.

▲

On that last score, it's important to realize that the "total current value" of your portfolio will be listed as either *long value* or *short value*, depending on whether the securities were purchased in the normal manner (long) with cash, or as a short position (short), meaning the securities have been borrowed from your broker, or on margin, using a loan. We're going to talk about another kind of security, called options, in Chapter 14, "Getting Into Options Trading," but it's worth noting here that options contracts that you purchase will show up in the long-value side of your balance sheet.

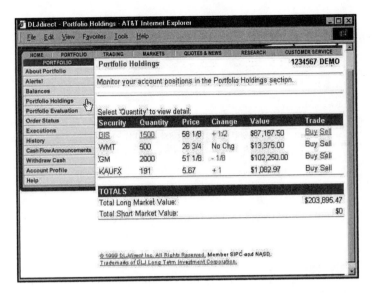

The current value display.

Gains

The preceding information will give you only the present value of all your holdings. In addition, though, you'll want to know whether you're currently making any money.

Either as part of the same display as "current value" or as part of a separate display, you should see columns listed as gains or losses, either realized or unrealized.

Realized gains or *losses* refer to money made or lost on an actual sale of assets. *Unrealized gains* tell you what kinds of gains you have earned on your assets up to the present, assuming you have not yet sold the securities in question. Obviously, if you're currently losing money on these investments, you'll be shown *unrealized losses*. Again, if you are selling securities short, the amount of gains or losses will reflect the ultimate price to be paid to your brokerage versus the value at which you have sold securities borrowed from your broker.

Here's how to read gains and losses:

▼ **Try It Yourself**

1. You should see the ticker and name of the security on the left-hand side, followed by a column labeled either Realized Gain/Loss or Unrealized Gain/Loss.

*The gains and
losses display.*

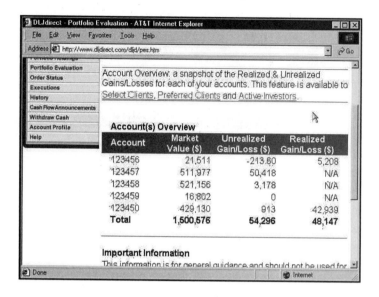

*The gains and
losses display.*

2. By clicking on the ticker symbol of the security or by scrolling
   to another point in the Web page, you should see a breakdown
   of the realized or unrealized gain figure. The following table
   shows how gains are generally computed.

Calculating Your Gains

Ticker Symbol	Principal	Cost	Gain/Loss
	(number of shares × current price per) share	(number of shares × purchase price, plus fees and commissions)	(Principal–Cost)

Example:

LU	100 shares × $ 50.00 = $5,000.00	100 shares × $ 25.00 + $ 20.00 = $2,520.00	$5,000.00 − $2,520.00 = $2,480.00

No Gain, No Pain

Gains may be one of the trickiest parts of tracking your portfolio. Typically,
gains reported in a portfolio tool on the Web will list strictly how much
your assets have made or lost in the time since you purchased them. This
is the last price at the time the stocks or bonds were cashed in (or the
price at the time unrealized gains were calculated) minus the original
amount you paid. However, as you'll see in Chapter 10, "Understanding
Your Taxes" you also want to subtract from that amount the fees that

you paid because your taxes will be charged based on the amount you actually made after subtracting fees, as well as the share price. For this reason, it's important to subtract fees when calculating gains for tax-reporting purposes. We'll talk more about this in the next chapter.

Managing Cash in Your Account

Understanding what you've won or lost is the simplest part of portfolio management. You can only trade so long as you have money to spend, right? For that reason, while you keep track of how your stocks rise and fall, you also need to keep a watch out for how your cash is moving in and out of your account. As you'll recall from Chapter 7, "Signing Up with an Online Broker," there are two main types of accounts: cash accounts and margin accounts. Again, we'll talk about buying on margin in Chapter 13, but you'll see information for both in your Balances section, assuming you actually have both kinds of accounts.

In brief, here's what you should see:

- Assets. This category lists the total current value of your stock and mutual fund shares and your bonds. It also lists cash you've deposited into the account, and money market funds if you've arranged to place unused cash in a money market fund. (Remember from Chapter 7 that you will have the option of putting your unused cash into a money market or mutual fund.) Note that this category lists both assets on which you may be losing money as well as assets on which you're running a profit.

- Liabilities. This category lists any amounts you owe your broker. The most common reason you'll see an amount listed for liabilities is because you've purchased shares of stock or mutual funds or bonds, and you have yet to send in the funds to cover those purchases. The amount you owe will usually be listed under Cash, meaning you have to send that amount in cash to your broker via check or wire transfer. Two other categories, Short Market Value and Securities Owed, pertain specifically to selling short. You can ignore these for the moment; we'll talk more about them in Chapter 14.

- Your total equity, which equals your assets minus liabilities. This is how much money you have over and above any cash or stock owed.

- Lastly, you may see an amount for how much you can spend on margin. This may be listed as Buying Power. (Buying power is explained in detail in Chapter 13.)

The basic asset and liability display.

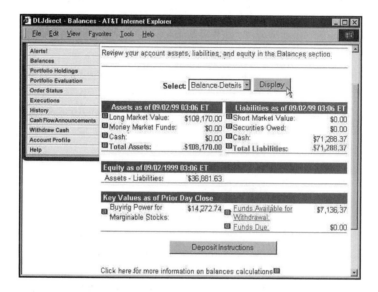

Income and Interest

In addition to computing your present assets and liabilities, you'll want to keep tabs on money that you're going to earn at a future date. If you own stocks that pay *dividends* or fixed-income securities that pay interest, such as bonds, you'll want to know how much money you can expect to receive from those securities down the line.

Dividends are regular payments you receive for each share of stock you own. In stock market talk, dividends are often referred to as "income" because they provide a regular annual gain over and above the appreciation of the stock itself. Dividends paid tend be small amounts, on the order of a few pennies to a few dollars per share per year.

You'll likely find this information listed in a separate part of the Web site as a section titled Cash Flow or Cash Flow Announcements. Here you should see a few different figures listed. These figures are time-dependent, meaning the amounts listed are expected to change depending on how far into the future you look. For that reason, the Web page will usually feature a drop-down dialog box giving you a few options of how far into the future you want to look. The figures listed include

- **Projected Principal**   This is the amount in cash dividends you can expect to receive for the next week, month, quarter, and so on.

- **Projected Income**   This is the amount in interest payments from bonds that you can expect to receive within the specified time period.

- **Total Projected Cash**   You'll see a listing of how much cash you can expect to have in your account when dividends and interest to be paid are added up.

- **Current Money Fund**   This is the amount of money currently in money market funds.

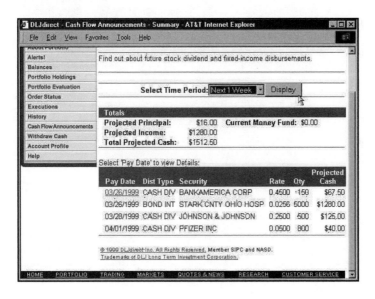

The basic dividends and interest display.

Divining Your Dividends

What's the easiest way to find out what kind of dividends your account is paying out? Look in the paper. Newspapers such as *The Wall Street Journal* list the amount of dividends paid out per share in the stock market tables. Likewise, the interest or "coupon" on a bond will be listed in the tables for bond price quotations.

The Disappearing Dividends

Dividends are not a certainty of investing. How much is paid out varies from stock to stock, and some companies pay no dividends to their shareholders. The interest in dividends, moreover, has varied quite a bit over time. In general, during periods of market speculation when investors are focused on catching the latest hot, fast-growing stocks, there is a focus on earnings and sales growth and a decreased interest in the dividends paid out by stocks. Also, with lower interest rates, and with the re-institution of the capital gains tax in the last decade, there's been a shift away from income by investors and a movement toward capital appreciation, in the form of capital gains, as the preferred means of investment profit.

Depositing Money

You don't necessarily have to put money into an online brokerage account in order to start trading. As mentioned in Chapter 8, "Placing Your First Trade," some brokerages will let you start trading with no cash in your account. However, you'll have to start making deposits to your account in order to pay for securities you've purchased.

Down to the Wire

A stock market rule called "Regulation T," established by the Securities and Exchange Commission (SEC), a federal regulatory body, states that investors must deliver funds to their broker to cover their securities purchases within three business days of when the purchase order is placed with their broker. That means that if you buy stocks on Monday, you have to get funds to your broker to cover the purchase by Thursday or your order will expire and you'll lose the shares. There is usually a two-day grace period in addition. If the third day arrives and you've not yet sent funds, you can still make the deadline provided you can get to your bank before it closes and wire the funds.

There are a variety of methods to deposit funds to your account. They are

- Send a personal check. Your account will be credited as soon as the check is received by your broker before the check has cleared. You can send a check by mail or by overnight mail. Usually, your broker will have different addresses for the two options.

- Wire funds. To wire funds to your broker you will have to complete a form at your bank, including information about the name and address of the bank branch where your brokerage receives wire transfers and your own name and brokerage account number. Most of this information should be available on your broker's site. There is usually a fee charged by your bank for this service, on the order of $15 per transaction.

- Transfer funds directly. Increasingly, online brokers are providing ways you can transfer money instantaneously from your checking or savings account to your brokerage. In most cases this will be an additional service of your broker, and though there probably won't be a fee involved, you will have to complete an additional application with your broker and wait for approval and activation of funds transfer privileges. Also, brokerages are increasingly offering traditional bank account products. If you open a checking account with your broker, you may be able to transfer funds easily and with no extra fees between your checking account, for example, and your trading account.

- Use credit cards and money orders. Many brokerages will not accept money orders or credit cards. Some may accept cashier's or bank checks for larger transactions—say, more than $10,000. Individual brokers maintain different rules about how large a transfer is sufficient for such transactions.

Withdrawing Money

Keep this simple fact in mind: The money in your account is yours. That means that at any time, you're entitled to withdraw the cash you've put into your account. Withdrawing funds from your account can happen in a few ways:

- Your broker can mail you a check. This is the slowest means.

- Your broker can wire funds to your bank account. This is a little quicker than a check—you can get funds the same day, in a matter of hours.

• Your broker can deposit funds into your checking or savings account. This is only the case if you open a bank account with an online broker offering traditional banking services. Obviously, this is the fastest option.

The easiest way to withdraw funds is by having your broker mail you a check, which you deposit into your bank account. In some cases, this is handled by calling the support line of your brokerage and asking the firm to cut a check to the address you give them. However, most e-brokers should provide a form online where you can request the check in a specific amount.

You can in many cases initiate a check request right from your e-broker's home page.

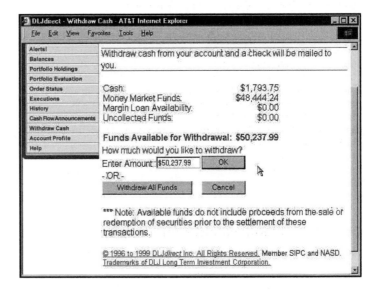

If you require the funds quicker, you can request a wire transfer from your brokerage account directly into your bank. This will usually get the money into your hands within a matter of hours. To do so, do the following:

Try It Yourself ▼

1. Assemble the following information: your name and the number of your brokerage account; the name and address of your bank; your name as it appears on your bank account records and your bank account number; and something called the "ABA routing code" for your bank. Don't worry what that is. You can get it simply by calling your bank.

2. List this information on a fax to your broker listing the amount to be transferred to your bank account.

3. Fax the document to the fax number provided by your broker. ▲

Brave New Banking

You may wonder why, if you're trading online, you still have to go to the rather clumsy extreme of wiring funds to and from your bank account to your brokerage account, or sending a check to cover your trades. The reason is that the commercial banks, which operate your checking account and your savings and IRAs, have evolved separately from the investment banks that have run the brokerages for the past 60 years. As a result of the Great Depression, Congress passed the Glass-Steagall Act in 1933, which formally separated these functions that had previously been performed as part and parcel of the same business.

In 1999, however, Congress repealed the Glass-Steagall Act. That means commercial banks are now free to open brokerage services, and investment banks are free to offer IRAs, checking accounts, and so on. The result for you, the online investor, is that you'll increasingly be offered traditional bank accounts as competitive offerings of online brokers. You should shop around to see what kinds of banking services brokers will offer you. Most brokerages with an offline, full-service presence (such as Schwab or DLJ Direct) will at the very least offer checking accounts and credit cards, although they may require a minimum account balance for such. An inevitable side-effect of all this will be the ability to move money effortlessly out of checking accounts and into your brokerage account, and vice versa, making the entire process of managing cash flow much easier.

Wire Early, Wire Often

If you're in a real rush for funds, make sure you find out the hours of the day during which your broker will process fund transfers. Many brokers will not process requests for wire transfers faxed after a certain time of the day until the following business day. Likewise, your bank has to be open during the time that your broker is wiring the funds.

Other Cash Management Features

Several things you can do with cash will require some further work on your part. They include

- Setting up a money market fund. As explained earlier, money in a cash account that is not being used to pay for stocks you've bought can be swept into a money market account where it will earn interest. Money market funds are usually a free offering of most brokerage accounts, but they usually require an extra set of paperwork to be completed.

- Individual Retirement Accounts. Brokerages are increasingly offering to place your cash balance into IRAs, many of them without the traditional management fee.

How Far Does Your Broker Go?

The extra services mentioned here may depend in some cases on how sophisticated your broker is and on the kind of account you've established. As mentioned in Chapter 3, "Selecting the Right Online Broker for Your Needs," services offered vary quite a bit from broker to broker and within brokers. You should keep in mind extra services such as IRAs and money market funds when considering which broker to go with.

- Margin loans. Margin loans are low-interest loans provided against assets in your account. Brokerages will allow you to borrow up to 50% of the value of the securities in your account. If you've built up a valuable position in certain stocks, bonds, or mutual fund shares, this is a quick way to obtain heavy borrowing power. To obtain margin loans, you must first establish margin account privileges, which will usually involve extra paperwork, and you'll most likely have to have a cash balance above a certain minimum.

Other Things You Can Do Online

At some point, you're bound to find the tools your broker offers rather limiting. There is a wealth of other online tools offered by online publications, specialty investment sites, and purveyors of financial software. Some of these sites are listed in Appendix A, "Useful Web Sites for the Investor." In general, additional capabilities you'll find at these sites include

- Tracking gains. Although we mentioned gains already, you may find that your broker offers incomplete or poor tools for analyzing how much your stocks, bonds, and mutual funds have increased or decreased in value versus their initial cost. In some cases, a broker may require that you maintain an expensive balance just to receive such information. Fortunately, the leading financial Web sites provide means to check the appreciation on your assets. All that's required in most cases is to plug the amount you paid, plus commissions, into an online spreadsheet.

- Comparing portfolios. An important feature of any online portfolio tool is the ability to compare how different groups of securities you own have performed relative to one another. You may, for example, want to see whether growth stocks you own have actually performed better than value stocks, and how both compare to your mutual fund returns. Or you may want to set up an imaginary portfolio and compare its returns with your actual portfolio. Or how about comparing your portfolio to the historical gains of the major market indices such as the Nasdaq Composite Index and the Dow Jones Industrial Average?

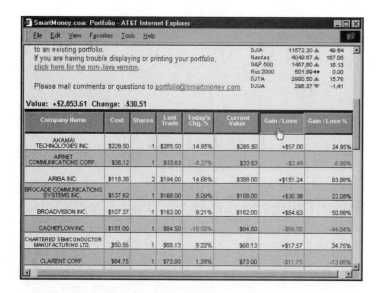

Online portfolios can display daily and total gains.

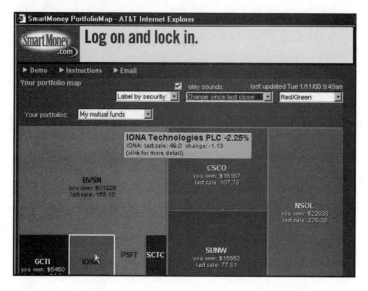

You can compare portfolios with some online sites.

- Understanding where your money is being spent and how you are allocating your assets. This is as important as tracking how much you've made and will help you better plan what to buy or sell next. You can understand in which classes of stock the majority of your money is invested, and run so-called "model portfolios" to plan how you might shift your investments to guarantee a better return on investment. We'll talk more about this in the next section.

Some online port-folios let you analyze asset allocation.

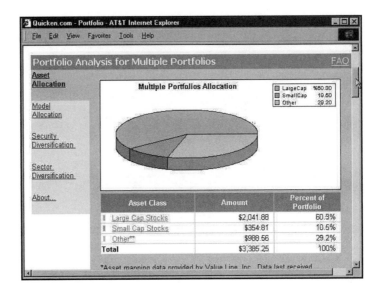

- Evaluating your securities. As stated in Chapter 1, "The Pros and Cons of Online Trading," being an online investor doesn't mean you have to think about stocks and bonds day and night. However, if you're particularly into researching individual securities, or if you consider yourself an active investor and you have the time to think about the securities in your account, you may want to seek out some tools to help you do more extensive research into your securities. Some Web sites will let you research particular characteristics of individual stocks, bonds, and funds, such as how much a particular stock has returned in the past or how much the company it represents is expected to earn in the current year. This can help you to evaluate whether an individual security is a good buy.

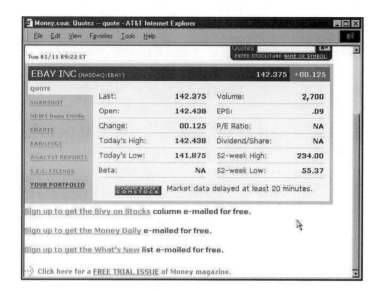

The ability to research and evaluate individual securities is another important feature of online portfolios.

To enjoy these features, you'll have to enter some data at the Web site where the portfolio tracking tool is being offered. Here's how it's generally done:

1. Surf to one of the financial Web sites listed in the appendix that offers portfolio tracking tools.

2. Start a new portfolio—usually by clicking on a link labeled New Portfolio.

3. Enter data for the share price at which you purchased the security, how many shares you purchased, the date on which you purchased the shares, and, perhaps, the commission or fees paid for the security.

▼ **Try It Yourself**

▲

Taking It with You

Rather than entering share data for your portfolio by hand, some Web sites will let you import data from your broker's Web site. Whether you can import data usually depends on whether your broker has a deal with the Web site that is offering the portfolio tracking program. Even in cases where you can import data automatically, you may be asked to enter the cash balance of your account by hand, as this cannot be directly imported.

*Entering data for
a new online
portfolio.*

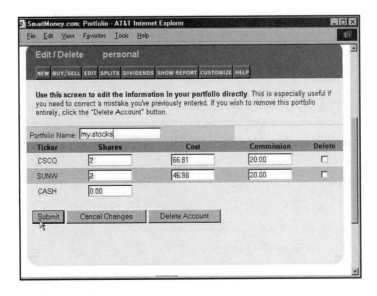

*You may be able
to import data
from your account
with some online
portfolios.*

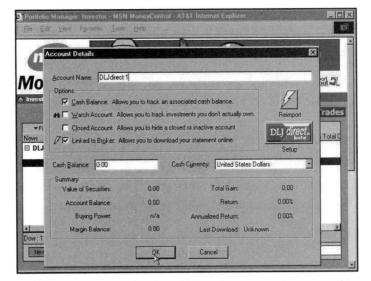

More Extensive Portfolio Tracking and Analysis

At some point the thrill of plugging in stock trades must yield to the realities of physics—like, for example, how much money you can reasonably afford to invest. That means you'll want to keep your brokerage account(s) in line with your checking, savings, and credit accounts. The easiest and the most thorough way to go about this is to purchase one of the more sophisticated offline pieces of software, such as Intuit's Quicken or Microsoft Money, both of which were discussed in Chapter 4, "Tools of the Trade: Hardware and Software Considerations."

Setting Up Offline Management of Your Portfolio

Programs such as Intuit's Quicken or Microsoft's Money will allow you to enter information about your portfolio holdings, as well as your bank account balances and personal assets such as home, car, and so on.

The basic steps for using these programs are as follows:

▼ **Try It Yourself**

1. Install the program software. Bear in mind that programs such as Quicken and Money may require additional updates after you have installed them, because changes in the program will have been made since the software was shipped to retail stores. Follow the specific instructions for your particular software.

2. Set up your brokerage and banking accounts. As with online portfolios, this can be set up manually by a fill-in-the-blanks process of copying your account data. However, the real advantage of using a program such as Quicken or Money is the ability to automate the process of account setup by importing data from your bank or your brokerage over the Internet. Follow the specific instructions in your program to download information from your brokerage or bank account.

What's in an OFX?

No, it's not an exotic jungle creature. OFX is an acronym for Open Financial Exchange, and you're likely to be hearing more about it as you work with your portfolio, both online and offline. Various Web sites and portfolio software packages such as Intuit's Quicken package use the OFX technology to exchange information about your portfolio. The technology was developed jointly in 1997 by Microsoft, Intuit, and a company called CheckFree for the purpose of reconciling bank account, brokerage, and bill payment data.

Connect to your existing broker-age account to import data to the program.

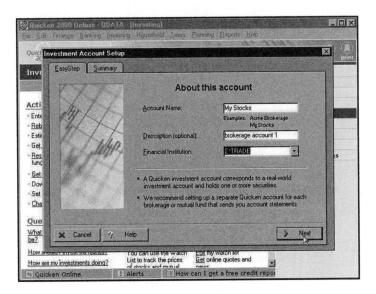

3. Step 2 may require you to complete an application with your broker or your bank to gain online, Web-based access to your banking or investment accounts. If you have already set up an account with a brokerage using this book, a few extra steps may be necessary to extend those privileges so that you can get access to your portfolio from the software program you are using. You may be able to find out what is required from within the software program you are using.

4. Once you have set up your account information, you can record transactions, such as ATM withdrawals and purchases or sale of stock. You can also view your checking balances and your portfolio information such as gains in your stock portfolio.

Issues Regarding Portfolio Software

There are a number of issues to keep in mind when using these programs:

• If you have applied to your bank to access your account electronically, you may have to wait a couple of weeks before you can actually check your accounts from within Quicken or other programs. This is because your bank must process the necessary changes to your checking account.

- Your bank may have to send you a special PIN number in the mail to use only with the software package. A PIN code is like the number you use at ATM machines to withdraw cash. Your bank may require that you use a second, separate code when checking your account from Quicken, for example, and it will have to provide this second code. Talk with your bank representatives for details.

- In addition to PIN codes, you will probably need a user ID for each brokerage or banking account that you are trying to connect to electronically. This can be a problem because Quicken and Money and other programs may limit the number of characters or numbers that can be used for this ID. If the user ID you currently use to log in to your brokerage account or the name on your bank account is too long, you may need to alter those IDs to fit with what Quicken and Money can handle. Procedures for changing these IDs will vary depending upon your financial institution.

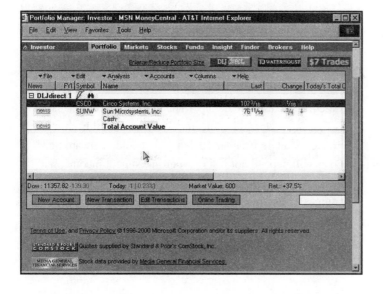

You can view your portfolio online.

Integrating Your Investments with the Rest of Your Finances

Once you've set up your trading portfolio and your other financial information in Quicken or another program, there are a few important things you can do to integrate your finances with your portfolio:

- Calculate your total worth. You want to know not only how much your stock or bond or mutual fund holdings are worth, but also the total value of all the various assets you hold. Quicken or Money can do this by combining information about your checking and savings accounts—as well as IRAs and so on—with data from your portfolio. The result will give you a combined figure representing your net worth.

Calculate your
total worth.

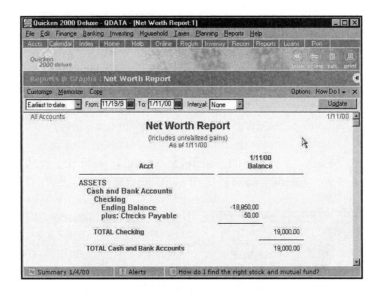

- Calculate taxes. Just as important as figuring your net worth is figuring your taxable income. We'll discuss this issue in greater depth in Chapter 10, but you should be aware that taxes will depend not just on your investment income, but also on how your investment income relates to the other sources of income you receive. Portfolio software is a way to calculate taxes based on all the money you receive in the course of the year, including payouts from sales of assets in your portfolio.

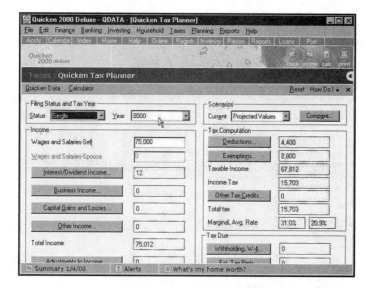

Figure taxes for your investments and the rest of your income.

- Plan your investment goals. By using the software to add up your net worth and calculating your ultimate financial goals—home purchase, car purchase, retirement, increased vacation spending—you can start to think more holistically about how you invest. One way the software can help is to tell you how much you can expect to have in investments over time, and to tell you if you need to move money into different kinds of assets or sell your existing assets.

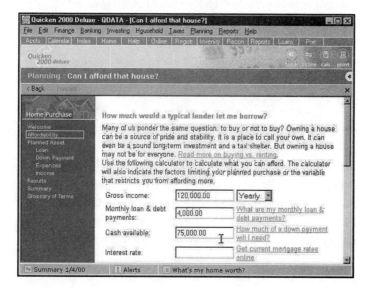

Plan how you'll invest and which assets to emphasize.

- Make a budget for investing. If you add up your expenses and calculate how much monthly income is left over, you can start to plan a regular program of putting money into the market.

Create a budget for investing.

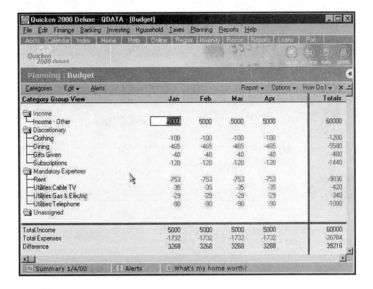

- Use programmed transactions and "dollar cost averaging." Once you've made a budget for yourself, you can program your software to automatically alert you when it's time to make payments, such as paying off loans. How does this pertain to your portfolio? One transaction you may want to make regularly is to buy shares of stock. You can tell the software to alert you as to when it's time to make a buy or sell based on broadly defined plans you have for investments. This can be an effective way to use so-called *dollar cost averaging* as an investment strategy.

Dollar cost averaging is one way to achieve what experts call portfolio diversification. *Diversification* means spreading your investment money around so as not put all your eggs in one basket, and thereby mitigating the effects of swings in the market. One way to diversify is to invest in many different stocks or other securities, and many different kinds of securities. Another way is to place money into a stock or another security on a regular basis, so that you effectively "average out" the highs and lows in the fluctuating price of the stock or bond or mutual fund. Hence the name.

As with the procedures outlined earlier for setting up your portfolio, these various tasks will require you to follow the specific instructions of Quicken, Money, or whichever software you happen to be using.

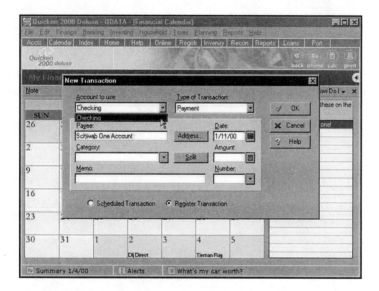

Set up alerts and automatic payments for routine transactions and dollar cost averaging.

What You've Learned

Managing your portfolio is a complex affair involving diverse activities. You must keep the cash balance in your portfolio up-to-date if you want to continue to trade on a regular basis. You want to keep track of how much you're making, and you want to plan for taxes and for your overall financial future. This chapter has hopefully helped you to start thinking about portfolio management by explaining

- What kind of information you can get from various portfolio tools.

- Some of the basic "lifeline" tasks you should learn to perform online and offline, such as depositing funds to your brokerage account or checking your portfolio balance on a regular basis.

- How to use some more advanced software packages to think about investments in the context of your other assets.

CHAPTER 10

Understanding Your Taxes

Sooner or later you'll realize, like all investors, that taxes only get more certain as you start to build your personal fortune through investing. Tax laws will affect how you buy and sell stocks and other securities. They'll affect what you decide to do when you close out an account, when you're redistributing your money between different kinds of assets or accounts, and when you are ready for retirement. This chapter presents some considerations and strategies for all of these circumstances.

It's a good idea to read over this chapter carefully before you do any trading at all. Some of the points outlined here are crucial for maximizing your return. You should memorize these key points and keep them in mind when you go to make your trade.

What's Good About Online Investing from a Tax Standpoint

We've talked a lot about various benefits of online trading in previous chapters. There's actually a big tax benefit to trading online as well. If you have your money tied up in a mutual fund, which many people do, you are at the mercy of the fund manager. If the fund manager decides to make distributions to you and other clients, there's nothing you can do about that.

Distributions are when a mutual fund manager or another person in charge of managing an investment takes a portion of that investment and converts it to cash to give to the investor.

Mutual fund Web sites usually post information about the kinds of distributions they are giving out to shareholders.

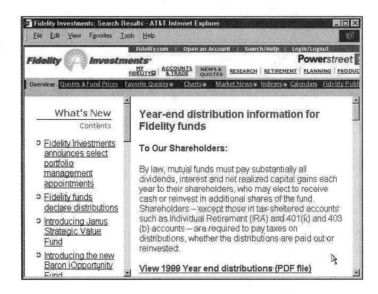

What that means is that you suddenly have to pay taxes because you've just been handed some profits from your investing (assuming your mutual fund is actually profitable).

The bad side of mutual funds is that they limit your control over how you manage investments with respect to taxes.

With online trading, you are in control of how and when you cash in your investment. In other words, you make your own distributions. As a result, you have tremendous power to do the following:

- Decide not to cash in your investments and let them continue to earn, thereby forgoing paying taxes.

- Choose a mix of different investments that may limit how much you end up paying in taxes when you do cash in your investments.

- Follow certain carefully constructed strategies to minimize your tax burden when you do finally cash in.

Using the power at your disposal, you may end up following quite profitable tax strategies that you might not have even considered. For example, rather than cashing out of your stocks every time you want to make a major purchase—a car, a first home, and so on—and getting hit with taxes, you might keep your investments in your portfolio. That way, they can continue to appreciate in value, and you can use your mounting paper wealth to obtain credit with which to purchase the things you need. (We'll talk more about this in Chapter 13, "Trading on Margin and Trading Options.") Treating your investments like a piggy bank is not necessarily the best idea; treating them like equity against which to borrow may be a better idea. Having control of your portfolio through online investing gives you the power to decide.

Deducting Your Online Obsession

While you're gaining more control over your tax situation, you can also be making tax deductions for some of the expenses that you incur to conduct online trading. Your computer and the monthly subscription fee for your Internet service account may be tax-deductible as "investing expenses." Check with your accountant.

Using margin loans can be a way to spend your mounting paper wealth while avoiding taxes on investments.

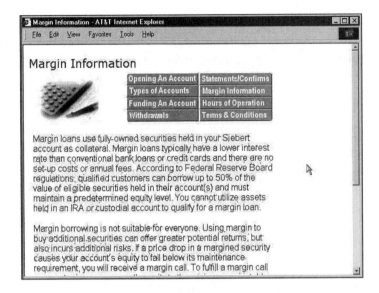

Margin Information

Margin loans use fully-owned securities held in your Siebert account as collateral. Margin loans typically have a lower interest rate than conventional bank loans or credit cards and there are no set-up costs or annual fees. According to Federal Reserve Board regulations, qualified customers can borrow up to 50% of the value of eligible securities held in their account(s) and must maintain a predetermined equity level. You cannot utilize assets held in an IRA or custodial account to qualify for a margin loan.

Margin borrowing is not suitable for everyone. Using margin to buy additional securities can offer greater potential returns, but also incurs additional risks. If a price drop in a margined security causes your account's equity to fall below its maintenance requirement, you will receive a margin call. To fulfill a margin call

A Few Tax Considerations for Mutual Fund Investing

Keep in mind that even with mutual funds, there are good tax strategies and bad tax strategies. Even as an online investor, you may end up making several mutual fund purchases. For that reason, it's good to remember the following important points about mutual fund investing:

- Buying into a fund after its distributions have been made is a means by which you can avoid paying taxes on that fund for the current year.

- Try to look for funds that tend to hold their investments for a long time, rather than funds that tend to buy and sell frequently. The less a fund cashes in its investments, the lower your taxable distribution will be in any given year.

- Holding a mutual fund in a tax-deferred IRA or 401K will let you avoid taxes on fund distributions altogether.

Tax Considerations While Investing

Planning for taxes as an investor is a process that takes place over many stages—before you invest, while you are managing your current investments, and when you are closing out positions in

securities you hold. This section discusses the twin concerns of
asset allocation (discussed in Chapter 2, "Is Online Trading Right
for You?"), and capital gains, which are basically the profits on
investments.

Tax Issues Affecting Asset Allocation

Several specific tax issues can affect how you apportion your
money on an ongoing basis, meaning your asset allocation:

- **Tax bracket**   Your tax bracket will affect how much money
  you want to maintain in cash (that is, savings or checking),
  and how much you want to plow back into shares of stock or
  bonds. You should check the tax Web sites listed in the back
  of this book. They have numerous online worksheets that can
  help you figure out the right balance. You'll also want to consult the asset-allocation sites listed in the appendix under
  Chapter 2. In general, you will want to adjust how much money
  you keep in shares of small- and large-cap stocks versus how
  much you put into fixed-income securities such as bonds.

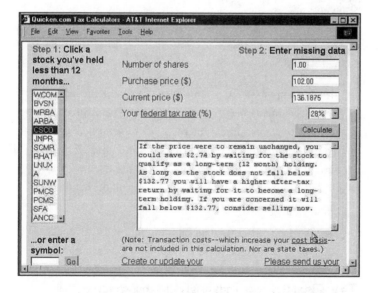

Tax worksheets
can help you plan
how and when to
cash out invest-
ments.

- **Tax-free holdings**   Investments that are not taxed until your
  retirement, such as Individual Retirement Accounts (IRAs)
  and 401K plans, will, again, affect how much you place in
  more aggressive, small-cap investments, and how much you

put in bonds. U.S. Treasury bills, for example, are subject to
all federal taxes, but they are not subject to state and local
taxes. Based on your tax bracket, the return on a U.S. Treasury
bill may be greater after federal taxes are taken out than the
return on shares of stock once those shares have had taxes
taken out. You will have to consult a table of personal income
tax to see how tax-free and taxed assets compare on this score.

*Tax-free invest-
ments, such as
U.S. Treasury bills,
may in some cases
offer you a better
after-tax return
than other, tax-
able securities.*

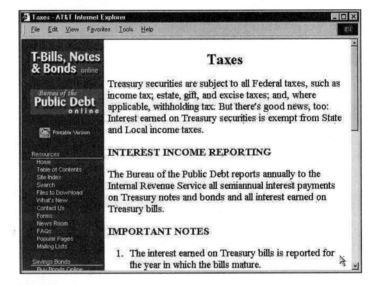

- **Interest expenses**   Certain interest expenses incurred on
  your investments may be tax-deductible. These are usually
  referred to as investment interest. *Investment interest* is interest paid on purchases of securities made on margin. You
  should invest with an eye to how you can offset taxes by
  declaring investment interest you have paid during the year
  and deducting this amount.

- **Invest wisely**   Rather than building up funds in your own
  account to send children to college, you may want to start a
  separate college fund for dependents and place stocks and
  bonds in those accounts as gifts to your children. That means

that when the children come of college age and cash in the account holdings to pay for college, the money will be taxed at your children's lower tax rate, allowing them to keep more of it.

Why the Roth IRA Is So Great

If online investing is your first pass at investing, chances are you're a young person who's just starting on a lifetime of savings. If you fit this profile, many experts recommend that some portion of your savings aside from stocks, bonds, and funds be put into tax-deductible assets, such as IRAs. The Roth IRA has emerged in the past few years as an ideal way for those earning less than $95,000 to $110,000 annually ($150,000 and $160,000 for a couple) to set aside tax-protected income that still allows you to spend for things like cars and homes. Unlike traditional IRAs, which let you deduct the money you pay into the IRA, the Roth IRA payments are not deductible. However, unlike other IRAs, the money you put into a Roth each year can be taken out with no penalties and with limited tax due at any time to cover expenses such as education. Also, the entire haul can be cashed in after age 59 1/2 tax-free, whereas traditional IRAs tax cash-outs after age 59 1/2 just like the rest of your income. With traditional IRAs, if you are withdrawing funds for expenses such as college, you must pay taxes on the entire amount withdrawn. Theoretically, the savings you get with a Roth IRA when you finally cash out more than make up for all the tax payments you didn't avoid in the years before.

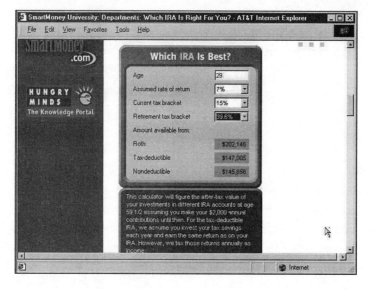

Worksheets such as SmartMoney University's IRA calculator can help you see how much return you'll enjoy from different IRAs.

A Capital (Gain) Idea

To calculate capital gains taxes, you first need to know what your gains are, of course. A good online broker should provide you with a display of your capital gains and, in some cases, a breakdown of your basis, showing share price and commissions paid.

Capital Gains

Any time you sell assets to cash in on your holdings, your profits will be taxed. In investing, this is known as *capital gains*. As a special class of rules that affect your asset allocation, capital gains are a complex subject. The basic definition is as follows:

Capital gains are what you have left over when you subtract the original cost of a security—say, shares of stock—and the broker fees you've paid from the current value of the security. In other words, it's your profit.

Just so you know, the total cost to you, including broker fees and commissions, and the actual price paid per security or per share of a security, is referred to your "basis." Thus, you can also think of capital gains as the difference between the current value of your investments and your basis.

Your online brokerage should give you a display of your gains on its Web site.

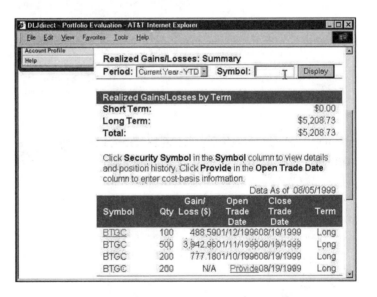

A whole complex style of investing has arisen to minimize or balance your exposure to capital gains taxes. This is definitely a subject requiring consultation with an accountant, but in general, there are a few basic rules to keep in mind about capital gains:

- Capital gains vary depending on when you cash in your investments. Investments less than a year old are taxed at your regular income tax rate, which can be as high as 39.6%, whereas investments older than a year are taxed at a flat 20% rate.

- Thanks to recent tax reforms, starting in 2001 it will be possible to reduce your capital gains tax by selling assets that you hold for five years starting in that year. If you want to do this with existing holdings, your broker must help you hold your shares of stock or bonds as if they had been sold and repurchased starting in 2001.

- Capital gains will affect how much of your portfolio you want to put into stocks and bonds and how much you want to put into non-taxable assets such as IRAs. For example, you may be able to hold onto more of your money by cashing in some part of a tax-deductible IRA as opposed to cashing out your investments and paying capital gains. That's because income tax on Roth IRAs, for example, apply only to the earnings part of the money you withdraw, not the part that counts as the original contribution you paid in. So an equal amount of IRA withdrawals and stock payouts will generate a different tax bill. You have to invest, in other words, with an eye to the relative burden of capital gains versus income taxes.

We'll explore the issues relating to capital gains a bit more in the next section.

Issues When Selling Assets or Closing Accounts

Quick: You've just opened to your portfolio to find that a stock you invested in eight months ago has doubled in value! But you're sure the stock is overvalued and you're afraid you will lose those gains if you don't cash out. However, being only eight months old, this particular stock will be taxed at a higher rate than if you waited just four more months until it's a year old. Do you wait, and risk the stock plummeting, or do you take the tax hit, losing a larger chunk of your gains, and get some sleep?

This kind of dilemma can come up again and again. Fortunately, there are ways to hedge your bets. That's why as an investor you have to think not only about how you apportion your assets between different investments, but also how you cash in on your winnings. The following sections discuss some points to consider.

Selling for Profit, Selling at a Loss

You're either selling stock for a profit or selling it at a loss. Good tax strategy says that you try to balance the amounts of profit and loss in any year to cancel out taxable gains. When cashing in shares of stock, there are a few strategic points to consider:

Know Your Basis

This is where it becomes especially important to keep records of your basis so that you will not overestimate your capital gains. If you know exactly how much you paid for each share of stock, and how much you paid in commission, you can pick out those shares that have given the least return and select them to cash out. This is another reason to follow the instructions on portfolio management in the previous chapter.

- The first step, profit, is clear: You're going to sell your stocks and rake in the profit you've made. We'll get to losses in a minute. If you're selling stocks at a profit, you ideally want to find stocks that are both the least profitable and the oldest in your portfolio. The less profitable your stocks are, the less profit there is to be taxed, obviously. And if stocks are older than a year, you pay only the 20% capital gains rate, not the higher income tax rate. You can specify the individual shares that have given you the least gain (or, said differently, the ones that cost you the most) and that are the oldest and request that these shares specifically be sold.

- You won't always be able to sell shares that are both older than a year and the least profitable. Sometimes you'll have to pick one criterion or another, at which point you'll have to do the math and figure out which is the more profitable route to go.

- Selling shares of mutual funds for profit is basically the same. It gets a little more complicated because you will have to sort through shares of the same asset to see which ones have the highest cost basis and therefore the lowest taxable return.

- The reason to sell stocks at a loss is because the loss you incur can protect the capital gains you receive on stocks you are selling at a profit from taxation. (Losses can even protect items such as real estate gains.) This is known as *capital losses*.

Using Capital Losses

Let's talk a bit more about how capital losses can shelter capital gains. Basically, any amount of capital loss in your portfolio will cancel out the same amount of capital gains in your portfolio, from a tax standpoint. What that means is that if you have $10,000 in losses and $10,000 in gains, you will not pay any taxes on the

$10,000 gain because it has been effectively negated by the comparable loss, at least from a tax standpoint.

If you have some losses left over after computing this balance, that loss can be used as a tax deduction, up to $3,000 annually. If you have more than $3,000 in capital losses left over, the rest must be carried forward and used in later years.

The example is mapped out in the following table.

Selling at a Loss: How It Works

While you add up your gains...	...You have to balance things out with losses
1. You sell some stock for a profit of $10,000.	1. At the same time, you sell some other stock at a loss of $13,000.
2. The $10,000 profit is canceled out by the equal loss, so no taxes are charged on the gain.	2. $10,000 of the $13,000 is used to cancel out the profit.
	3. Of the $13,000 loss, $3,000 in losses remains. That $3,000 can be deducted from the rest of the investor's taxes.

Don't Be a Washing Machine

If you are selling shares of stock at a loss, the IRS has a clause that can trip you up if you're not careful. Called the "wash sale" law, this rule says that if you buy shares of the same stock 30 days before or after selling those shares at a loss, you will not be able to claim that loss until you sell the new shares you've just bought. So make sure you're 31 days clear when you claim a loss on a particular stock before you buy again.

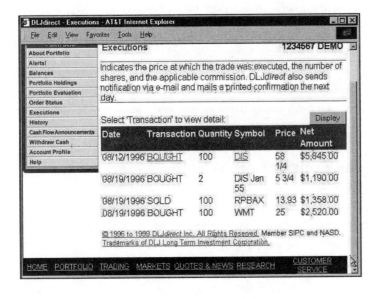

Be mindful of when you sell securities at a loss if you are considering repurchasing those securities.

Try to Lose Early

If you're going to use losses to shelter gains, you should look to sell securities that are less than a year old. That is because these short-term losses can be used to protect short-term gains, meaning those taxed at the normal high tax rate. Long-term losses, meaning losses on shares of stock held for more than a year, can only be applied to long-term gains, meaning profit on shares of stock held for a year or more. But sheltering such long-term gains should only be a last resort because those gains will already benefit from a lower tax rate. So remember, always look to shelter short-term gains first to eliminate the higher tax penalty.

Gifts and Donations

There are a few clever tax-avoidance strategies relating to making gifts and donations:

- Assign shares of stock to dependents as gifts. This was previously mentioned in relation to college savings, but it applies to protecting your own gains as well. Stocks and bonds given to dependents will be taxed at a far lower tax rate, letting you hang on to more of your gains. Likewise, shares of stock given to charity are a tax write-off, which is a savings if you were going to make a donation anyway.

- There's even more tax gain to be had by heirs who inherit your portfolio. If you leave stocks, bonds, or mutual funds to heirs, all the money earned on those holdings up until the time they are passed along is tax-free; only when they fall into the hands of heirs are they considered to start earning taxable income.

Tax Considerations with Respect to Your Broker

There are several points to check with your e-broker before you make any purchase or sale of securities. These points will have continuing tax consequences for your portfolio:

- Make sure your brokerage can provide information about the original price at which you purchased stocks and other securities. This is important for calculating your capital gains obligation.

- Inquire whether your broker offers the range of tax-free instruments you are considering. Many brokers offer Roth IRAs; some will offer bond funds that invest in tax-free U.S. Treasuries or U.S. Savings Bonds.

- You may want to borrow against your holdings in order to make large purchases rather than cash in your assets and take a tax hit. You should carefully consider what terms your e-broker maintains for letting you borrow on margin against the value of your holdings.

- If you plan to invest in mutual funds in addition to stocks, make sure your online broker will allow you to identify specific blocks of fund shares when it comes time to receive distributions. That is because just as shares of stock held for a longer period of time are taxed at a lower rate, individual shares of mutual funds will be taxed at different rates depending on how long they have been held.

What You've Learned

Obviously, there are a lot of different ways to play the tax game. You should talk with your accountant to match up your tax strategy with the kinds of investing you'll be doing based on your own investing profile as discussed in Chapter 2. This chapter has given you just a little taste of

- The potential tax benefits of being in control of your portfolio.

- Things to think about while choosing what to invest in.

- Some of the strategies for cashing out, including what you need to know about your broker.

CHAPTER 11

Troubleshooting and Ending Your Online Trading Relationship

Stocks go up, stocks go down, and somewhere in between you may lose some money trading. Hopefully, on balance, you'll earn more money on your investments over time than you would in a savings account. But as careful as you may be in trading stocks, bonds, and mutual funds, there may be times when something goes wrong through no fault of your own, for a variety of reasons. The Internet is an inherently unreliable medium of communication at this point in time. For that reason, it's important for you to understand what can (and probably will, at some point) go wrong when you invest online as opposed to going through a traditional broker. This chapter outlines some things to be careful of, how to deal with problems you may encounter, and also one of the most important technical issues of an online trading account, namely how to close or transfer your account.

Before You Start Trading, Get Information

Trading securities is complex enough without disaster and scandal thrown into the mix, and it's difficult to anticipate things that can go wrong when you're diving into something for the first time.

Nonetheless, you owe it to yourself to read the materials offered for investors at the Web sites of the various regulatory agencies before you do any trading—even if you don't completely understand the materials posted. Reading the tips and suggestions on these sites, which are geared toward beginning investors and which are mostly in simple language, may mean that something valuable will stick in your head when you sit down at your computer to make a trade for the first time.

Following are a few of the Web sites you should consider visiting. They were mentioned earlier, but it's worth reviewing them again:

Try It Yourself ▼

1. The Securities and Exchange Commission (SEC) site at *www.sec.gov*. This should be your first stop. Aside from advice on how to get into online trading, there's a lot here in the way of simply worded instructions on how to deal with fraud and with trading volatility. There are also speeches by the SEC chairman, Arthur Levitt, that very often set the tone for the way the securities industry thinks about certain practices.

The SEC Web site.

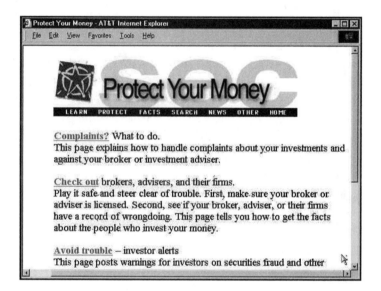

2. North American Securities Administrators Association (NASAA) at *www.nasaa.org*. This group is a voluntary organization composed of state securities regulators. The NASAA works to define guidelines for proper practice by securities firms. The NASAA is where you'll find the address and phone number of the securities regulator in your home state.

The NASAA has special information about "blue sky" regulations, meaning the rules of compliance for securities to trade in each state, and also ongoing information about day trading firms that is especially important if you're considering using a day trading firm.

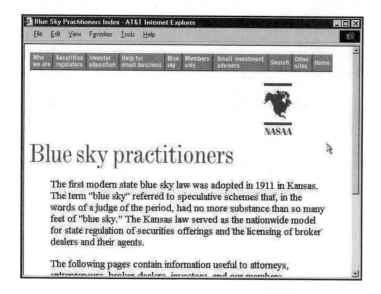

The NASAA Web site contains information about local state securities regulators.

3. The regulatory site for the National Association of Securities Dealers (NASD) at *www.nasdr.com.* Remember, this is the industry body that oversees the Nasdaq stock market and the OTC bulletin board on which small stocks are listed. The NASD regulation site is good to browse because you can see some of the "talking points" on which the NASD is briefing its members, the brokerage firms, in regards to online to trading. You may want to be familiar with these talking points before you start trading. You can find a summary of the NASD's recommendations to brokerages regarding online trading at *www.nasdr.com/pdf-text/9911ntm.txt.*

*The NASD regula-
tion Web site
includes advice on
avoiding scams
and talking points
about Internet
fraud.*

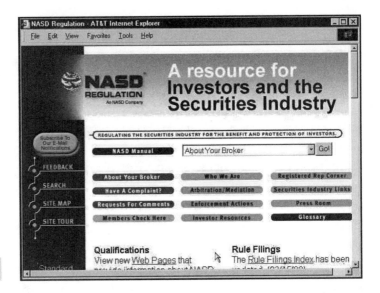

What will you find at these sites? You'll find suggestions about common problems that can occur in online trading and about more serious types of fraud. Let's look at the common problems first.

Things That Can Go Wrong When Using an Online Broker

Not every matter justifies an immediate call to the cops or the lawyers. First of all, it helps to know exactly what you're entitled to as an investor. You should check out something called the Investor's Bill of Rights at the NASAA's site (*www.nasaa.org/ investoredu/billofrights.html*). These rights include

- The right to ask for and receive information from a firm about the work history and background of the person handling your account.

- The right to receive account statements that are accurate and understandable.

- The right to access your funds in a timely manner and receive information about any restrictions or limitations on access.

Bear in mind that, as mentioned in Chapter 2, "Is Online Trading Right for You?", there are certain features of a full-service brokerage that you give up when you trade online. In fact, when you sign up for your online account, you may be asked to consent in the application process to the waiving of things such as the right to "Receive recommendations consistent with your financial needs," as the NASAA site puts it. The Investor's Bill of Rights is an important set of guidelines, but you have to realize that going online means some compromises in what you can expect from your broker.

How to you proceed if you feel one of your rights has been violated? The SEC posts a few rules about how you should approach situations where you think your brokerage firm has wronged you. The general sequence of steps goes as follows:

1. If a problem arises, first call your broker. Ask for an explanation of how the situation occurred. Make careful notes of the answers you receive from your brokerage, so that you have a record of its excuse.

   ▼ **Try It Yourself**

2. If you are not satisfied with the answers given by your brokerage, write directly to the compliance office at the main branch of your broker's offices. Explain the situation and tell the firm how you would like it to resolve the matter. Instruct the firm to respond to you within 30 days.

3. If you're still unhappy with the situation, or if you receive no response within 30 days, write to one of the following, enclosing copies of your original letters: The Investor Education Office of the Security and Exchange Commission; the National Association of Securities Dealers (which runs the Nasdaq stock market); or your state securities regulator. These steps are detailed at *www.sec.gov/consumer/jcompla.htm.*

   ▲

*The SEC posts
guidelines about
how to deal with
broker problems.*

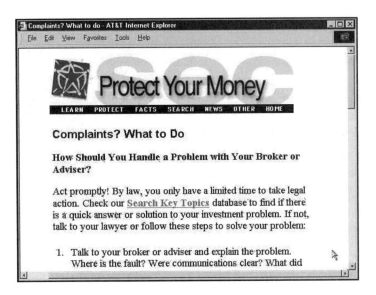

Step back and think about what you do when you invest online, from a 3,000-foot perspective, as it were. The most basic problems you'll encounter while trading are

• You are unable to connect to your broker's Web site when trying to enter a trade.

• A trade is not processed.

• You end up paying a different price than you expected for a trade.

• You enter the wrong trade and then cannot cancel your order.

• You can't get confirmation of the trade onscreen.

You Are Unable to Reach Your Broker's Site to Place Your Order

There are many reasons why a Web site for an online broker can become suddenly unreachable. It's important to realize that the Internet is composed of many computers and many telecommunications lines, and any one of those elements can be the weak link. That means that the problem could be with your brokerage's computer or its connection to the Internet, or the problem could be with your own connection to the Internet. As mentioned in

Chapter 3, "Selecting the Right Online Broker for Your Needs," companies such as Keynote Systems (*www.keynotesystems.com*) make a business of telling you which sites are more or less reliable.

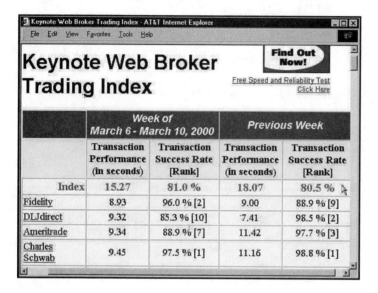

Keynote Systems is among the firms that can give you relative performance ratings for brokerages.

The SEC doesn't mandate that any site be reachable at all times; if the site has poor performance, it may be a poor product, but you probably can't sue your broker over it. What the SEC does say is that brokers cannot make false claims about the availability of their Web site. If you sign up with an online brokerage based on certain claims about its ability to process your trade and you find that in practice the brokerage does not live up to its claims, you may have a legitimate case of fraud that you should take up with your state securities regulator. The NASD is actually quite firm about the requirement that members not mislead investors through public statements. Specifically, the NASD states:

> *"Misrepresentations or omissions of material facts in public communications violate National Association of Securities Dealers, Inc. (NASD) Rule 2210 as well as Rule 2110, which requires members to observe high standards of commercial honor and just and equitable principles of trade."*

The NASD also mandates that member firms have adequate capacity to handle high volumes of Web orders:

> *"NASD Regulation reminds member firms of their obligations under Securities and Exchange Commission (SEC) Staff Legal Bulletin No. 8 to ensure that they have adequate systems capacity to handle high volume or high volatility trading days."*

However, the best way to protect yourself from the consequences of slow or unreachable Web sites is to find out in advance whether your broker allows you to place a trade via alternative means, say, by placing a phone call.

Find out whether your broker provides phone trading and what the numbers are.

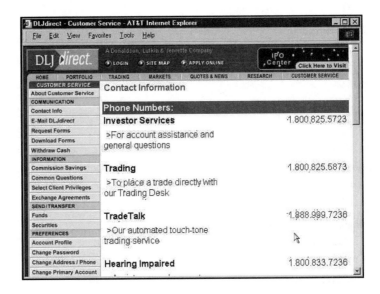

Most brokers will allow you to trade by phone, and most maintain an informal (that is, not a written) promise that they will honor the price quote you found online at the time that you were trying to place your order. However, brokerages may also maintain an informal policy of allowing only so many of these types of calls from your account. If you frequently call and demand that orders be processed at prices you saw quoted over the Web earlier, you may find your broker drawing the line at some point over whether he or she will honor those requests.

Also, make sure to check your broker's phone capabilities. Not all brokers have the same level of phone support, and if you want to be covered in the event of an Internet problem you don't want to find that your broker's telephone-based service rep is also off the hook.

A Trade Is Not Processed

Perhaps more disturbing than not getting through at all to your broker's site is submitting a buy or sell order, walking away confident you've made that trade, and finding out later the order was never received by your broker. The most obvious precaution here is to make sure you receive a confirmation after placing your order. *Never walk away from the computer until you've seen your order confirmation!*

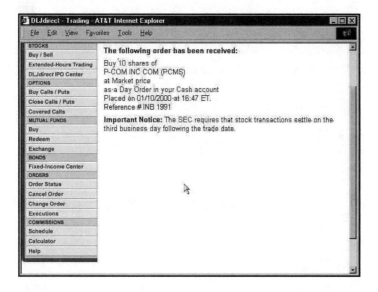

Make sure you see the order confirmation screen.

If your order cannot be processed—because of computer malfunction or overwhelming order volume—and your broker informs you of this, there may not be much recourse but to dump your broker for one with better reliability. However, if you've received confirmation and later find that the order did not go through, you may have a genuine grievance to make with the state securities regulator and with the SEC. The NASD states quite clearly that online brokers must make clear when their computer systems may not be able to process trades. The NASD states:

"[F]irms should provide adequate, clear disclosure to customers about the risks arising out of evolving volatility and volume concerns and any related constraints on firms' ability to process orders in a timely and orderly manner."

You Don't Get the Price You Expected to Pay

This happens most often when you enter a market order, expecting that the current price in the market when your order goes in is the price you'll end up paying. In fact, you may end up paying a different price, and sometimes the gap can be quite large if trading is especially volatile. You may not realize this until you go to check the order execution records on your broker's Web site or until you receive confirmation of a trade via email. There's always a risk with market orders that the price you end up paying will be different from what you're expecting, perhaps substantially different.

Know Your Limits

Recall from Chapter 8, "Placing Your First Trade," that a limit order is an order that will be processed only if prices can be found in the market matching the conditions you specify. That may mean that a limit order will not be filled at all. Therefore, understand that a case of a limit order not being processed is more than likely a normal operating situation and not an error on your broker's part.

Order execution may show a price that's different from what you thought you'd be paying.

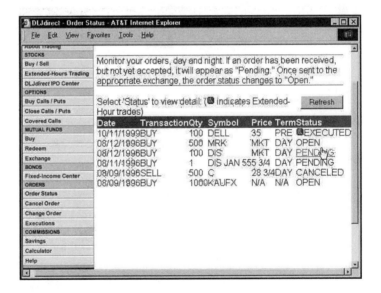

Unfortunately, you are mostly on your own here. If you end up paying a different price than what you last saw quoted for the security on your screen, there are no immediate grievances you can bring against your broker. SEC regulations do not require brokers to transact your order within any set amount of time, although it is generally expected that your order will be processed with all due haste. (And as in the case of Web sites that cannot be reached, the SEC does say that brokers must not make false claims about the speed or efficiency with which they can execute trades.)

And of course, your broker is not required by securities regulators to process your trade at a particular price for a market order, but simply to get the best price possible at the time.

That being the case, the best thing to do is to be mindful of the risks before you place any orders and to take the necessary precautions:

- If it's a wild day on Wall Street and prices are zigzagging up and down, use a limit order. The limit order is designed to protect you against unforeseen price swings, and you should become familiar with how to use it.

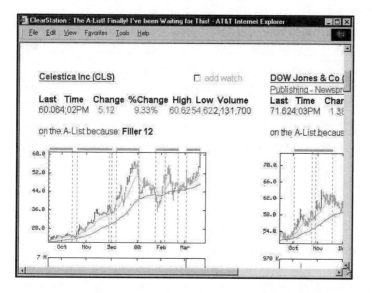

You should check the day's stock chart before placing any trades to get a sense of the degree of volatility.

- Try to avoid periods of known volatility. As most experts will tell you, the first half hour of trading, and in general the early morning, can be the most volatile periods of daily activity. Prices are more likely to swing at this time than at any other point in the day. Not only that, but your market order may

well be delayed due to the high volume of transactions. If it
takes several minutes for your order to be processed, the
price may move against you and it could cost you dearly.

- Likewise, try to avoid the rush mentality around special
developments. Be very careful about situations where you are
trying to play off of news about a stock, or speculating on
significant developments in the underlying company.

A typical example might be a write-up in the Sunday papers
about a company offering a wonder drug that's sure to boost
sales. Monday morning, everyone rushes to place an order to
buy the company's stock, thinking they're the only ones to
find this hot tip. The result: Your order is one of thousands
that push the stock price into stratospheric levels, resulting
in a hugely inflated price for you and everyone else.

- You can sometimes direct where your order is "executed." As
mentioned in Chapter 6, "Understanding the Basics of Stock
Trading," orders to buy or sell stock are executed, meaning
filled, by being sent to a market such as NYSE or Nasdaq.
Also mentioned were the new Electronic Communications
Networks, and you may under certain circumstances be able
to send your order to that market. (We'll talk more about this
in Chapter 17, "After-Hours Trading and Electronic Communications Networks.") Why is this important? The more
markets you have access to, the better the price you may get.
The SEC suggests that you find out where your electronic
brokerage is processing your orders and whether you can
enter a request to have your order sent to a different market.

On this last score, the SEC chairman, Arthur Levitt, has stated
that investors have a right to know how their trades are being executed and what an online broker is doing to process trades in the
best manner possible. You can check out Chairman Levitt's comments in full at the SEC Web site, *www.sec.gov/news/speeches/
spch315.htm.*

Directing your order to a particular market can have an impact on how well your order gets filled.

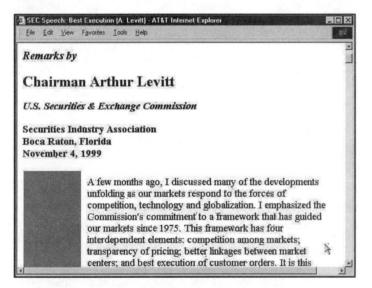

SEC chairman Arthur Levitt issues important guidelines for proper conduct in the market by brokers and investors.

Strength in Numbers

Keep in mind that in some cases you may not be the only party affected. If there are substantial problems with your broker's Web site, you may be just one of many clients who end up with strange order results that are clearly at variance with what happened. In such instances, broker-ages have been known to honor complaints from clients and to reset orders to market prices at the time the client claims to have placed the order. So read the papers and watch the financial news: If there is a widespread problem with a broker's Web site, you may be able to find out about it and join the throng of investors demanding restitution.

Entering the Wrong Order and Problems with Canceling Erroneous Orders

Investors love the direct quality of online investing: Once you've opened an account, it's so simple to start popping trades into a Web page. Suddenly, the Web has removed enormous obstacles to most investors gambling their life savings away by making the process of buying and selling stocks as easy as ordering books at Amazon.com.

The supermarket nature of the Web trading screen makes it easy to get careless with a trade.

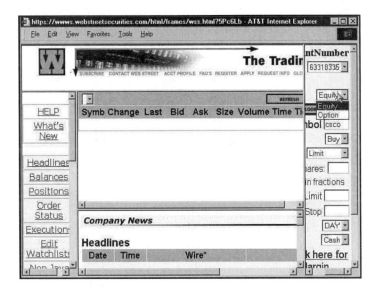

One of the biggest problems, then, is that it's so hard to undo what you've done when you place an order for stock. If you buy a book at Amazon.com, you can go back to your shopping cart and start pulling things out if you change your mind. Unfortunately with trading securities, your brokerage house is under mandate from securities regulators to process your order as swiftly as possible. When you go to cancel an order, you are basically racing against a computer system that should be racing to get your order placed with the market.

For that reason, in many cases you won't be able to cancel an order. Some trades are harder than others to cancel. Remember from Chapter 8 that limit orders usually wait in a queue behind market orders. For that reason, a limit order may afford you slightly more time in which to place a cancel request. But don't count on it.

In some cases, you may be able to explain the situation to your broker. But deciding whether to let you off the hook for a trade is pretty much at your broker's discretion. The attitude of many brokers is that to have completed a trade on the Web, you will have had to go through an order review screen and possibly an order confirmation screen, signaling your assent in each screen.

Brokers like to insist that because you are required to go through numerous screens when placing your trade, you should be fairly mindful of what you're doing. Again, limit orders may receive different consideration than market orders. It's easier to enter a market order because there are fewer points of data to be entered into a Web form. With a limit order, by contrast, you must enter the price at which you want to perform the trade. Most brokers consider it next to impossible to accidentally enter a limit order wrong, and for that reason they may be less willing to give you the benefit of the doubt in the case of an erroneous limit order than in the case of an erroneous market order.

Good Money After Bad?

The only thing worse than not being able to cancel an order is thinking you've canceled the order and going on making additional stock trades with money you may not be able to spend. You should know whether you have successfully canceled an order before you try to enter a new order. Some Web sites are developing order types called "cancel and replace," which will allow an investor to place a new order only if the old order has been successfully nixed. These sorts of improvements are not mandatory in the industry, but you may want to look for brokers who have added such features.

Not Receiving Confirmation of a Trade on Screen

The reverse of walking away without checking for an order confirmation is placing an order and receiving no confirmation at all. This is simply a case of poor Web site design, and the rules here are somewhat fuzzy given that the art of designing an informative, responsive Web site is still evolving. However, if you place a trade but you are not able to find out if the trade has been put through, you may have a legitimate grievance to make with securities regulators, especially if you can make the case that the inability to confirm your order cost you money.

In the meantime, though, self-defense is your best policy. Therefore, if you have any doubt as to whether your order was received,
make sure to check the section of the site where your order history is listed. Check this section to make sure there's a record of
the order just entered.

*If you have any
doubt about your
trade, check the
order status or
order history sec-
tion of the site.*

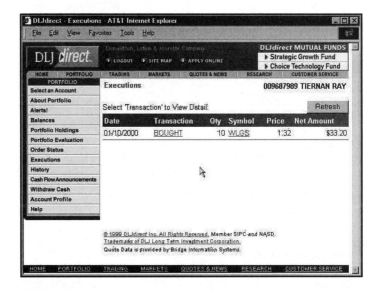

Your Right to Know

Remember that even if your broker is not legally bound to confirm
receipt of an order on the Web page, he or she is bound by securities
law to inform you in a timely manner of whether or not your trade has
been processed successfully. Any failure to do so—by email or regular
mail—represents a violation of securities regulations that you should
bring to the attention of the SEC and your state securities regulator.

Fraud

Obviously, fraud is a much more serious matter than problems
with your broker's Web site. In an age where everyone wants to
make a million dollars, it's all too easy to be led astray by the random chat room denizen who's touting securities that will soon
soar or exotic investment pools that don't really exist. The easiest
way to stay out of trouble when investing is to realize that investing means planning your financial future and placing your money

in securities for the long term. The more you focus on the careful
work that needs to be done to build your investments, the less
likely you will be to chase after dubious propositions.

The SEC gives the following general tips on avoiding fraud:

1. Make sure any securities you hear recommended are actually ▼ **Try It Yourself**
   listed on an exchange. Unlisted securities are a good tip-off
   that a stock you hear being talked about is actually part of a
   scam. If you can't find data on the company by searching the
   Web, you may also want to check with your state securities
   regulator, which, again, you can look up at the NASAA's site.

2. If someone is offering to sell you securities directly, find out
   if he or she is licensed as a broker or broker-dealer. Again,
   you can find out this information by calling your state securities regulator, or you can look up the brokerage firm on the
   NASD regulation site, as mentioned in Chapter 3, at
   www.nasdr.com/2000.htm.

3. Lastly, and this is somewhat subtler, be wary of brokers that
   seem to offer too much freedom to trade. There are rules discussed in Chapter 13, "Trading on Margin and Trading
   Options," about trading with borrowed funds, for example.

   Margin trading is an important feature of any brokerage
   account that will enhance your ability to invest. However, it
   can also get you into debt quickly if your broker is not strict
   in the requirements placed on margin accounts. If a broker is
   offering to give you unlimited ability to borrow money in a
   margin account, he may be doing you a serious disservice,
   not to mention violating securities law. While this may or
   may not legally amount to fraud, you should be wary of irre-
   sponsible brokers who can lead you into trouble simply by
   failing to impose proper discipline on your trades.   ▲

The SEC offers tips
on avoiding fraud.

Internet Fraud:
How to Avoid Internet Investment Scams

October 1998

The Internet serves as an excellent tool for investors, allowing them to easily and inexpensively research investment opportunities. But the Internet is also an excellent tool for fraudsters. That's why you should always think twice *before* you invest your money in any opportunity you learn about through the Internet.

On October 28, 1998, the SEC announced charges against 44 stock promoters caught in a nationwide enforcement sweep to combat Internet fraud. These promoters failed to tell investors that more than 235 companies paid them millions of dollars in cash and

Common Types of Fraud

Some of the most common types of fraud include

- Blind pools. You may be contacted by organizations that sound like mutual fund firms, offering you a chance to pool your investment money with a group of other "lucky" individuals. The firm will not say what investments your and the rest of the group's funds will be put into. That's the first tip that the firm may be running a so-called "blank check" scam, in which your funds will be invested in any number of bogus vehicles, such as using the money to buy a private company that is trying to go public but that cannot meet SEC requirements for public stock.

- IRA approved investment opportunities, meaning those touted as legitimate individual retirement accounts (IRAs). A common tactic is to cite an investment as being approved by the IRS for purposes of building a retirement nest egg. This is a fraud commonly perpetrated against older investors. Individuals are coaxed into placing their retirement nest egg in investments that may be touted as the perfect vehicle to save for retirement. Officials caution you to remember that the IRS does not endorse any specific investments whatsoever, so any such claims are automatically false.

- Boiler room brokers. Like most people, you probably hang up on cold callers who try to reach you during the most inopportune moments of the day. In the event that you do take a call from a stockbroker trying to sell you his or her product, securities regulators point out that you should distinguish between the legitimate brokers who will harass you and the "boiler room" brokers—fly-by-night types who are looking for a quick hit-and-run profit. Real brokers are trying to build a base of clientele, and they will take the time to ask you questions about your investment goals and to explain their offerings to you. Boiler room brokers are simply trying to sign you up as quickly as possible, and will try to pressure you into accepting their products. The distinction may not mean much in practice, but it's good to keep in mind nonetheless.

While you're fending off the cold callers, you should be aware that any securities dealer calling you on the phone has to obey certain Federal laws regarding cold calling that are designed to protect your rights. The SEC points out that investment professionals calling you on the phone must observe the following rules:

- They may only call between 8 a.m. and 9 p.m.

- They must state their name, their firm name and address, and their telephone number upon request.

- They must explicitly state that the purpose of the call is to offer you investments.

- They must put you on their "do not call" list if you request that they do so.

- Though it may seem obvious, Federal laws stipulate that cold callers must not threaten or intimidate you or use obscene language.

- They must get written permission to transfer any funds from any account you may hold, in the event that you agree to invest.

- Lastly—and, again, this should be obvious—cold callers must not lie.

If cold callers fail to comply with any of these guidelines, you should inform them that they are breaking the law and simply hang up. The SEC keeps a Web page listing these rules and how to deal with cold callers in general at *www.sec.gov/enforce/alerts/coldcall.htm.*

Online Fraud

In addition, regulators point out a few new scams that have cropped up with the advent of online investing:

- Brokers with online brokerages selling their own services on the side. These are cases in which a broker employed by a legitimate brokerage may be posting offers of online trading services on computer bulletin boards. In the cases highlighted, the broker posting the message was working outside the knowledge of his firm and was making extraordinary claims about celebrities being involved in the brokerage and other come-ons.

- Email pyramid schemes. A chain letter in the form of an email message is sent in a mass mailing—dubbed "spam"—to investors. The addressee is told to send a dollar to various names contained in the email and then told to send the letter onto several other individuals and encourage them to also send money and forward on the message. In each case, the message is sent with the promise of thousands of dollars in profit.

- Pump and dump schemes. The stock of a troubled, obscure over-the-counter company is touted in online chat boards and through email messages as being on the verge of some breakthrough or significant profit development that is supposed to boost the stock. After investors buy in, the stock collapses. The scenario usually mentions something along the lines of new diamond mine discoveries or significant gold contracts.

What sets these scams apart, according to regulators, is the fact that the scams can spread rapidly thanks to email and online chat room postings. As mentioned in Chapter 5, "Researching Stocks, Bonds, and Mutual Funds Online," chat rooms and message boards often contain a lot of dubious advice and recommendations. The SEC and other officials suggest that investors be especially mindful of stock touts who use these venues to push "sure thing" stocks.

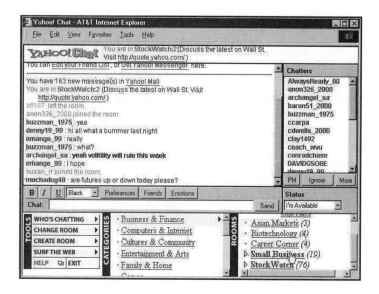

Chat boards are important resources, but you should be careful whose advice you follow.

Be mindful of attempts at manipulation, in other words. Securities officials warn investors to also be especially wary of exotic investing tips, such as stocks of companies with obscure technologies or wild development schemes like ostrich farming or viatical settlements (the purchasing of life insurance policies from individuals as a speculative investment).

Bold New Mail Fraud

Keep in mind that if you receive a proposition through email to participate in something that's fraudulent, the perpetrators may be open to charges of federal fraud for using the U.S. postal system to solicit. Avoiding email offers altogether is probably the best thing you can do, but if you receive messages at any point during your dealings with brokers or those soliciting participation in an investment, hang on to the original emails—they may end up being important pieces of evidence.

The NASAA offers a few tips for how to avoid the most common
online scams:

- Don't approach investing with a get-rich-quick attitude. The
  more you look at investing as speculation for a quick gain,
  the more likely you are to be led astray by promises of enormous short-term return from wild investment opportunities.
  Deals that sound too good to be true probably are.

- Don't assume the online service is monitoring or moderating
  chat rooms and message boards. Again, the Web is a wide-
  open meeting place. Most interactive forums you'll find are
  free-for-alls with no real administration as far as content. Don't
  assume that what you read is being screened for accuracy or
  appropriateness.

- Always be suspicious of anonymous postings of information,
  as well as claims of inside knowledge. Postings made by
  unnamed individuals or postings made by someone using
  an alias who claims to have special insider information are
  common tip-offs that something's fishy.

Most of this should sound like common sense. If it does, then
congratulations, you're on your way to avoiding the scam artists.
But check this section every once in a while just to think about
how you're interacting with information on the Web. It helps to
check yourself now and then to make sure you're not lingering
too long where touts and boiler room brokers ply their trade.

Ending Your Online Trading Relationship and Transferring Accounts

At some point you may choose to close your online account—
either to move to a different broker or because you've decided to
move all of your winnings out of the stock market and into something more reliable, such as a South Seas island resort franchise.
Checking out of your existing brokerage account doesn't have to
be a complicated matter. The most important thing to remember is
that *the assets in your brokerage account belong to you*, just like
the money in an ordinary savings account. You can take cash and
stock out of a brokerage account and put them under your pillow
if you like. It's up to you. You do have the right to take those
assets when you want.

The steps involved are as follows:

▼ **Try It Yourself**

1. Call your broker's telephone service line and inform them that you will be closing out your account. If you are not immediately transferring your money to another brokerage account, you will have to have funds paid out to you, which can be performed like any other payment. You can either have your broker send you a check or you can arrange for a wire transfer to your bank account. Unless you're in quick need of money, it's best to take a check because the funds transfer will cost you a fee. Certificates should be sent to you in the mail for the securities in your account.

2. If you are transferring an account directly to another broker-age, you shouldn't close out your old account immediately. It will be several days before you can trade the securities in your new account, and so the old account may be the only way you can trade those securities if you find you need to trade. Instead, hang on to your old relationship while you begin the transfer process. You will need to obtain your new bro-ker's transfer form and a copy of the most recent statement from the account you are closing. (You can usually request the transfer form, which is a paper form, from the Web site of the brokerage to which you are transferring.) Complete and send the transfer form and the old account statement to your new brokerage firm. It is possible to complete the transfer at the same time that you are opening the new account

3. The transfer of the account may take up to three weeks; this is to allow for a variety of paperwork to be completed by your old broker and your new broker. In the first few days after you file the transfer paperwork with your new broker, you can continue to trade the securities in your old account. After a few days, there will be what's called a "blackout period," in which you will not be able to trade the securities in either your old or your new account. After a few days, the blackout period will pass and you will be able to trade the securities in your new account. However, you may want to hold off until the transfer is confirmed in the order history window of your new account. That is because if you start to

trade securities while they are still in the process of transfer, there is a chance your new broker will become uncertain of the exact nature of the securities being transferred and the transfer will be rejected.

Scarier Than a Blood Transfusion

Given the complex exchange of paperwork and the possibility of transfer rejection, it may be best to plan the transfer of securities for a time when you can afford to simply refrain from trading those securities, just to make sure all goes smoothly.

4. Once you receive confirmation in the order history section of your new account, it should be safe to close out your old account.

Fortunately, there shouldn't be any special tax considerations with an account closeout. Closing out your account is not the same as closing out your position on individual securities. You still own those securities, and so you are not collecting taxable income that you must figure for tax purposes.

However, it's important to hang onto your old account records; you will need them when tax time rolls around. In fact, you might want to make a printout of the various sections of your broker's Web site that display account balances, order history, capital gains, and so on.

You should make printouts of online account records, including transaction history and account balances, for tax purposes.

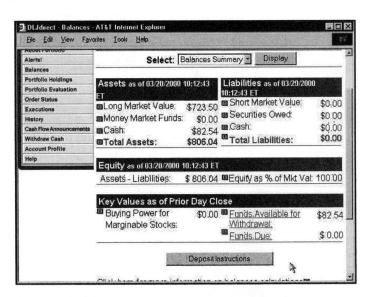

Know What's Coming to You

Make sure to check your balances statement online before closing out your account. You should know exactly how much in cash and securities your broker is supposed to send you or transfer to your new account. In fact, it's not a bad idea to print out the Web page containing your balances statement so that you may avoid any disputes down the road.

What You've Learned

The most important elements of keeping out of trouble when online are hanging onto your own common sense and avoiding the quick buck approach to investing. Hopefully, this chapter has given you a sense of some of the specific pitfalls to avoid in the evolving world of online trading. You should now have a sense of

- What can go wrong in the course of a normal trading session and how to deal with it.

- More serious types of fraud that can be perpetrated against you, and how you should respond to them.

- How to manage canceling or moving your online account.

PART IV

Special Trading Situations

CHAPTER 12

Getting Into IPOs Online

Perhaps by now you've grown tired of following the latest high-tech momentum stock. You've mastered completing your tax return and you've had all you can take of stock discussions in the online chat forums. What you want is a little adventure at the cutting edge of investing. There couldn't be anything more daring than plunking your money into a young, risky company that's just coming onto the market. This chapter explains the how-tos and the wherefores of investing in new companies through what's called the *initial public offering*, or IPO.

What You'll Learn in This Chapter:
- ▶ What is the initial public offering?
- ▶ Why are IPOs so hot?
- ▶ How to trade in IPOs.
- ▶ Other ways to go about investing in IPOs.

The Initial Public Offering: A Definition

Thousands of new companies are born every year. Long before they ever go public, when they are just starting out, most companies are self-funded—they receive money from their friends and families or founders' life savings. Or, they may seek money from private investors, called venture capitalists, who act as money managers for well-endowed universities, corporations, and wealthy individuals.

Sooner or later, though, these same investors seek to cash out and they need to sell their investment to someone else. The company they've backed will need access to more funding if it is to continue to grow. The solution is to make the private company a publicly traded company. The initial public offering is how that's done.

The IPO, or *initial public offering*, is a first public offering of stock for a young company. It can also be thought of as the process by which a company "goes public."

The actual offering of stock is a multi-stage process in which the company and its investors seek out an underwriter to help support the issuing of public shares.

The *underwriter* is an institution, usually an investment bank, that helps organize the offering of new shares.

Underwriters such as Morgan Stanley are responsible for bringing companies public.

The investment bankers actually have a number of specific responsibilities:

- The bankers help the company decide how many shares of stock to sell based on the company's capital needs and the banker's sense of how much of an appetite there is in the market for the company's stock.

- Investment bankers determine the price at which the new stock will be offered, based on a series of calculations involving how much cash the company is expected to generate down the road and, again, what kind of demand there is in the market. The price they decide on is called the *offer price*.

  The *offer price* is the price at which shares of stock are offered to the public.

- The investment banker helps to organize a "road show," in which the company's executives travel to meet with potential shareholders to pitch the value of the business.

- The investment banker helps to draw up a prospectus of the company, officially dubbed an "S1," which must be submitted to the Securities and Exchange Commission and be approved prior to the offering going forward.

  The *prospectus* is a formal report listing the amount of shares offered and their value; the company's historical revenue and earnings; a description of its business and market; its management team; and the major shareholders and their percentage holdings of the company's outstanding stock. Before the prospectus is approved by regulators, it is usually referred to as a "red herring" to distinguish it from the final version of the S1.

- The retail and institutional brokers at the underwriter go to work selling the offering to their clients.

Never Too Old to Go Public

IPOs are commonly associated with relatively young companies, but there's no hard and fast rule about that. In fact, in 1999 a little brokerage by the name of Goldman Sachs went public 130 years after its founding. Goldman was the last private investment house on Wall Street to sell shares in the company to the public. Although the move to bring in public investors was hotly debated within Goldman given the firm's focus on returning profits to its partners, the need for new capital to compete with other, larger banking houses finally pushed Goldman to make an offering.

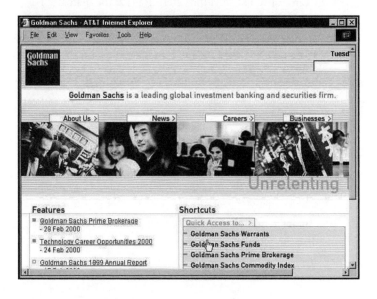

Goldman Sachs went public in 1999, 130 years after its founding.

The Race to Get Into IPOs

How big is the IPO phenomenon? Big and getting bigger all the time. Technologic Partners, which publishes *VentureFinance*, a magazine covering the IPO market, says that in 1999, 397 new high-tech companies offered their stock for the first time on public markets—a record, and way above 1998's total of 127 or even the previous record, 371, back in 1996. The public offering market can fluctuate in popularity year to year. Generally, when investors are eager to find new places to put their money, as in strong economic times like the present, IPOs will get a good hearing.

Recently, though, investors have taken to IPOs as a kind of get-rich-quick scheme. Why? It's often true that buying the stock of successful companies when they first begin to trade can lead to dramatic percentage returns over several years.

For example, a thousand dollars invested in shares of Cisco Systems stock in 1990, when the company first began trading publicly, would be worth approximately $580,000 today, a return of 58,000%. If you had invested four years later, in 1994, you would have enjoyed a return of 2,600%. That's not bad, but obviously far less on a percentage basis.

But that's not why people get into IPOs. Getting into IPOs is all about the difference between the offering price for shares of new stock and the price on the first day of trading.

- When people talk about getting into IPOs, what they mean is getting hold of shares at the price set by the underwriter, before the stock actually begins to trade on its first day. Most investors expect that they will be able to turn around and sell shares on the first day at a profit because they expect the price to rise above the initial price set by the underwriter.

- Most IPO shares are usually reserved for select customers, which means that the average investor can't get shares of IPOs before they start trading. Instead, most investors buy IPO shares by purchasing them on the first day of trading, just like any other stock.

This is a crucial distinction. When people talk about getting into IPOs, they mean getting in on the ground floor at the price set by the underwriter, not the price on the open market.

Why? Easy profit is why. During a period when IPOs are popular, shares purchased at the underwriter's price can be sold for enormous profits on the first day of trading. Recent examples abound. On December 9, 1999, a four-year-old company named VA Linux Systems began trading with an official price of $30. The stock jumped by 967%, a first-day record, to $320 dollars before finishing the day at $239. Obviously, those who were able to sell shares purchased at the offer price of $30 stood to make a fortune.

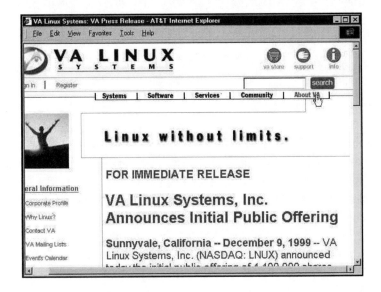

VA Linux Systems had a record bounce on its first day of trading.

The No-Flipping Clause

There's an important note to all the excitement about buying into IPOs at the offer price. Even though you may feel privileged, you won't enjoy the status of a pure insider. While the underwriter and special clients may sell on the first day, your online broker will likely request that you hold your shares of stock for anywhere from 30 to 60 days after the first day of trading. This is called the no-flipping clause, because it prevents you from "flipping" your shares on the first day and profiting from the difference between the offer price you paid and the price in the market—just exactly what you'd hope to do! Some brokers will practice a soft no-flipping rule. They will allow you to sell at any time, but if they notice that you keep flipping IPO shares, they may curtail your participation in IPOs at their discretion.

These policies should be clearly stated in the information on your broker's site regarding IPOs, so make sure to check those postings and keep the no-flipping rule in mind if you are expecting an easy profit from IPOs.

Are IPOs Fail-Safe?

Getting in on the offer price of an IPO sounds great, but it's not always profitable. In fact, most are a failure in the first year after trading. A study by *SmartMoney* magazine found that two-thirds of all initial public offerings trade below their offer price in the six months following their IPO (although they may of course increase in price after that). That means that even if you are lucky enough to get in on the IPO at its offer price, you could still lose money more than half the time unless you sell right when the stock begins to trade. It's even possible for IPOs to trade below their offer price on the first day.

Risks of Buying in Above the Market Price

You should keep in mind the other side of investing in IPOs: buying at prevailing market prices on the first day of trading. If you're not able to get shares from your broker at the offering price, you could be one of the people paying extraordinarily high prices if a stock does jump on its first day. In fact, one of the most unfortunate investment mistakes in times of IPO fever is to enter a market order before the stock begins to trade.

As mentioned in Chapter 8, "Placing Your First Trade," the first hour of trading on any day is the most volatile part of the day. If there is pent-up demand for an IPO, the volatile start of trading is when shares are likely to jump far above their offer price. If you enter a market order the day before, expecting to pay the offer price, you may be surprised to find you have actually paid far more when things take off.

For this reason, it's good to take the following precautions:

- As with any volatile stock, avoid submitting orders to be transacted at the opening of trading the next day.

- If you are going to bid on an IPO at the opening of trading, always submit your bid as a limit order. This way, if the price jumps far above the offer price there is a limit to how much premium you will pay.

A Better Way to Invest Early?

Once you start looking into IPOs and all the hassles involved with getting shares or, worse, the consequences of buying at market prices on opening day, you might ask why you can't just put some money into companies when they are still private. Investing in private companies, what's commonly known as a "private placement," has numerous regulations placed on it by the SEC that usually limit participation by ordinary investors. Banks are allowed to offer shares either to large institutions or to individuals who qualify as "accredited investors," meaning they have a personal net worth of $1 million and income of at least $200,000 in the last two years (or $300,000 for a couple), and they can reasonably be expected to continue earning that level of income in the future. Brokers may also offer shares to up to 35 people who are not accredited investors, but they must make sure that the investment complies with those individuals' experience and goals as investors, and they must have an existing broker-client relationship with those investors. Still, there have been many attempts to give investors access to private placements. A recent example is a group known as OffRoad Capital, which for a $1,000 one-time membership fee and a $250 annual fee to renew membership, will send you prospectuses of private companies that have registered with OffRoad. Some online brokers, among them Schwab, are beginning to offer this service to their clients in partnership with OffRoad. OffRoad says it tends to recommend investments to its members of at least $25,000. Similar ventures are starting to pop up, such as E*Offering, from Web broker E*Trade.

OffRoad capital gets investors into private placements.

Trading IPOs

As previously mentioned, what is generally meant by "trading IPOs" is purchasing shares of new offerings at their offering price. IPOs are not an automatic privilege of having an online trading account. Unfortunately, if you're a new investor, IPOs may be beyond your reach. Not all brokerages offer IPO trading, and those that do reserve IPOs as a special service for their most valuable customers. You may be required to do the following:

- Have a minimum balance of $100,000 in equity in your account before you can begin trading.

- Complete an evaluation form asking certain questions about your investment background. Because new, young companies are inherently more risky than investing in companies that have been public for some time, brokers want to know that you are not an absolute neophyte and that you have some investing experience. You will likely be asked to state your investment objectives. Usually, candidates for IPO trading are expected to declare a "speculative growth" approach to investing or something similar.

- Have funds in your account to cover the number of shares you intend to purchase. You may not need to have these funds in your account when you first place your order, but you must deposit these funds into your account once you're given shares, just as with normal stock purchases. (IPOs cannot be traded on margin. See Chapter 13, "Trading on Margin and Trading Options.")

Not every broker will let you order IPOs online. Some may require that you phone in your order. Generally, you will not have to pay a fee for ordering IPO shares because the normal brokerage commission is paid to the broker by the issuer of the IPO as a percentage of the total value of the offering.

With those brokers that do provide trading of IPOs, the process goes something like this:

- You must first find the section listing upcoming IPOs that you can participate in. This may be in a section titled IPOs, or it may be in a section broadly titled "new issues."

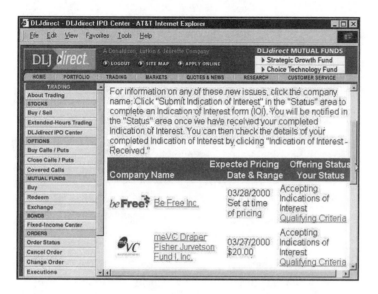

Find the section for new issues.

- You must follow the link for the prospectus. Reading the prospectus is a condition of participating in the offering, and you will be asked when you go to make your bid for shares whether or not you have read it.

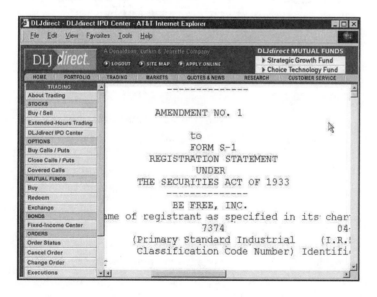

Find the prospectus for the offering.

- After reading the prospectus, you can make what's called a "conditional" offer to purchase shares. Your bid is conditional on the offering being approved by officials and proceeding as planned.

- When the initial, unapproved prospectus, or red herring, is filed, the final offer price for the offering will be undecided. Instead, a range of possible prices will be listed. As with other stock purchases, you may enter market orders, indicating your willingness to purchase shares at whatever the offer price may be, or you may enter limit orders, indicating that you will only purchase shares up to a certain offering price. You'll be asked to state the number of shares you're interested in as well.

- Just as with any order, you should receive a confirmation notice after submitting your order indicating that your expression of interest in the offering has been received.

- You will be contacted by email the day before the offering has been made official by the SEC and asked to reconfirm your conditional offer. The day the IPO is made official is sometimes referred to as the pricing date, because it is on that day that the underwriter announces not just the date of the IPO, but also the price at which it will be officially listed. If you can't be reached by your brokerage, your conditional offer may be pulled and you will miss the IPO. When reconfirming your conditional offer, you have the opportunity to change the number of shares you are interested in receiving.

- Once you have reconfirmed your conditional offer, the allocation of shares to you and the other interested investors will start on the pricing day. In most cases, there will be a limited amount of shares withheld for brokerage customers. For that reason, you and other clients of your online broker will typically be entered into a lottery for shares. Any leftover shares will be granted on a first come, first served basis.

Keep in mind that brokerages don't have to offer shares to anyone. They can and sometimes do decide to reserve shares or not to offer shares at all. Or, your broker may limit the total number of shares that you can purchase. Just because there's a prospectus on your broker's Web site doesn't mean you're necessarily entitled to shares.

If your order for shares has been accepted and you've been allocated shares, you'll be informed of such via email, and you should be notified when the final version of the prospectus shows up on the Web. Keep in mind that when you first submit your conditional order, you'll see the order in the status window of your IPO section. Likewise, once your order is accepted and shares are delivered to your account, you should see them listed in the normal portfolio display. It's important to remember that as with normal purchases, you will have three days to deposit funds to your account to cover the purchase.

IPO shares in your account can be sold via the normal process, but be careful to observe the no-flipping rule previously mentioned.

Getting Information About IPOs

Given that there's less information publicly available about new, young companies, it's good to arm yourself with as much information as possible. Consider the following information sources:

- Your first task is to find out about a new offering. If you are interested in the overall market for new offerings, and not just those offered through your broker, you can get notification of new offerings from third-party sites that specialize in IPO information. Several of these are listed in the appendix of Web URLs at the back of this book. They include sites such as IPOHome.com and IPO.com. There are more of these popping up every day, it seems. Very often these sites will boil down the essence of a prospectus, which can give you a quick read of what a company is about. (Some third-party sites may charge annual subscriptions, which in some cases can be several hundred dollars.)

- In addition to checking third-party sites, be sure to check the news section of the Securities and Exchange Commission's Web site. This site lists new prospectuses the day after they are filed.

Coming to Your Town

Keep in mind that not all IPOs can be traded from every state in the U.S., not even over the Internet. Companies that are filing to go public must comply with something called the "blue sky laws" regarding proper disclosure as defined by each state. It's possible for a company to be cleared in most states, but not in your state, in which case the IPO will go forward but you will not be able to participate.

Third-party sites, such as IPO.com, give you up-to-the-minute filing information.

The news section of the SEC's Web site lists the previous day's prospectus filings.

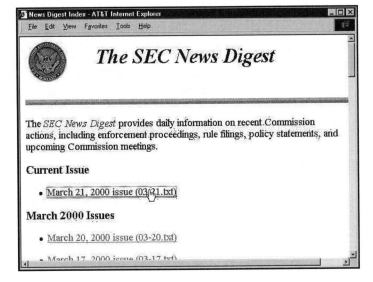

- To keep track of upcoming IPOs, you'll want to check an IPO calendar on a regular basis. If your brokerage supports online trading of IPOs, it will likely offer a calendar of IPOs on the site.

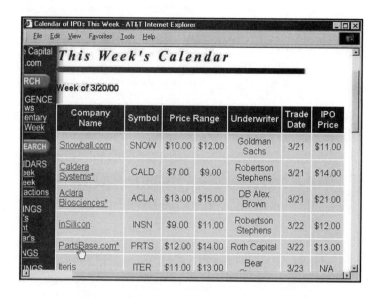

Consult the IPO calendar to keep up with new offerings.

- Reading the prospectus at your broker's site is, of course, a must before you make any trades.

- You may want to look at historical data on how similar IPOs have performed to get a sense of what your chances are of holding a turkey or a winner in six months' time. Again, third-party IPO information sites usually offer performance data for IPOs from previous years.

Third-party sites such as IPOHome.com can give you historical data for comparable IPOs.

- Of course, don't forget to check the Web site of the company you are investing in. While you may find the material somewhat bombastic, you should take advantage of basic product information and information about the company's management.

Company Web sites will give you some basic, if biased, information about products and management.

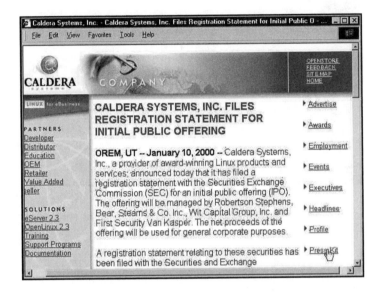

Alternatives for Investing in IPOs

If IPOs are what you care about most in investing, you may want to consider a brokerage that specializes in them.

William R. Hambrecht, the founder of a prestigious San Francisco investment firm, Hambrecht & Quist, started a new venture in 1999 called WR Hambrecht & Co. designed to bring IPOs to the average investor. You can open a standard cash or margin account with Hambrecht and trade stocks per usual.

In addition, though, Hambrecht holds what's known as a "Dutch auction" for IPOs. In the Dutch auction, both large institutional investors and individuals are invited to submit bids for as much as they're willing to pay for each share of stock, plus a request for the total number of shares they want. All bids above a certain minimum are accepted, and those bidders are given as many shares as requested. Bidders at or below that minimum get a percentage of the shares left over.

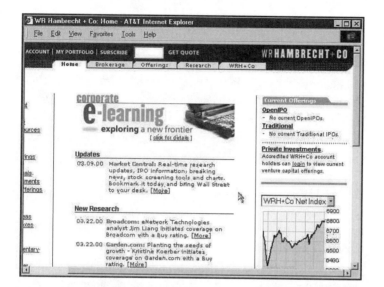

WR Hambrecht is trying to change the offering process.

The Dutch auction at Hambrecht may be a more equitable way of allocating IPOs.

The point is that by letting each bidder vote exactly how much he or she thinks shares are worth, there may be less of a chance that those with overwhelming capital assets can dominate the IPO process. That's the theory, at least. WR Hambrecht & Co. is young and the auction is unproven, so stay tuned.

You'll have to apply for the auction as a separate procedure after you've already been approved for a WR Hambrecht brokerage account. The OpenIPO requires no minimum deposit beyond the basic $2,000 initial deposit for your brokerage account. But as with other IPOs, you must purchase the shares you bid on with cash, as opposed to buying them on margin.

In addition to the OpenIPO auction, Hambrecht offers participation in traditional offerings underwritten by other firms that do not use the auction method. For these offerings, you will need to go through the usual approval process with Hambrecht. You will also need to maintain a $25,000 balance.

Public Venture Capital

There's one last option to consider that may be the safest way to play the new issues market. Even if you can't get into a private placement and you don't want the risk of playing Hambrecht's Dutch auction, you can still put some money into public companies that specialize in investing in and taking public private companies. These firms, which are multiplying rapidly, are commonly referred to as public venture capital companies because like the venture capitalists who back young private firms, these publicly traded money management companies put money into outfits that are have not yet gone public, but that could bring a big return when they do go public.

An example of a public venture capitalist is CMGI, based in Andover Massachusetts, which itself went public in 1996.

CMGI has invested in several prominent Internet companies in the past few years and taken many of them public at record valuations, including Lycos, the Internet portal site, and Geocities, a company that offers home pages on the Web and that was subsequently bought by Yahoo!, the Internet search engine. Investors in CMGI benefit from the company's investing savvy by seeing their shares of CMGI stock appreciate. Since the time it went public in 1996, through the end of 1999, CMGI stock rose 7,000%. That kind of success has spurred competitors, and there are now other prominent public venture companies, such as SafeGuard Scientific. Investing in these companies is an interesting way to follow the private equity market and the public offering process at arm's length.

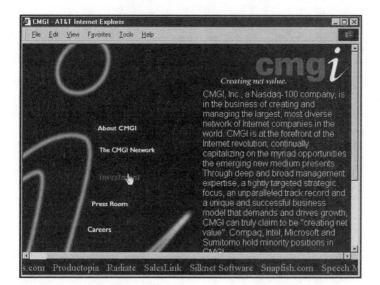

CMGI is one of the new breed of public venture capital firms that let you get in on IPOs indirectly.

What You've Learned

If your interest in IPOs is piqued, hopefully this chapter has given you the basic information you need to start examining the world of new issues. You should have learned

- What an IPO is, how the IPO process works, and how you can get involved.

- How to place trades for IPO shares with your online account.

- Sources of information on new offerings.

CHAPTER 13

Trading on Margin and Trading Options

So you're bored already just trading high-tech stocks and stuffing your portfolio with bonds? At some point you will of course hear people mention casually that they are trading like a demon with "margin privileges." Or they may say that they've been selling short several shares of a highly speculative, hot growth stock.

Welcome to the world of margin trading, where your ability to purchase securities increases dramatically. Margin is nothing more than a loan from your broker: Just as you use home loans or auto loans to make significant life (or lifestyle) purchases, you may at times find that your investing goals can only be met if you have more cash at your disposal to put into securities right away. What's more, as you become a more aggressive investor, you may want to try the practice of short-selling, meaning trading in securities you don't own. You cannot sell securities short without margin privileges, because selling short is basically a form of borrowing securities from your broker. This chapter will help you understand how to obtain and how to use margin privileges. But beware: As discussed at the end of this chapter, margin trading takes you into a whole new world of risk and potential loss. If you're not an experienced investor, trading on margin can be a quick route to financial ruin.

What You'll Learn in This Chapter:

▶ What margin borrowing is and how it works.

▶ How to trade on margin.

▶ The margin call.

▶ What options are and how they work.

▶ How to trade options.

How Margin Borrowing Works

Margin borrowing is an alternative to going to the bank and taking out a personal loan, an education loan, a car loan, or any other borrowing you might do for major purchases. A primary benefit is that your broker will offer you interest rates lower than the standard bank rate. But that's not all. Banks won't give you money with which to gamble on the stock market, so margin loans from your broker are the only way to make further investments beyond the cash you have at hand. What's more, when you use margin loans to purchase stocks on margin, your broker will in some cases float you funds that can effectively double the amount of spending power you have. It's a special feature that goes beyond the ordinary lending process.

The main benefits of margin accounts are

- Low-interest loans. Margin accounts are not just for trading. One big advantage in margin accounts is the ability to get low-interest loans for car purchases, home purchases, or any other major investment for which you need extra capital. Rates on margin borrowing can be quite low. For example, some brokers will offer margin loans at rates as low as 7%–9%, versus a bank loan offering 12%–13% interest.

- Flexible payments. Margin loans, unlike commercial loans, usually have no repayment schedule and no due date. That means that unlike most other loans, you don't have to make payments in any regular fashion, and you can keep the loan outstanding for as long as you are willing to allow interest to build up. (However, as mentioned at the end of this chapter, margin loans can backfire if your broker requests early payment of your debts, which can happen. See the section "Risks of Margin Lending," later in the chapter.)

- Leverage in trading. Using a loan from your broker, you can actually generate additional credit with which to purchase securities. The result is that you can end up with far more money to invest than if your bank were to simply lend you funds to place in the market. The result, in the best cases, is a larger return on investment. Using a margin loan to purchase securities at half their price means you'll get double your return on investment versus paying the cost of the securities up front. Of course, you will ultimately pay the full price of the security plus interest when you repay your loan, but in the meantime you have used less money for an equal return on investment.

- Ability to sell short and to trade in certain options. In fact, you cannot sell short without a margin account. Selling short involves trading stocks you don't own, so you'll need margin privileges to borrow the shares. While you don't need margin privileges to trade in options, you will need them to do what's called writing uncovered or "naked" puts and calls, which are a more risky form of options trading. We'll talk more about this in the next chapter when we talk about options trading in general.

- Unique home loan offerings. Some brokers have gotten into the mortgage business and they will offer you unprecedented mortgage terms. For example, some brokers may allow you to finance 100% of the cost of your home using the securities in your account as collateral. That's a nice way to get around some of the more restrictive terms of traditional mortgage lending, but it also opens you up to risks that extend beyond just losing your investment money, as we'll discuss at the end of the chapter.

How to Obtain Margin Privileges

Assuming you are applying online, there are a few simple steps to follow to set up margin trading privileges:

1. Send an email to your broker's margin trading department, following the instructions in the customer service section of the Web site. In your email you will make a request of the sort, "I would like to set up margin privileges for my account." You will be asked to include your username and account number.

   ▼ **Try It Yourself**

2. You should hear back within 24 hours of submitting your request. You will receive an email asking you for certain additional information about your economic profile. The requested pieces of information will most likely include

   - Current employment status, including self-employed individuals

   - Annual income

- Net worth (see Chapter 9, "Managing Your Portfolio")

- Source of income, including salary, pension, interest income, IRA, mutual fund distributions, and so on

3. You can simply reply to the email message, filling in each blank.

4. Once you've sent your reply, you should hear back from your broker via email within a few business days telling you if you've been accepted or rejected for margin privileges.

▲

Qualifications for Margin Privileges

Realize that by asking your broker to open margin privileges, you are asking him to vouch for your fiscal health because he will be buying securities in your name with the brokerage's money. Brokers must believe you can repay the loan at some point. Moreover, you're not automatically entitled to margin privileges, so granting of such is ultimately at your broker's discretion.

Factors according to which you can be approved or turned down for margin privileges include the following:

- You must have a minimum amount of equity in your account. The actual amount you're required to maintain will vary from broker to broker. $2,000 in equity is standard, but some brokers may require more. Bear in mind that the equity can be in the form of either securities or cash or both.

- You must have sufficient investment experience. How experience is defined and judged will vary from broker to broker, but it's ultimately at their discretion whether you are acceptable material for margin trading.

- You have to have the right investment goals. If you have informed your broker that you're pursuing a conservative strategy of protecting the wealth you have through, say, fixed-income investments with low risk, then your broker may legitimately decide that taking out margin loans doesn't fit your financial objectives and he may turn you down.

- You may also be judged on what kind of assets you maintain aside from the securities and cash in your e-trading account. If you're not making enough in annual salary, it's conceivable you could be declined for margin privileges. Again, this is at your broker's discretion.

On the last point, it's important to note that you're not automatically out of the running for margin privileges if you've been turned down for other credit, such as for a credit card. Even if you have a history of bad credit, you may still be granted margin privileges from a broker, so it doesn't hurt to try.

It's important to note, too, though this may seem obvious, that you must have some securities in your account against which to borrow. Even if you have $2,000 in your account to meet the initial equity requirements, you will not be able to start borrowing if you don't have securities against which to borrow.

How to Trade on Margin

Margin lending is simple if you're using the money to buy a car or a home or some other major life purchase. The amount of cash you have to withdraw from your brokerage account simply increases by the amount borrowed. You'll see this in the Balances display we discussed in Chapter 9. You can then get access to the cash in the same way you normally take cash from your brokerage account—that is, through fax request for wire transfer, by having your broker send a check, or by having money directly transferred if your broker offers some sort of electronic banking service.

Using your loan to trade in securities is a little different. For all intents and purposes, your margin privileges should be transparent as you buy and sell securities. You can purchase stocks on margin, but also mutual funds, bonds, and some types of options. You can enter normal market orders and limit orders and, as you'll see in the next chapter, you'll be able to enter options orders, which you would not be able to do otherwise. However, you should understand the basic rules of margin trading because they will affect what you can spend to buy new securities.

Marginal Differences

Remember from Chapter 3, "Selecting the Right Online Broker for Your Needs," that some brokers will scrutinize you before they'll let you sign up for an account. Well, that fact relates to margin accounts as well. In some cases, a broker may not ask you any questions regarding your fiscal soundness. That is because the broker has already evaluated your financial profile at the time you opened your account. In other words, if you passed muster the first time around, you won't be scrutinized a second time for margin privileges. You'll simply have to complete some extra paperwork.

How to Calculate Your Buying Power

Trading on margin is primarily a way of increasing your buying power, meaning the amount you can spend to buy new securities. Your buying power is a factor of how much your broker will lend you against the assets in your account. In the basic case, you can borrow half the total value of the securities already in your account and 100% of the cash in your account. Your buying power is calculated in the following manner:

1. Take the total value of the securities in your account.

   You can borrow up to some percentage of that amount. It might be 50%, it might be less.

2. You can use the money borrowed to purchase up to half the value of any security.

Let's break it down with an example. Your entire brokerage account consists of $10,000 worth of IBM stock. You want to buy $10,000 worth of Microsoft stock. You can borrow up to half of the total amount of IBM stock, or $5,000. You then use the $5,000 to purchase the Microsoft stock, paying the balance—$5,000—from the cash in your account.

In practice, the entire transaction will be transparent in the sense that your purchase of Microsoft shares will be the same as any other purchase of securities. The only difference is that when you go to pay for the securities by depositing funds to your account, you will only need to deposit 50% of the total purchase price, not 100%.

Marginability

That's not hard to understand, is it? Margin lending simply lets you borrow half the value of your stocks and trade with that money. But there's another factor to take into account called *marginability*. Marginability refers to both securities in your account and securities you want to buy. How much you can borrow to trade depends on the concept of marginability.

A stock is *marginable* when you can borrow against it. Basically, securities are marginable only if they are relatively stable investments that are not likely to fluctuate wildly in value. Your banker doesn't want to be holding highly risky stocks or mutual funds as collateral for your loan, so he or she may declare certain securities "unmarginable." The total amount you can borrow is proportional to the amount of marginable securities in your account. If you have $10,000 in marginable securities in your account, it means that $10,000 worth of the shares you hold are suitable to serve as collateral for the margin loan. As mentioned previously, up to $5,000 can be borrowed, assuming you can borrow 50%, as mentioned above.

But there's a second part to this. Marginability also refers to the stocks you intend to buy with the money. If the stocks you intend to buy are marginable, you can increase your buying power up to twice the amount you have borrowed on margin. That means that if you have $10,000 in marginable securities, you can buy $10,000 more in marginable securities.

This leads to the following rules of thumb:

- You can buy half-again as much in non-marginable securities with borrowed funds as the total amount of marginable securities already in your account.

- You can buy as much again in marginable securities with borrowed funds as the marginable securities in your account.

When buying marginable securities, your broker is in effect lending to you twice: once based on the marginability of the stocks in your account and a second time based on the marginability of the stocks you are trying to buy. The result is that you can double your portfolio's value without having to spend a penny. In practice, you won't have to deposit any funds to cover the purchase price of securities bought in this way.

How Buying Power Can Vary with Marginability

Depending on how much of your assets are marginable and how much of the shares you are buying are marginable, your total buying power will vary. Here's how to think about it:

- You can only borrow against the total amount of marginable securities. That means that if you have $10,000 in securities in your account but only $5,000 are deemed marginable by your broker, you can only borrow against that $5,000. With $5,000 in marginable securities, you could borrow up to $2,500.

The Case of the Disappearing Marginability

You might wonder what happens if you open a margin account and then you sell all your marginable securities and end up with a portfolio filled with nothing but non-marginable securities. Will you lose your margin account? No. Your margin account will still be active, but you will not be able to borrow any money until you fill your portfolio with some marginable securities against which you can borrow.

- If the new securities you want to buy are themselves margin-able, you can figure your total buying power by dividing the total amount of your margin loan by what's called the "margin requirement" of the securities you are trying to buy.

What is a margin requirement? Not all marginable stocks were created equal. Securities have different margin requirements, which means the amount of their value that can be borrowed. In the best cases, securities will be 50% *marginable*, as they say. That means that if you divide your loan amount by .5, the normal maintenance requirement, you will come up with double your loan amount. To return to the preceding example, if you have $5,000 in marginable securities in your account and you are able to borrow $2,500 in margin loans, you can purchase up to $5,000 worth of securities that have a 50% margin requirement. $5,000, then is your new buying power, the amount you can spend on securities.

If, however, the securities you are trying to buy are deemed more risky, for whatever reason, the margin requirement will be a higher percentage—say, 70%. That means you will have to divide your loan amount by .7 instead of .5. To continue with our original example, if you have $5,000 worth of marginable securities in your account, and you borrow $2,500 and you try to purchase securities with a 70% margin requirement, you will only be able to purchase $3,571 on margin before you have to put up some cash. Your buying power, in other words, is $3,571 instead of $5,000 as in the previous case.

Your buying power is always expressed by the following formula:

$$\frac{(\text{value of marginable securities} / 2)}{\begin{array}{c}\text{margin requirement of securities}\\ \text{you are purchasing}\end{array}} = \text{your buying power}$$

The following table shows an example of how your buying power might be calculated.

Calculating Buying Power in a Special Situation

Total value of your securities	$50,000
Total value of marginable securities	$20,000
Total amount you can borrow	$10,000
Maintenance requirement of the security you are buying	70% or .7

Divide the margin amount you are borrowing by the maintenance requirement	$10,000/.7
To get your total buying power	$14,285

As you can see from the table, $20,000 worth of marginable securities can be used to buy up to $14,285 worth of new securities if those securities have a slightly higher margin requirement, in this case 70%. If the security in question were a normal marginable security, the margin requirement would be 50%, or .5, and the total amount you could spend on margin—your total buying power—would be $20,000, the exact same amount as the value of the marginable securities in your account.

In the first case, you would end up holding $64,285 worth of securities in your account if you used your entire buying power; in the second case, where you're purchasing securities with the less restrictive 50% margin requirement, you would end up with $70,000 in securities in your account if you used your entire buying power.

Some Marginability Is Better Than No Marginability

In general, it's less likely that securities will have exotic maintenance requirements than that they will not be marginable at all. That means that in most cases, your buying power will be either exactly half the total value of the your marginable securities in your account or exactly the same as their total value, not in between. And that means that most of the time you shouldn't have to go through the exotic calculations listed above. What a relief!

Knowing Your Marginability

Your account balance will usually tell you what amount of your securities are marginable. Remember the discussion of the portfolio balance display in Chapter 9? Once you've signed up for margin privileges, if you go back to your portfolio Balances display, you should see a display for margin buying power.

The Balances display shows your margin buying power.

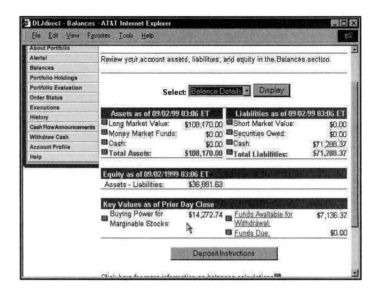

Likewise, when you go to make a trade on your Web page, you will be notified if you are about to purchase a marginable security or if there are different maintenance requirements for the security.

You'll receive a flag if the security you are about to buy is non-marginable.

Generally, brokerages do not post reasons for a particular security to be non-marginable. The reasons themselves may be changing. In general, there are a few reasons why stocks may not be marginable:

- Recently public stocks. If a security only began to trade publicly in the past few months, it may not be marginable.

- Highly volatile stocks. Stocks or mutual funds that fluctuate wildly may not be marginable.

- Stocks that cost under $5 per share. These stocks are simply too small to be margined.

Maintaining Your Margin Account

What happens after you've purchased on margin?

- Your account balance will show the total amount of the securities purchased on margin in the liability, or debit, section, rather than the asset section where securities you own are usually displayed.

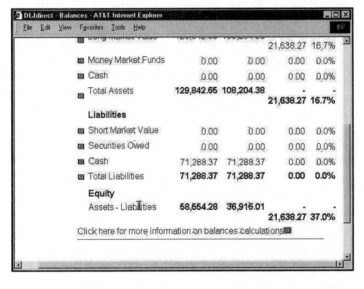

Your Balances section will show the amount spent on margin in the debit column.

- The amount spent on margin will be a debt that you owe your broker, and you will pay interest on that debt at your broker's specified margin lending rates.

- If you spend any amount on securities over and above your total buying power, you will owe that amount to your broker in the same way you must pay your broker for normal trades made in a cash account. That means that you will have to deposit cash to cover that purchase within three business days following the trade.

The Margin Call

Okay, you've bought some stocks on margin and you're reveling in your margin buying power. But the trick with margin trading is that if your securities don't perform the way you hope, you could receive a *margin call*.

Remember that some initial amount of equity must be deposited into your account in order simply to be approved for margin privileges. It turns out that you must also maintain a certain amount of that equity in your account or you will be in violation of your margin privileges.

A *margin call* means that the combination of stocks you actually own and cash in your account, referred to as your equity, has dropped below a certain allowable percentage of your portfolio. This can happen because the marginable securities against which you've borrowed have dropped in value, making the equity in your account a lower portion of your combined equity and debt.

The amount of equity you are required to keep in your account varies from broker to broker. A typical requirement is that your equity must equal at least 35% of the total combined value of the stocks you own and those you are holding on margin. This percentage is termed the *maintenance requirement*.

The *maintenance requirement* is the amount of securities owned and cash that you must maintain in your account as a percentage of the securities both owned and held on margin (or borrowed, as is the term in the case of securities sold short).

How a Margin Call Unfolds

With a margin call, the original equity pledged for your margin loan has fallen below the maintenance requirement. For example, suppose you own $10,000 worth of securities and you purchase $2,000 more by taking out a margin loan. Your equity (the $10,000 in securities) represents a healthy 80% of the total value of the securities you hold, including the original $10,000 worth of securities and the $2,000 you've purchased on margin. However, if by some terrible catastrophe that original $10,000 in stock you own falls in value to less than 35% of the value of securities you hold—in this case, if it dropped to $1,000 and your $2,000 worth of stock purchased on margin didn't change in value—you'd suddenly be below the maintenance requirements and have to add funds to bring your equity back up to 35%.

You can reestablish your maintenance requirement in the event of a margin call by doing the following:

1. Deposit cash or marginable securities. You would do this in the normal fashion.

2. Sell some securities and deposit the proceeds into your account.

What happens if you can't do either of these things? If you can't deposit funds and you can't decide which of your assets to sell in order to raise cash, your broker will make that decision for you, selling whatever he or she feels is necessary to bring your equity in line with maintenance requirements.

Calculating Your Equity

Chapter 9 discussed the concept of equity. It's useful to review how equity is determined for the purposes of margin privileges. The formula for margin equity is as follows:

$$\text{equity} = \frac{\text{(the long value of your securities} +}{\text{cash in your account)} - \text{(debit balance)}}$$

Another way to state this is that your equity equals what you have left over in assets after subtracting your outstanding liabilities. Stocks, bonds, and mutual funds actually owned will be listed under long value, while the value of the securities you have purchased on margin will be counted as part of your debit balance.

It's important to realize that equity is not the same as marginable securities. If you have a combination of $5,000 worth of securities owned in your account and $5,000 in cash and you don't owe any money to your broker, then you have a total of $10,000 in equity—the value of your assets over and above your liabilities. If you purchase $2,000 worth of stock on margin, that $2,000 will be subtracted from your $10,000 in equity, leaving you with $8,000.

Maintain the Maintenance

It's especially important to keep track of your equity when you consider the fact that your broker is not required to notify you if your equity falls below the maintenance requirement. In fact, the margin lending agreement you sign when you apply for margin privileges usually includes a clause that will allow your broker to begin the liquidation process if you fall below the maintenance requirement *without ever issuing a maintenance call*. In practice, honest brokers will in fact give you a margin call and will leave it up to you to meet the maintenance requirement. However, as a defensive strategy, you should try to make it your business to keep on top of how well your equity position is meeting the maintenance requirement.

Risks of Margin Lending

Margin lending can be a powerful way to increase your purchasing power, especially with respect to securities. However, it can also get you into a lot of trouble if you cavalierly pursue margin loans without considering the consequences. It's good to keep in mind some of the risks of margin lending before jumping in whole-hog:

- Given the ease with which you can take out money, it's easy to imagine that a margin loan is simply a revolving cash account. Don't get carried away spending the easy money that comes from margin lending. Every time you purchase securities on margin, you are essentially racking up more debt that has to be paid back at some point in the future. Racking up debt with the low interest rates of margin loans can be more dangerous than going to town with your credit cards.

- Purchasing stocks on margin is fun until your positions start to decline and you receive a margin call. Remember that by purchasing on margin you are setting up the expectation that the securities in your account will remain stable in order to serve as collateral. If the long value of those securities begins to decline, you'll have to put new money in to meet margin calls, whether or not shelling out the cash is convenient to you at the time. Even worse, consider the case of a margin loan that is used to purchase some important asset, such as a car or a home. It's one thing to have to sell securities. Consider the case of a new home that is financed 100% through a margin-backed mortgage. It's always conceivable that if your equity declines sufficiently, your new home could be the only piece of collateral left to collect. Your broker can in fact put a lien on that mortgage, which would require you to sell your home to make payment to your broker.

- With increased buying power, you may be tempted to speculate more frequently in the market, and that can lead you to be less careful about the kinds of investments you are making. If you get careless about your investing in the rush to exercise your purchasing power, you'll run a greater risk of ending up with dogs in your portfolio.

Graham Frowned on Margin Investing

The legendary securities analyst Ben Graham frowned upon the use of margin lending for securities purchases for the very reason that investing discipline, he felt, was cast overboard. His thinking was that investors using margin were more likely to make impatient, short-sighted decisions in an attempt to speculate, rather than long-term decisions based on sound investment. As Graham wrote in his landmark 1934 book *Security Analysis*, "...The margin trader is necessarily concerned with immediate results; he swims with the tide, hoping to gauge the exact moment when the tide will turn and to reverse his stroke the moment before. In this he rarely succeeds, so that his typical experience is temporary success ending in complete disaster."

- Lastly, if you use your margin borrowing abilities to write options contracts, or to sell short, you can quickly rack up a mountain of debt in your account that dwarfs the problems of margin calls on ordinary stock purchases. Selling short is actually much riskier than buying securities on margin in the normal manner. With the short sale you are selling securities borrowed from your broker and hoping that you can buy them back at cheaper price. But there's no guarantee that's the way it will work out and, in fact, there's no limit to how much more you may end up paying to buy back the shares for your broker. Writing options contracts runs a similar risk. As discussed in the next chapter, both short selling and writing options contracts expose you to the potential of unlimited risk. And if you think that sounds bad, it is—*very bad!*

Further Considerations of Margin Call Issues

There are a couple of fine details to keep in mind about how the margin call works, too. When you receive a margin call, you've got to effectively "bail water" in your account to bring your equity back into alignment with the maintenance requirement. Not only is that an unhappy occurrence, it can have a far-reaching effect on your investment success. As an investor, you are being asked to sell securities whether or not you can make money off of them by the sale. You may have to sell securities that are losing you money, rather than holding onto them until they reach profitability. Or you may have to sell really good investments that you should stay in for the long term.

Meeting a margin call, in other words, hinders your ability to make good investment decisions and can seriously harm your investing strategy by making you cash out of positions at inopportune moments.

And it gets worse. As mentioned, your broker is not required by law to give you a margin call. Although most honest brokers will do so, it's conceivable that a broker could simply start liquidating your assets. At that point, you have absolutely no say over what your broker will decide to sell, which is obviously not good. As part of this practice, your broker is entitled to sell whatever he must to meet your maintenance requirement. In some cases, your broker may actually sell more securities from your account than is in fact required, but he is unfortunately not required to return the difference to you.

What's more, although you can hold a margin loan indefinitely, a quality that makes them highly desirable, your broker retains the right to demand payment at any time in full. Again, most honest brokers won't capriciously demand that you settle your account, but they will retain such rights as part of the terms of granting your margin privileges.

Lastly, consider that no matter how vigilant you are about your maintenance requirements, your broker reserves the right—again, as part of the fine print in the margin agreement—to raise your maintenance requirement at any moment in time. You could be at 35% one day, and 50% the next. Again, an honest broker won't pursue such capricious activities, but it's something worth keeping in mind when you're signing up for margin borrowing.

What You've Learned

This chapter should have given you some idea of how margin lending, and trading on margin, differs from getting an ordinary loan. Margin lending is an important tool to give you leverage in building your portfolio. But it's also one that involves subtleties, such as marginability and maintenance requirements, that take time and thought to master. All too often investors rush for the pot of gold held out by margin borrowing, as if it were a gift. Pay close attention to the risks and downsides outlined in this chapter and plan your finances and your goals before you take on any margin. At this point, you should understand

- The advantages of margin borrowing over typical bank loans and how trading on margin can dramatically increase your securities purchasing power.

- How to obtain margin privileges and how to calculate buying power given the basic rules of marginability.

- The unfortunate consequences of out-of-control margin borrowing.

CHAPTER 14

Getting Into Options Trading

Welcome to the wild frontier of securities trading. Options are part of a larger class of financial instruments known as derivatives, and the history of this type of investment has been steeped in scandal for as long as financial markets have been around. In the simplest sense, a *derivative* is the right to purchase or sell a security at some future point in time at a specified price that is fixed. Traders buy and sell these rights just as they would ordinary shares of stock, shares of mutual funds, bonds, or other securities. As such, derivatives are part of the rich history of speculation in financial markets.

Speculation means purchasing a security solely on the expectation that that security will increase in price at a future date, as opposed to investing, where the investor expects the asset itself to increase in value.

Just like initial public offerings, which we covered in Chapter 12, "Getting Into IPOs Online," and day trading, which we'll talk about in Chapter 16, "Day Trading Online," options are probably more complexity than you're interested in. Nonetheless, they are an interesting phenomenon in their own right and knowing something about them can give you perspective into your own investing.

An Overview of Options

Options are a form of derivative that allow a speculator to purchase the option to buy or sell a security at a specified price at some time in the future. The term "option" is apt because the owner of the option has the option to execute the contract on the date of the option, or to let the contract expire worthless.

Speculators buy options contracts because they believe the price of a stock or another security will move up or down by a certain amount in the weeks or months following their purchase of the option. By buying the option, they lock in the right to purchase the stock or bond or other security at a fixed price on the date that the contract comes due. The hope is that the price on that date will be either above the price at which the contract will allow the speculator to buy the security, or below the price at which the contract allows the speculator to sell the security. If that happens, speculators make money on the difference between the price they are entitled to buy or sell at and the going rate at that time.

For example, a basic option purchase might work like this:

Try It Yourself ▼

1. You buy a contract that entitles you to sell some shares of Microsoft stock on a specific date several months away at a price of $150 per share.

2. When the date arrives, you check the price of Microsoft stock in the market. If the price of Microsoft stock is less than $150, your option to sell at $150 will enable you to get a better price for your shares of Microsoft stock than the going rate.

3. You exercise the option to sell Microsoft shares at $150 per share. You don't have to have own the shares of Microsoft in question when you buy the contract. If you do happen to hold the Microsoft shares in your account, you simply sell them and collect the $150 per share. If you don't already own the shares of Microsoft stock, you would simultaneously purchase those shares in the market at the going rate and then sell them for $150 a share, per the contract, pocketing the difference.

▲

How Options Work

The preceding example is rather simplistic. There are important details concerning how the contracts for options are bought and sold, and how you act on your options.

Options are traded on many different securities markets. The largest clearing of options contracts happens on the Chicago Board Options Exchange (CBOE), but options can also be traded

on the New York Stock Exchange and other markets. Options are
purchased just like other securities, but the nature of what is bought
and sold—the contract—is different from a share of stock or a
bond. Following are the basics of how options are bought and sold:

- Someone offers to buy or sell an options contract, which is a
  right to buy or to sell shares of a certain amount of a stock or
  a certain amount of bonds.

- The contract is offered at a certain price, which varies from
  moment to moment just like the price of stock, and there is a
  strike price specified for the contract and a date on which the
  contract expires.

  The *strike price* is the price at which the shares of the security covered by the contract can be bought or sold. The strike
  price is usually different from the market price of the security
  at the time at which the contract is sold.

- The person buying the contract can choose to hold it until the
  expiration date, like holding shares of a stock, or he or she
  can sell it before the expiration date.

- If the speculator chooses to hold the options contract, he or
  she has a choice of exercising the option any time on or
  before the expiration date or just letting the contract expire
  without being acted upon.

There are a few things to keep in mind about the preceding arrangement. First, the option is something separate from the underlying
security to which it pertains. The holder of the contract owns a
right to buy the underlying security, but simply buying the options
contract is not the same as actually owning the underlying security
itself.

Second, the option gives its owner either a right to buy the underlying security or the right to sell the underlying security, not both.
This is specified in the nature of the contract, which is termed
either a *put* contract or a *call* contract.

A *put* is an options contract that gives its owner a right to sell a
security at some point in the future at the specified price. A *call* is

an option that gives its owner the right to buy a security at a certain price. Therefore, when buying an options contract, a speculator is said to buy either a put or a call.

A third point to keep in mind is that the options contract has its own price, which is not the same as the price of the security to which it pertains. Prices of options fluctuate throughout the day as the contracts are bought and sold on the exchange. Pricing an options contract is determined by two things, namely the difference between the strike price and the current price, and a little bit extra that's added on top, called the *time value*.

Time value refers to how far away the exercise date of the option is from the date on which it's purchased. Basically, the further away the exercise date, the more chance there is that the gap between the strike price and the actual price of the stock will widen, giving the holder of the option more potential profit. For that reason, the time value is deemed higher for an expiration date further in the future. An options contract that expires 90 days into the future will be more expensive than a contract with an expiration date that is nearer in time—say, 30 days away—all other things being equal. (But not always, as you'll see.)

Notice, too, that unlike common stock, the number of shares of the underlying security that can be purchased in an option is fixed by the contract. Usually, the amount is 100 shares, though it may vary.

The price of an options contract listed on the exchange is not the total amount you'll pay to buy the contract. Rather, the total amount you'll pay is the listed price multiplied by the number of shares specified in the contract. In other words, a $2 options contract will actually cost you $200 if it represents an option to buy or sell 100 shares. This is often referred to as the *value* of the contract.

The value of the options contract is different from its price. The *value* of the option is its price multiplied by the number of shares of the underlying security specified in the contract. Thus, a contract with a price of $35 giving the buyer a right to purchase 100 shares of a stock has a value of $35×100, or $3,500.

The strike price of the option—that is, the price at which the contract holder may buy the underlying security—may be higher, lower, or equal to the price of the security at the time the contract is purchased. For example, if stock in Cisco Systems is trading at $105, the option may offer the contract holder the right to buy or the right to sell Cisco stock at $105, at $110, at $100, or at some other price different from the current price.

If you choose to sell an option before it expires, you may get a better or worse price than what you paid for it, just like with shares of stock, bonds, or any other security you might trade. That's because the time value is always changing, and generally it will go down over time, bringing down the value of the option.

How Do You Make Money on This?

Now that we've discussed some of the intricacies of the options contract, we can talk about how you make money on an option. There are at least a few ways to make money on options:

- If the price of the underlying security moves in a favorable direction with respect to the market after the contract has been purchased, you can exercise your right to buy (in the case of a call option) the underlying security or to sell it (in the case of a put) and make money on the difference in price.

- If the price of the options contract itself moves in a favorable direction, you can turn around and sell the contract itself at a profit. Remember that the price of an option is the difference between the strike price and the current price of the underlying security (plus a little bit for the time value). If the gap between the two prices starts to widen, the price of the options contract itself will naturally increase as investor interest in owning the contract increases. As interest increases, the price of the contract can be expected to increase in the market, the same way stock goes up in price.

- Lastly, there's a whole world of additional kinds of derivatives, where you can buy and sell options on options. This introduces a new level of speculation because you're gambling on the change in price of the underlying option, which in turn is changing according to the change in the underlying security. The mind reels!

The third scenario is beyond the scope of this book. Suffice it to say that if there's a security that can go up or down, be it a stock or an option on that stock, or an option on the option of that stock, somebody's thought of it, and they're probably trading it!

However, we will talk a bit about the first two situations.

Making Money by Exercising the Option

Let's take a couple of examples. In the first instance, you make money on the change in the underlying security by exercising the right granted to you in the options contract. Let's return to our Microsoft example to see how this is done:

Try It Yourself ▼

1. On December 15, you purchase put options contract XYZ, granting you a right to sell 100 shares of Microsoft stock for $150 on or before January 7. The current price of Microsoft stock is $115 and the price of the option is $36 for each of the 100 shares, for a total price of $3,600. It should be clear that $35 of the price represents the difference between the strike price and the current price, while the balance of the price, $1, is the time value of the option.

2. January 7 arrives and, lo and behold, Microsoft stock has dropped $3 per share to $112 per share. You exercise your right to sell 100 shares of Microsoft stock for $150 each, and at the same time you buy the shares on the market at the going rate of $112 per share.

3. The difference between what you've sold each share for, $150, and what you had to pay to buy each share on the market, $112, is $38 ($150–$112=$38). After subtracting the cost of the options, $36 per share, you've got a profit of $2 per share of Microsoft stock. The contract is for 100 shares, so you've just made $200 in profit.

The preceding transaction is summarized in the following table:

Options Profit Model for a Microsoft Put Option

	Category	Amount
1.	Strike price of options contract less	$150
2.	Microsoft share price at exercise	– $112

	Category	Amount
3.	Equals profit from exercise of put option	= $ 38
4.	Less the cost of options contract	– $ 36
5.	Equals net profit from exercise of put option contract	= $ 2
6.	Multiplied by the total number of shares covered under put option contract	× 100
7.	Equals the total value at exercise of put option contract	= $200

As you can see, two fundamental features of options are important for making money in the preceding example:

- You must be able to sell something you don't already own.

- The only way you can profit from exercising the option contract is if the price of the underlying security at the time you exercise the option is lower than the strike price by an amount greater than the amount you paid for the put contract itself.

On the first score, the owner of a put option (a right to sell shares), must sell shares he or she does not already own and then turn around and buy those shares in order to capitalize on the difference in price. How can you sell something you don't already own? By borrowing the shares from your broker. This is known as *selling short*.

Selling short is the process of borrowing shares to sell and then buying those shares to pay back the party from whom you borrowed the shares. One of the functions of a broker is to lend shares to his or her clients so that they can sell short. The clients will then buy the shares, hopefully at a price lower than what they paid, and give those shares to their broker. We'll talk about this a bit more in "What Options Trading Isn't: Short Selling," later in the chapter.

The second point is that the difference in actual price and strike price has to be sufficient for you to clear a profit. Look again at the preceding table. The profit earned in line 5 is a direct result of the fact that the profit from the exercise of the option on line 3,

$38, is greater than the original price of the contract on line 4, $36. That is a result of the fact that the difference between the strike price and the price of Microsoft shares has widened in the time since the option was purchased. In fact, the difference between the two has widened so much that it has erased the $1 premium you paid for the time value of the option when you first bought the contract.

Making Money by Selling the Options Contract at a Profit

In the second example of options profit, you make money by selling the options contract at a profit without actually exercising the right to buy the underlying security. Taking again our Microsoft example:

Try It Yourself ▼

1. On December 15, you purchase put options contract XYZ, granting you a right to sell 100 shares of Microsoft stock for $150 on or before January 7. The current price of Microsoft stock is $115 and the price of the option is $36 for each of the 100 shares, for a total value of $3,600.

2. The very next day, December 16, Microsoft stock drops $2 to $113 per share. Speculators, sensing weakness in Microsoft shares, start to bid up the price of your XYZ options contract, betting that Microsoft stock will go even lower and your contract to sell Microsoft shares at a high price will soon be worth even more. You notice that the price of your XYZ contract has increased by $2 to $38. You sell the contract for $3,800.

3. The difference between what you paid for the options contract, $3,600, and what you've sold it for, $3,800, is a net profit to you of $200.

▲

Notice that in this second example, there was no actual buying or selling of the underlying security. The only thing bought and sold was the options contract itself.

Benefits of Options

Obviously, you can make some money off of options, just as you can make money trading in securities. So what's so great about options? Three things:

- Limited downside

- Hedging

- Leverage

We'll now talk a little bit about each.

Limited Downside

Limited downside basically means that there is a limit to how much you will be on the hook for if the price of an underlying security of an option contract moves in an unfavorable direction. Think about the cost and the potential payout of an options contract:

- The only money you're guaranteed to have to pay out is the price you paid for the options contract itself. If the price of an underlying security moves in the wrong direction, you can simply let the option expire rather than take a loss. If you buy an option to purchase Microsoft stock at $115 when it is trading at $120 and by some strange fluke the price of Microsoft shares drops to $100, you won't lose the $15 per-share difference. Instead, you simply let the contract expire without exercising your option and you're only out the money you paid for the contract.

- If, on the other hand, the price of the security represented by the options contract moves in the proper direction, there is no limit to the amount of upside you could enjoy. Again, if you buy an option to purchase Microsoft stock at $115 when the stock is trading at $120, there's no limit to how much money you could make depending on how high Microsoft shares go before your contract expires.

For this reason, it's commonly said that options contracts have "limited downside and unlimited upside." However, as you'll see in the "Risks of Options" section later in the chapter, there are some downside aspects to consider.

> **For Whom the Call Tolls**
>
> You might wonder, if you have limited downside, who's left holding the bag when you make money off of a put or a call options contract. After all, if you're making money, someone else has got to lose in the market, right? In fact, every contract is originated by another party called the "writer" of the contract. It is that party's responsibility to sell shares if you decide to exercise a call option to buy the shares. Likewise, the writer must agree to buy shares if you exercise your right to sell shares with a put options contract. We'll talk about this a bit more in the section "Writing Options Contracts: Covered Calls and Naked Puts," when we discuss how you can become the writer of an options contract.

Hedging

The second advantage of options is closely related to the first point. Because there is limited downside risk to put and call options, investors can sometimes use them to hedge the risk they are carrying on a traditional securities investment.

Hedging is the process of using one investment to limit the risk on another investment.

Let's consider how you might use options to protect your downside risk with a traditional investment in Microsoft shares.

Try It Yourself ▼

1. You purchase 100 shares of Microsoft stock at the going rate of $115 per share.

2. At the same time, you purchase a put options contract to sell 100 shares of Microsoft at a price of $115.

3. The put options contract has a price of $3.50 per share of the underlying security, for a total cost to you of $350.

4. Ten days later, shares of Microsoft stock fall to $105. They are now below the price you paid, $115. At this point you have a loss of $10 per share, or $1,000, on the books. But by using your put contract, you can still sell the shares for what you originally paid for them, $115, and recoup your investment. You then have a loss of $350, the cost of the options, versus the $1,000 you would have paid if you had to sell your Microsoft shares at a loss. A put contract used in this way is

▲   sometimes called a *protective put*.

Realize, too, that in the last example as Microsoft shares drop, the value of the put contract itself may have increased because it is now what traders call "deep in the money"—that is, the strike price at which you can sell has risen above the current price of Microsoft shares. Speculators betting that Microsoft shares will fall further might be willing to purchase that put option at a higher price than you paid for it, on the belief that Microsoft shares will continue falling. What that means is that you have a choice of selling your money-losing Microsoft shares, or else selling your put options contract at a profit and holding onto the Microsoft shares in case they start to climb back up. Either way, you've hedged your losses in the underlying security, Microsoft shares, by using the put option.

Leverage

The third benefit of options is leverage. Think about the two examples of options trading in the previous section: the case of exercising the Microsoft options and the case of reselling them for a profit. You did not use your own money to buy the underlying securities covered by the option in either case. In the first case, you had to spend $3,600, the cost of the options, to make $200. Assuming the shares of Microsoft stock sold using the put option were purchased on margin, you didn't have to put up any money for the actual shares of stock, only for the options contract cost. In the second instance, you again spent $3,600 to make $200, and that time you didn't have to trade shares at all. If you had to actually purchase the shares of Microsoft stock covered by the options in each example, you would have spent, at a minimum, $115 per share, the going rate on Microsoft stock, or $11,500. In other words, you spent a lot less money to make money.

The point is, speculating in options can be substantially cheaper than purchasing the underlying security and hoping it will increase in value. This kind of cheap speculation in securities is the essence of leverage.

Leverage is the ability to spend less money for an equal or greater return. In the case of options, rather than buying shares of stock, you spend only the money required to purchase the options, which will always be less than the price of the stock at the time you purchase the options.

The result of spending a smaller amount of money is that the relative return on investment with leverage is greater. Consider the Microsoft example one more time. Suppose that instead of using options, you had purchased Microsoft stock at the going rate of $115 and the price had risen by two dollars per share to $117 the very next week. You would then be able to sell the stock for a profit of $2 per share.

But at $2 per share, your total profit of $200 is only 1.8% of your $11,500 investment. As a percentage of the cost of the options contract ($3,600), on the other hand, the $200 profit is 5.6%, more than three times as much.

Because you can spend less on options than on stock and receive the same or better return, options contracts are sometimes characterized as a means for the small investor to gain an advantage over those with more capital at their disposal.

In-the-Money and Out-of-the-Money Options

To understand leverage properly, it helps to understand a concept that distinguishes options from one another. Options can be *in-the-money* or *out-of-the-money*. You'll recall that that the strike price of an option can be more than, less than, or equal to the current price in the market of the underlying security. The terms in-the-money and out-of-the-money refer directly to this fact about strike prices.

In-the-money options are options whose strike price would yield a profit at the current market of the underlying security. That means that for a put option to sell a security, the strike price is higher than the current price on the market. Likewise, for a call option the strike price would be below the current market price.

In the example of Microsoft stock, the put option is in-the-money because the strike price, $150, is instantly higher than the current price of Microsoft stock, which means that it would yield a profit if exercised immediately.

Out-of-the-money options are options whose strike price would yield no profit at the current market price of the underlying security. That means that for a put option to sell a security, the strike price is less than the price of the underlying security. Likewise, for a call option the strike price would be higher than the current market price for the security.

In the case of an out-of-the-money option, exercising the put and call options would yield no profit, or perhaps even a loss, because

- In the case of a put, exercising the option would mean selling the underlying security at less than the current market price, which would mean a loss when you have to buy the shares at the current market price to cover the short sale.

- In the case of a call, exercising the option would mean buying the underlying security for more than the current market price, which means that when you go to sell the security, you would incur a loss.

So how do these terms affect leverage? Remember that the price of an option is made up of the difference between the strike price and the current price of the underlying security. In the case of out-of-the-money options, the difference between the two is either negative or zero. In either case, the value of the options is considered zero. This means that the price is solely the time value, or the chance that the option will increase in value over time.

As a result, out-of-the-money options are usually extremely cheap compared to in-the-money options. For example, consider the following table, which lists the prices for call options on Microsoft stock at various strike prices, assuming a current price for Microsoft stock of $115.

Comparison of Microsoft Call Options when Microsoft Stock is at $115

When the Strike Price Is	The Price of the Option Is
$100	$15 3/4 (in-the-money)
$105	$10 1/2 (in-the-money)
$110	$5 1/2 (in-the-money)
$115	$1/2 (break even, sometimes called "at the money")
$120	$1/8 (out-of-the-money)
$125	$1/16 (out-of-the-money)

The options strike prices in the left-hand column are listed in descending order from most in-the-money to most out-of-the-money. For example, the $100 strike price at the top is "deep in-the-money," because if it were exercised based on the current price of Microsoft shares, $115, it would yield a profit of $15. In contrast, the strike price of $125 at the bottom is "deep out-of-the-money." If exercised immediately, it wouldn't give any profit at all, but rather a deficit of $10 per share.

The prices of the options reflect this difference in value. The in-the-money options have the most potential value, and so they are the most expensive; the out-of-the-money options have the least potential value at the moment, so they are the cheapest. The price of the $100 option, for example, is $15 3/4 versus $1/16 for the $125 option.

What does this mean? The out-of-the-money $125 option can be bought cheap—it costs only $6.25 for the option to buy 100 shares, as opposed to the $100 in-the-money option, which would cost $1,575. But if Microsoft stock were to jump $11 or more from its current price of $115, to, say $126, the holder of the cheap $125 call options would instantly be in-the-money and could expect a profit of $1 for each share, or $100—less the $6.25 cost of the options contract, of course.

This ability to buy out-of-the-money options dirt cheap, relatively speaking, is the key to gaining leverage and the key to cheap speculation. Rather than spending thousands to buy the actual securities, options traders who buy out-of-the-money options can spend a few hundred dollars on the off chance that the security's price will move in the right direction and the option they hold will suddenly move "into the money," giving them a profit.

You've probably figured out by now that a put option works the same way. Put options that are far out-of-the-money, meaning puts on which the strike price is far too low to be sold at a profit, are going to be far cheaper than puts with strike prices that are in-the-money.

A Final Word About Time Value

We've left out one factor that makes cheap, out-of-the-money speculation slightly more complicated, and that's time value.

You'll recall that the time value is higher and an option gets more expensive the further out its strike price is. Likewise, even an out-of-the-money call or put can become steadily more expensive the further out its expiration date. The following table compares $125 out-of-the-money call options for Microsoft at $115 per share, with three different expiration dates.

Out-of-the-Money Call Options on Microsoft with Different Expirations

When the Expiration Date Is	The Price Is
January	$1 3/8
February	$3 3/8
April	$6 3/8

Thankfully, many of the intricacies of options pricing can be solved by simply checking any of a number of online options calendars. These devices allow you to plug in time value and other considerations and then they spit out options prices.

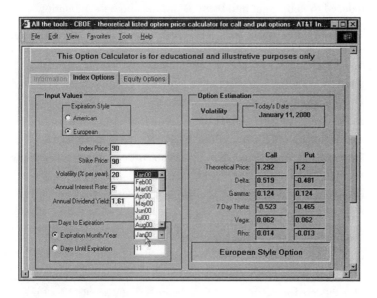

Use an options calculator and skip the mental effort of options pricing.

Risks of Options

Options are an extremely risky proposition. As you can probably tell from the preceding discussion, the contracts themselves are extremely complex animals to understand. Once you get into the intricacies of pricing options, and understand how time value varies and whether options are in-the-money or out-of-the-money, you'll have a lot of different variables to juggle. This is an especially hard science for the amateur to pursue. Moreover, experts caution that even the most experienced speculators lose money on options. It's easy to see why when you consider the risks of options. The primary risks are

- Overspending on out-of-the-money options

- False security of in-the-money options

- Failure to use limit orders and other risk-reducing strategies

- Failure to consider commission charges

Let's talk a bit about each.

The first issue, out-of-the-money options, are sort of a case of "your eyes are bigger than your stomach." Because out-of-the-money options are a relatively cheap way to speculate, you might be induced to jump right into them. But think about the mounting costs of buying several options. Even an option trading at a listed price of 1/16 will have an ultimate cost of $6.25. Given that such options usually don't make it into the money, there's a real risk you'll be induced to spend money on these contracts the way you might at the slot machines: willy-nilly. How many $6.25 contracts can you afford? 100? 1,000? As Nelson D. Rockefeller used to say, at some point that's real money! And if the price of the under-lying security doesn't move in a favorable direction, the money invested in the options contract is basically money down the drain. Unlike shares of stock held, the investment cannot be converted back into cash.

In-the-money options have a similar issue. Just because some-thing is in-the-money doesn't mean you'll automatically make money off of it. The market makers who price options run com-plex models for where they think the underlying securities will trade, and they are not in business to give away money. Therefore, it takes real movement in the underlying stock to give you any kind of profit over and above the cost of the option, including its time value component. Still, many speculators will be led to load up on in-the-money options because they offer limited downside and unlimited upside.

Because they reflect a difference between the strike price and the current price, in-the-money options are more expensive than out-of-the-money options. So, you have to ask yourself the same question as in the first point above, namely, how many options contracts with a total cost of $50 can you afford? 100? 1,000? Like out-of-the-money options, if you don't resell the options or exercise them, but rather let them expire, the money spent on them is money down the drain. Think about that when you see a deep in-the-money option that seems to offer $50, $100, or more in potential profit based simply on its strike price.

The third problem is a case of not following ordinary, proper trading procedures. As mentioned earlier, options contracts are securities just like any other. Their price fluctuates throughout the day, moment to moment. You have to protect yourself from overpaying by accident. In some cases, the price of options contracts can be inherently more volatile than regular shares of stock or bonds or other securities.

Volatile basically means something that is likely to make wide, erratic changes between different states. Think of a pendulum. A volatile security would be one whose price is like a pendulum that swings quickly and perhaps unpredictably from one extreme in its arc to the other.

In particular, out-of-the-money options tend to become more volatile as the option gets closer to its expiration date. Because the out-of-the-money options are getting cheaper and cheaper, demand can soar on the part of speculators looking for a cheap bet, and this can cause the price of the option to swing wildly. Obviously, this means an investor has to be careful to use the normal means of limiting his or her exposure to wild price changes, such as limit orders. We talked about these in Chapter 8, "Placing Your First Trade." If you're purchasing a put or call option close to the expiration of a contract, it's important to consider using limit orders. If you simply input a market order for the best available price, you may end up getting stung if the price of an out-of-the-money option soars.

Lastly, you may forget in the rush to speculate that you've got to pay a commission to your e-broker for trading options, just like with regular securities trades. Options usually cost more than other kinds of trades, too. A broker that charges $19.95 for the typical stock trade may charge $35 for an options trade. And because you can buy several contracts at the same time from a Web trading screen—say, 10 Microsoft puts of 100 shares apiece—you'll also usually be charged an additional amount for each options contract that you are buying. Commissions become especially important in the options market because in many cases you will be trying to make money off of the hair-thin margin resulting from a favorable change in price.

In the example of options on Microsoft stock, we did not calculate the fees and commissions that will have to be subtracted from the $200 profit you gain off the basic exercise of the option or the sale of the contract. In addition, if the option is exercised, you must factor in both the commission for purchasing the option in the first place, and the fees you will pay to your broker to trade the actual shares of Microsoft stock in exercising the option. Commissions on options, unlike with purchases of stock or bonds or other securities, will often vary according to the dollar value of the options contract. However, as with other securities, fees for trading options online over the Web are usually cheaper than through a full-service brokerage.

We've covered a lot of material so far. Before reading on about how to trade options through your existing account, you may want to read up on some of the material we've covered at some of the options information sites listed in the appendix of Web URLs.

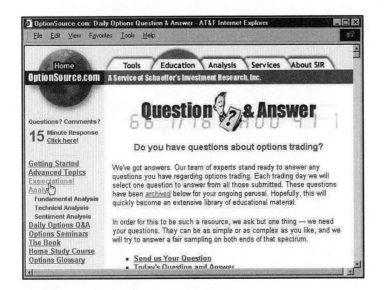

Sites such as OptionSource.com cover basic points about option investing.

Getting Started in Options

If after hearing both the good side of options and the substantial downside you are still interested in trading options, there are a few things you should do to set yourself up:

- You must complete an options application for your broker.

- You must have funds in your account other than margin to cover options contract purchases.

- You may want to have margin account privileges.

- You may want to have marginable securities in your account.

You don't need to have margin privileges to trade options, but you will have to complete an options trading application. In some cases, you can open a margin account and set up options trading privileges with the same form.

Most brokers will not let you purchase options contracts on margin. For that reason, you should be prepared to have funds in your account to cover the cost of options contracts. (Check with your broker regarding requirements.)

Even though you don't need margin to trade options, it's not a bad idea to get margin privileges first. If you don't have a margin account, you will have to have enough money in your account to cover the cost of the underlying securities if you decide to exercise put options. Obviously, if you want to enjoy the benefits of margin privileges, you must also have marginable securities in your account in order to use your margin privileges.

Also, you will, in fact, need margin privileges to do what's called writing options contracts, which we'll talk about in a little bit.

The Options Application

Usually, the options application will be a paper form; brokers will not let you apply online. In some cases, you can use one form to complete both the application for margin privileges and the application for options trading.

The options application will usually request the following information:

- Your investment objectives. Even if you have already answered these types of questions when signing up with your broker, they will be raised again in the context of the options application.

- Information about your financial background. You'll be asked to list your annual income, your net worth, and so on.

- Your investment experience, including the number of years you've been trading, the number of trades you make per year on average, the size of the transactions you make, the date of your most recent trade, and a self-estimation of your level of knowledge of trading (that is, from limited to good).

Lastly, you'll have to sign certain legal agreements specifying how trading of options will be handled. For example, a broker may reserve the right to sell your options contracts if the expiration date arrives without your having sold the contract or sent instructions for it to be exercised.

Trading Options

Next we'll talk a little bit about how options are traded because it varies a bit from typical securities trading, as you might imagine.

But first, a brief word on a potential point of confusion: short selling. Short selling sounds a lot like options, but it's not the same.

We mentioned at the end of Chapter 13, "Trading on Margin and Trading Options," that short selling is a kind of speculation tied to buying on margin, and that it has its own peculiar risks. Let's talk a little bit about how short selling works and how it differs from options.

What Options Trading Isn't: Short Selling

In the short sale, you sell securities that you don't own by borrowing the securities from your broker. You'll actually see an option to "sell short" when you go to the trading screen. The idea is that you can later buy the securities at the going rate and repay your broker for the borrowed shares. You assume that the price of the securities in the market will have dropped by the time you go to buy the securities, allowing you to profit by pocketing the difference. Selling short in practice is just another option that you specify on the trading screen where you enter the stock symbol, price, number of shares, and so on.

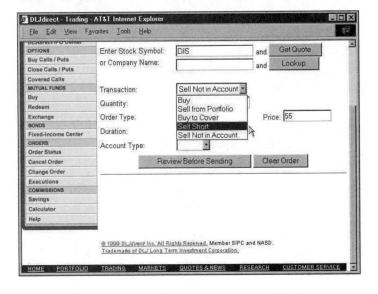

Selling short can be performed as an option within the normal trading screen.

Short selling in this way is very different from exercising a put option to sell at a certain price:

- With the put options contract, if the price in the market moves against you, you can simply let the contract expire and you're only out the money you spent on the contract itself.

- With the short sale, in contrast, you have already sold something you don't own. That means you are on the hook to come up with the shares to reimburse your broker for the shares borrowed. If the price in the market starts to climb above the price at which you've already sold the shares, there is no limit to the amount you could lose by having to purchase the shares on the open market. In other words, short selling has unlimited loss potential in contrast to the limited loss of trading puts.

Of course, the advantage of short selling, and the reason many people engage in it despite the unlimited risk, is that it requires little or no up-front capital at all. The shares to be sold are borrowed, just like buying on margin, which means that in most cases you'll pay 50% of the value of the shares. In some cases, if you have enough in marginable securities in your account, you can purchase the shares at no up-front cost whatsoever. The cost to purchase the shares later, when you must hand them over to your broker, is covered by the proceeds of the sale, while you pocket the difference. (Assuming, of course, the share price doesn't rise in the interim, in which case you're on the hook to pay extra to buy the shares.) Unlike with options, there is no contract to purchase and therefore no up-front cost.

The Procedures of Options Trading

There are a few basic steps to buying, selling, and exercising options. First, we'll look at the case of purchasing options.

Try It Yourself ▼

1. Go to the section of your broker's Web site that's set aside for options. Usually, this will be labeled as such.

2. There will be a form to enter the name or ticker symbol of the security for which you're interested in purchasing options.

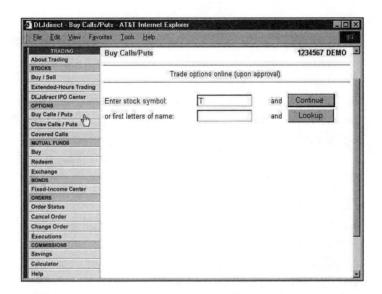

Go first to the section for put and call trading, where you'll be able to search options by underlying security.

3. Next, you'll see a chart listing the options contracts for that security that are available for purchase, sorted by strike price.

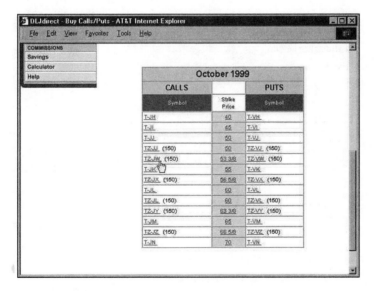

When you click Search, you'll be given a list of the options for that security by strike price.

4. Select the options contract you want by clicking on the link.

5. You should then see a summary of the option you've requested. You'll be asked to specify how many contracts you want to purchase and whether you're submitting a market order,

a limit order, and so on. These steps are basically the same as the steps you follow in submitting the usual securities purchase order.

A Contractual Obligation

It's important to remember when filling out the order form that the blank for Quantity refers not to the number of shares covered under the options contract, but rather the number of individual contracts you want to purchase. For example, if you're buying a put option to sell 100 shares of Microsoft, you can buy 1 of those put options, or 10, or more. In each case, though, each contract carries total cost equal to the price of the contract multiplied by the underlying number of shares. So a Microsoft put for 100 shares at a price of $5 will cost you $500. If you then buy two of those contracts, you'll be on the hook for $1,000, and so on. The worst thing you can do, then, is to confuse quantity with the number of Microsoft shares covered by the contract and erroneously enter "100" on the order form. At $5, you would be on the hook for 100 contracts with a total cost of $500 a piece, for a total of $50,000! This is important to keep in mind because the trade confirmation you receive when you enter your order won't necessarily tell you the total cost of your order. It's up to you to do the math and be vigilant.

Select the options contract and you'll be shown an order screen where you will fill in the standard order parameters.

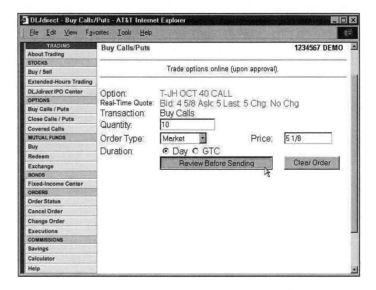

6. Finally, the Web page will display a summary of the options purchase order you've submitted and you'll be asked to confirm that the order is correct and to submit the order by clicking the submit button.

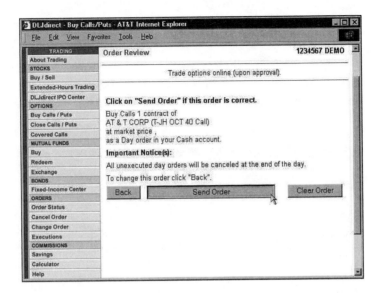

Next you'll be asked to review the details of your order.

You should receive a confirmation onscreen after submitting your order, just as with any other stock trade, showing the order you've submitted.

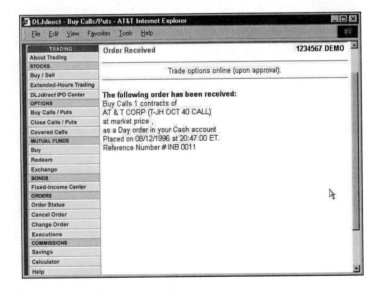

After submitting the order, you'll receive a confirmation that the order has been received.

Puts and calls that you have purchased will be displayed in your portfolio in the same manner as other securities you hold. If the options contracts have been purchased on margin, they will be displayed as a debit in the liabilities side of the balances display.

If the options orders were purchased with cash, they will show under assets. (Again, some brokers may not allow you to purchase options contracts on margin.)

When selling the option, in turn, you will be given a selection of options contracts currently in your account and asked to select which you want to sell.

To sell puts and calls, select the contract from your portfolio.

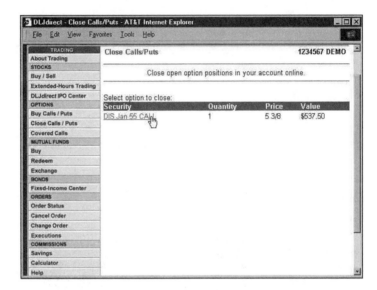

From there you will follow the same steps as you would when selling other securities in your portfolio.

You'll be asked to enter the terms of your sale into the order form.

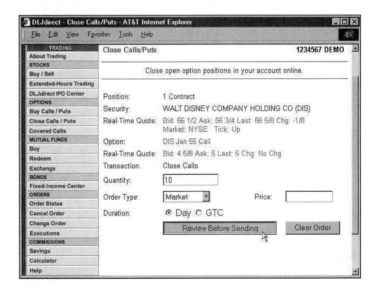

Getting Price Quotes on Options

Aside from the quotations you get at your broker's Web site, you might want to cruise some other information sources to find the latest options prices:

- You can check the newspaper daily for options quotations from the previous day. The *New York Times* and *The Wall Street Journal* carry listings of options that will tell you the closing price of puts and calls, how many contracts traded hands, and the expiration and strike price of each contract.

- You can get similar information in a real-time fashion from some software tools such as the Bridge Workstation from Bridge Information Systems.

There's a Limit to Limits

Bear in mind that some brokers may not allow you to enter limit orders or stop orders when purchasing or selling options contracts. You should check with the brokerage before signing up for its options trading service.

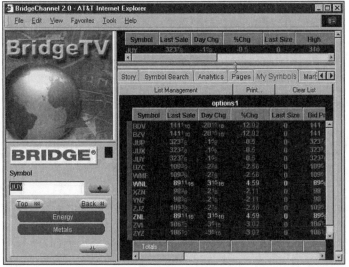

You can get real-time options prices from special software such as Bridge Workstation.

- If you want to research historical quotes for options, you can purchase a subscription to Dow Jones's Dow Jones Interactive Web site. A simple-to-use form on the Web site will allow you to look up options according to the underlying security and then trace the price back weeks or months.

You can get historical options price quotations from Dow Jones Interactive.

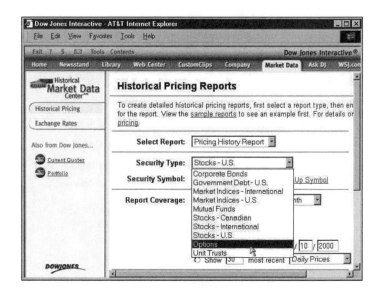

- The online version of *The Wall Street Journal* will give you quotations for the previous day's closing price on all options. Surf to the part of the site called Markets Data Center and look for the link to Listed Options. You will need a subscription to *The Journal* to use this database.

The daily edition of The Wall Street Journal *Online lists prices for all options contracts from the previous day.*

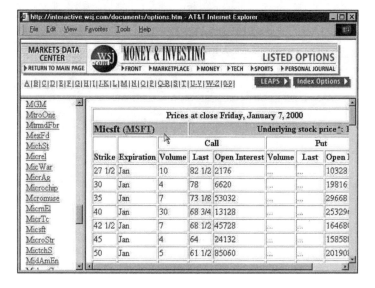

Exercising Your Options

Exercising options cannot be done online. The basic reason is that the operation is too complicated to be completed through a Web-based form. The standard procedure is to call your brokerage and talk with a live customer representative who can execute your order to exercise the options. Keep in mind a few important facts about exercising options:

- Your online brokerage won't remind you when the expiration date is coming up for a particular contract. You'll have to keep track of the contracts' expiration dates on your own.

- If you fail to send instructions to your broker regarding an option, the broker may choose, at his discretion, to exercise those options or to sell them. Rules about how this is done vary from broker to broker.

- You'll have to have buying power in your margin account to purchase securities on margin when acting on a call option. Remember that in Chapter 13 we defined buying power as the total amount you can spend to purchase new securities, including margin loans. You can use margin loans when exercising a call option to purchase securities, and the securities you are purchasing should have their normal margin requirements, such as 50%, and so on.

- When exercising a put option to sell securities at a given price, you can purchase the security in question, if you do not already own that security, at the same time that you are exercising the option. Your broker can help you arrange both the purchase of securities and the sale using the put option with one phone call. Again, the rules of buying power come into play for purchasing securities to be sold. Bear in mind that securities sold short to exercise a put option have their own unique margin requirements. In some cases it may be 50%, in some cases more.

Writing Options Contracts: Covered Calls and Naked Puts

Most of this chapter has been about how to trade options contracts. But as noted in the section about options benefits, the only reason you can purchase options in the first place is because someone has "written" an option contract offering a put or call option. In fact, you can act as the writer of an option contract if you want. Once you have been granted permission to trade options, you will also be authorized to originate those options contracts.

There are two kinds of options contracts that can be created, or written:

- **Covered**   In a covered call, the underlying security for the contract is already held in your account or otherwise paid for. Puts can also be designated "covered."

- **Uncovered**, or **"naked" options**   These are options where the underlying security is not in the option writer's possession. Both calls and puts can be uncovered.

In a covered call, you are granting someone else the right to purchase shares of a stock that you already hold in your account. The arrangement offers some protection against downside. For example, you would purchase shares of Microsoft at $115 for your account and in turn give the buyer of your option the right to purchase those same shares from you for $115. If the price of Microsoft shares rises, you won't lose any money as long as the increase in Microsoft shares is less than the money you earn from selling the option.

In an uncovered call, you would again write a contract giving the bearer the right to purchase Microsoft stock from you at $115. However, you would not hold the shares in your account because you are gambling that Microsoft shares will rise no higher than the price of the option and the option will not be exercised by the person to whom you sold it. If Microsoft stock does rise higher, you'll have to purchase the shares of stock necessary at a new, higher price in order to service the request by the option's holder to purchase those shares.

Likewise, with a naked put, you would grant the individual a right to sell you Microsoft shares at $115 at some time in the future. You're naked if you have no complementary call option that allows you to turn around and sell the shares at a fixed price if the option should be exercised.

Obviously, the latter of these two arrangements, the naked call or put, represents substantially higher risk. In fact, there is unlimited risk in the case of a call option because the price can continue to rise indefinitely above the strike price of the call option. Likewise, if the stock underlying a naked put has fallen in price at the time the contract is exercised, you must purchase that stock from the holder of the put and face having to sell it on the open market for much less, leading to potentially vast losses. With the naked put option at least, unlike the uncovered call, you have a limit on how much you can lose. You know the stock can't fall lower than zero, after all!

Reasons for Writing Options Contracts

Why would you bother engaging in any of this? Writing options contracts is purely a way of speculating on stock price movements. However, if you already own the underlying stock or you have an outstanding short position, as is the case in covered options writing, it's also a way to make some money off of your stocks immediately, before they rise in value. Let's take two cases:

- Covered calls can give you near-term income on your investments.

- Covered puts can be used to generate additional income from short sales you've already made.

The first point, income from covered calls, is not so hard to understand. If stock is sitting in your account, you can generate money just by selling a call option on the stock. It's a quicker way to enjoy a return on your investment than simply waiting for the underlying security to appreciate in value. In the event that the call option is exercised and you're assigned to satisfy it, you already own the shares so you won't risk having to buy them at the current price.

The only drawback of this is that if shares continue to rise, you've locked yourself out of catching the wave because you have pledged to sell only at the option's strike price.

The second point, using put contracts to make more money off of a short sale, takes a little more thought. Think back to the discussion of short selling. When you are selling securities short you are borrowing shares and selling them at the market price, expecting to buy them back later at a better price. By writing a put contract with a strike price below the price at which you've sold a security short, you're locking in a kind of maximum you'll pay to buy the shares back later on. You know you'll make a profit this way. In addition, you're generating some income off of the sale of the put contract. Of course, if the price of the stock in the market drops really low, you may end up overpaying if you have to honor the contract and buy the stock from someone at the strike price. That's because the put will only be exercised if it suddenly becomes in-the-money, meaning the strike price is more than the going rate.

How to Write Puts and Calls

Your online broker's Web site will provide simple forms for writing puts and calls. Take the example of a covered call, the most common type of option writing you'll do through an online broker. Here's how it might be done on one broker's Web site:

- You'll surf to a section of the broker's site labeled Covered Calls within the Options section.

- You'll be shown a list of the securities in your account against which you can write puts and calls.

- By clicking on the link for one of these securities, you'll be taken to a page listing the various possible call contracts for that security, sorted by strike price.

- By clicking on one of the strike prices listed, you'll be taken to yet another screen that lists the different expiration periods for that contract. For example, if you want to write call contracts for someone to buy Microsoft shares from you at $115, you could assign a date of January or February or April as the time frame in which the contract can be executed. It's up to you to decide.

- At this point you can click on the symbol for the contract and you'll be taken to a page listing the contract where you can enter the order details. Writing the contract is really like selling a security. You'll have to note how many contracts you're selling and for how much you want to sell the contract, including whether you want to sell it as a market order or as a limit order.

- You'll then proceed to the usual confirmation page, where you'll be asked to review the details of your options contract before submitting your order.

It's especially important to review the terms of the contract you are writing in this last screen, because you are taking the extra risks that come with options.

Funding Requirements for Options Contracts

Depending on your broker's individual requirements, you will have to make sure your account balance has the necessary funds to back your options writing. At a minimum, brokers will require that you have enough funds in your account to cover the total cost of the option your are writing, plus fees for writing the option, as well as some percentage of the total value of the underlying securities based on the current market price at the time you write the contract.

In addition, some brokers may require a sizeable minimum account balance before you write any options. Minimum account balances of $50,000 are not unheard of for options writing. Note too that, as mentioned earlier, you absolutely must have margin privileges to write options contracts.

Assignment

Don't forget: If you're writing options, chances are someone out there will try to exercise them. "Someone" is exactly right: The put or call you write may change hands many times in the marketplace before someone exercises it. What that means is that there is no direct relationship whereby the option holder can get in touch with you. Instead, your broker will choose your name in a sort of random drawing from among its clients who have written options contracts matching the specifications of the contract being executed. If your name is chosen, you'll be "assigned" to satisfy the terms of the options contract. If the contract is a call option to purchase shares of Microsoft at $115, you'll have to be ready to sell the number of shares specified in the contract at $115 per share.

Writers Need Not Apply

Bear in mind that not all e-brokers will let you write options contracts. Some brokers will let you write covered and uncovered options, but most will only let you write covered calls, which are much less risky. Some will let you do all of these, but only if you sign up for each privilege separately. Some brokers may grant you privileges to write covered options contracts and then request that you make separate applications to write uncovered contracts. Some simply don't offer it as a feature at all. Generally, you'll find that e-brokers geared toward a Mom and Pop crowd, or the lowest common denominator of investor, won't offer options writing. If writing options will be important to you, you may want to look for an e-broker that markets itself as a more "premium" service, or one that charges a higher minimum balance. This is another factor to keep in mind when going through the steps in Chapter 3, "Selecting the Right Online Broker for Your Needs."

What You've Learned

If you thought this was one of the hardest chapters in the book, you're right! Options are an incredibly deep subject, with subtleties that take years to master. Hopefully, this chapter has intrigued you. If you're interested in getting into options for real, it's highly recommended that you read as much as you can and seek professional investment advice before you start writing naked puts and calls.

You've covered the basics in this chapter, though. You've learned about

- What options are and how they work.

- How options contracts can be useful to you as an investor or a speculator, and how they can have serious pitfalls.

- And you've started to think about the specific steps involved in trading and writing options contracts.

CHAPTER 15

Trading Bonds and Mutual Funds Online

Hopefully, you've been enjoying the first flush of financial success and the thrill of placing a few stock trades. At some point, you've got to own up to the fact that the reason you bought this book was to learn how to organize your finances simply and easily online, not just to play stock jockey all day long. (That is why you bought this book, isn't it?)

When you get serious about investing online as your ticket to your financial future, you'll want to consider setting aside some money for bonds and mutual funds. Both types of securities can bring tremendous benefits to your portfolio that betting on individual stocks doesn't provide. They can reduce your overall risk, make sure you stay fully invested at all times, and give you greater return on investment in some cases. This chapter shows you how.

Differences Between Bonds, Mutual Funds, and Stocks

In the most important regard, mutual funds and bonds are no different from stocks. All three make money for you to the extent that you enjoy a return on the principal invested in them. The terms *principal* and *return* have already been discussed, but let's review them briefly.

Principal is the initial investment that you make in the bond, and that is expected to be repaid at the time the bond is due to be paid out.

Your *return*, also referred to as the *return on investment*, is the amount you expect to earn at the end of the bond's life over and above the principal invested.

What You'll Learn in This Chapter:

▶ How bonds and mutual funds are different from stocks.

▶ What's different about buying and selling mutual funds.

▶ Trading mutual funds with your online account.

▶ What's different about buying and selling bonds.

▶ Trading bonds with your online account.

▶ Tax considerations.

However, all three instruments behave slightly differently. While shares of common stock can be sold for a profit based on the increase in the share price over the price you paid, mutual funds and bonds perform in the following manner:

- Your return on mutual funds consists of both the appreciation in the value of a share of the fund and payments made to you by the fund.

- Bonds return a fixed amount of money at the end of a specified time. Your return on a bond is the value of that fixed amount of money as a percentage of the amount you paid for the bond (unless you decide to sell the bond at a profit).

Let's take a more detailed look at how mutual funds and bonds are different from investing in common stock.

Unique Aspects of Buying and Selling Mutual Funds

Making money on mutual funds is not all that different from investing in shares of common stock. A mutual fund pools the investment dollars of many investors and places that money in a group of stocks (or bonds, if the mutual fund is a bond fund). Some of these fund companies, such as Fidelity, have become household names among investors, as have their most renowned fund managers, such as Peter Lynch.

Fidelity is one of the many fund management firms that pools investor money.

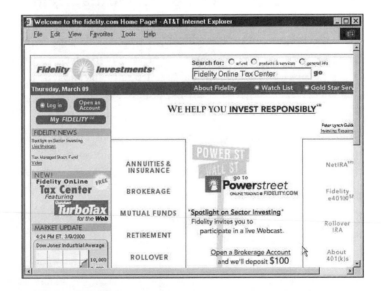

As the stocks in a mutual fund increase, the mutual fund's total assets rise by a certain percentage. You benefit from that by either

- Regular payments to you for the money the fund earns from selling its holdings at a profit.

- Actually selling your investment in the fund at a profit.

In some cases you can enjoy both benefits, collecting payments over a certain time period and then selling the mutual fund at a profit. In this way, buying and selling funds is quite similar to investing in shares of common stock. The profit of funds should track the increase in share price of the securities held by that fund.

Still, there are some critical differences that make investing in funds a different process. The following are the major points to keep in mind:

- First of all, remember that mutual funds are traded as part of a family of funds. Each fund is its own separate security, but it is designed by a fund company (such as Fidelity Investments, Inc., which maintains lots of funds).

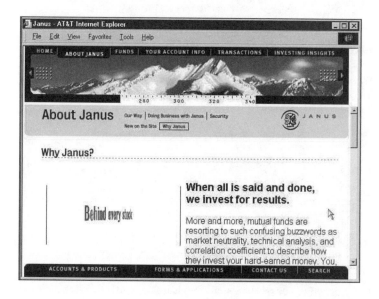

Janus is a fund firm that offers a selection of different mutual funds.

That means you'll have to be sure to separate the fund you want from the other funds in the family. Your broker will have tools for finding the specific fund you may be interested in, but you can also use third-party Web sites such as Yahoo! Finance.

Brokerage sites will offer tools you can use to research different funds.

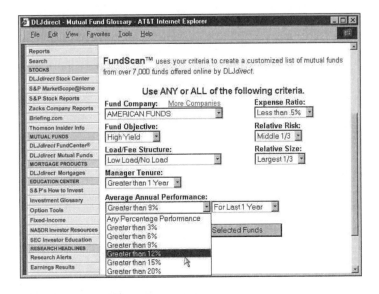

Using Yahoo! to search for mutual funds.

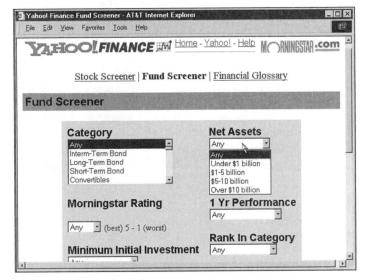

- Unlike shares of listed common stock, where you can buy odd lots (sub-100 shares) down to 1 or 2 shares, funds come with a minimum investment. That minimum is not expressed as a number of shares, although it does in fact grant you a certain number of shares. A common minimum might be $1,000, and you will usually specify the amount you want to pay at the time that you order.

- Again, unlike shares of common stock, most of which these days do not pay dividends, mutual funds have regular dividend payouts to investors, which let the fund distribute both the dividends that the fund receives on the securities it holds, as well as any short-term capital gains resulting from the sale of securities held by the fund. (Remember from Chapter 10, "Understanding Your Taxes," that short-term gains are gains on securities held for less than a year.)

  You can have these dividends reinvested by your broker. You will usually be asked when you place your order for the mutual fund if you want to reinvest the dividends that will be paid out.

- In addition to dividend payments, you will also receive annual distributions. These are payments for the longer term capital gains that the fund realizes by selling securities held in its portfolio for more than a year. These are usually labeled "capital distributions."

- Unlike bonds and stock, brokerage funds create their own mutual funds in addition to offering you funds from mutual fund firms.

- In addition to any brokerage fees you might pay, mutual funds have their own fees. According to Morningstar, Inc., about half of all funds charge something called *load*, which is a sales fee figured as a percentage of the total amount of money you are investing. In addition to load, there may be fees for cashing out your shares of a mutual fund, which is known as *redemption*.

  Redemption is when you sell shares of a mutual fund from your portfolio to clear your position in a mutual fund.

- Purchasing funds through an online brokerage will make the fees that you pay to participate different from what they would be if you purchased the fund directly from the fund company. In many cases, the usual fees for a fund will be waived for you through a special arrangement between your e-broker and the mutual fund firm offering the fund.

Tracking Funds in Your Portfolio

Although you will pay a lump sum to join a mutual fund, you need a way to measure the improvement of a fund's assets. That measure is the *Net Asset Value*, commonly cited as the acronym NAV.

Net Asset Value represents the total worth of a fund's investments divided by the number of fund shares outstanding. The increase in NAV is a common measure of fund performance.

At any moment in time, the appreciation on your investment in a mutual fund is equal to the percentage increase in the NAV, less the fees you pay to invest in the mutual fund.

You should see shares of mutual funds held in your account listed alongside stocks in the portfolio tracker at your broker's site. In this sense, tracking mutual funds is similar to the process mentioned in Chapter 9, "Managing Your Portfolio."

Keep in mind that as with stocks, you may or may not see a display of your gains on mutual funds, but instead only the present value of those holdings. That means you may want to use another third-party portfolio view to track gains in your fund holdings.

Kinds of Funds

Just as different stocks promise different kinds of return on investment, funds have their own profiles offering different investment goals. The main categorization is by the type of security. Funds are broken down into two categories that are self-explanatory—stock funds and bond funds—and one other category, money market funds. Money market funds focus on short-term debt securities such as T-bills and certificates of deposit that mature in days, weeks, or months as opposed to years in the case of bonds. Money market funds generally offer higher rates of return than bond funds.

There are important variations within these three categories:

- Growth funds focus on common stock of established companies that offer above-average earnings growth, which usually translates into above-average returns.

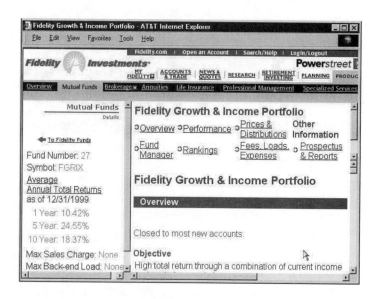

A Growth & Income fund follows companies with above-average returns.

- Aggressive growth funds focus on younger companies that may be growing faster than the companies in a growth fund, but that are riskier holdings.

Aggressive growth funds track risky, fast-growing companies.

- Equity income funds focus on the stocks paying dividends, which means they may not result in as high a capital gain, but they do offer the investor a steady stream of dividends and they are less risky than growth or aggressive growth funds.

Equity funds offer investors income through dividends.

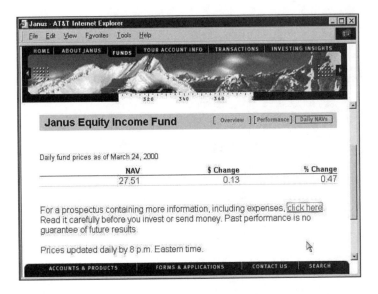

- Among bond funds, there are funds for all the different kinds of bond offerings, including municipal bonds, corporate bonds, and taxable municipal bonds, among others.

Bond funds are a simpler way to play the bond market.

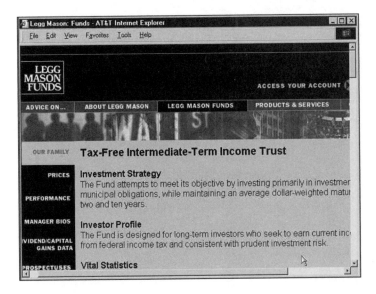

- It's also possible to find all kinds of funds with various "approaches." There are sector funds, which invest in different corners of a given industry such as technology funds. There are regional funds that may invest only in securities in a certain part of the world.

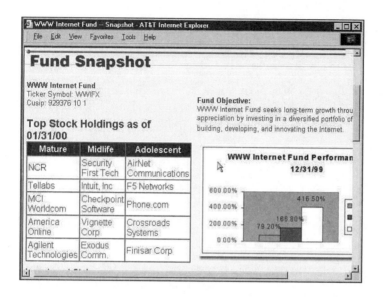

The Internet fund is one of the new, special funds that have cropped up in recent years to capture investor interest.

- Index funds allow you to own a piece of every stock making up one of the various stock market indices, such as the Standard & Poor's 500. Index funds are generally recommended as a low-risk way to guarantee yourself a return on investment that will track the average return in the stock market. For that reason, they may be a balance to more risky investments in your portfolio.

An index fund invests in the components of the various stock indices in order to mirror the perfor-mance of those broad measures of stock growth.

Benefits and Risks of Mutual Funds

There are several good reasons to make mutual funds part of your portfolio. The main benefits include

- Leverage. This is a term we'll return to in later chapters—it is a fundamental concept to understand in investing. As previously mentioned, when you buy shares in a mutual fund you are pitching into a general pool of investment money from several people. By doing so, you can participate in investments that might otherwise be out of your reach, but that promise a greater return.

  For example, suppose you want to purchase 100 shares of Microsoft stock, 100 shares of IBM stock, and 100 shares of Cisco Systems stock. If each share costs $100, you would end up having to spend $30,000 to buy all three. That's a lot to drop all at once, and on your own you might have to buy one stock at a time and more later. That means you might miss buying shares when the prices are best and end up paying more.

  With a mutual fund, you can make a minimum investment of $3,000 or $5,000 and your money will be used along with the funds of a lot of other investors to purchase not just hundreds but possibly thousands of shares of Microsoft, IBM, and Cisco. As a fund investor, you enjoy the returns from those stocks without having to put up $30,000 of your own money. You have greater buying power as a member of the pool.

  Leverage is the ability to invest less money for an equal or greater return.

- The second great thing about mutual funds is that you have professional investors selecting your investments. A mutual fund is run by someone called a *portfolio manager*. Portfolio managers usually have years of experience at picking stocks and bonds and they are generally selected for their investing acumen. Moreover, they have an entire team of experts at their disposal to assist with stock picking. Some of these portfolio managers, such as Jeffrey Vinick and Peter Lynch, mentioned above, have become legends in the last decade or so.

- Another important advantage of mutual funds is the ability to instantly diversify your portfolio. We spoke a little bit about this in Chapter 6, "Understanding the Basics of Stock Trading." A basic principle of investing is that you should spread your money among a number of different securities so that it is not dependent on the performance of any one security. Because mutual funds place the collective assets of their investors into a number of different kinds of stocks and bonds, there is more diversity to how your money is invested.

- Mutual funds can help you to invest on a regular basis. That's because the dividend payments made by mutual funds can be automatically reinvested for you. This is known as a *DRIP*, or dividend reinvestment plan.

  Under a *DRIP*, dividend payments that would normally be sent to you as a check will simply be rolled back into the mutual fund to purchase new shares for you. Bear in mind that while you can avoid taxes on dividend income by using DRIPs, you will have to subtract the normal mutual fund fees because you are purchasing new shares.

- Lastly, it may sound mundane, but you could be very grateful when tax time rolls around if you have only the payments from your mutual fund to account for, as opposed to accounting for capital gains and (possibly) dividends from multiple securities. Mutual funds simplify your bookkeeping, in other words.

Risks

Despite the long list of positives, there are certainly risks associated with mutual funds just as with any other kind of security. Before you buy any fund, you should track its return on investment in recent years. The Securities and Exchange Commission requires standard disclosure of fund performance, and you can visit sites on the Internet to see performance reports on various funds. A prominent source of fund ratings is Morningstar, Inc., which maintains a searchable database of fund performance.

In addition to the risk of bad performance, there are two other risks particularly associated with mutual funds:

- The investment style of the fund may not live up to its billing.

- The fund itself may face a credit risk.

On the first score, remember that what kinds of securities you invest in always depends on what kind of investor you are. It was mentioned a little while ago that different funds promise different kinds of risk and return. A so-called "aggressive growth" stock fund will focus on buying stocks of companies that have strong earnings growth, while more conservative "value funds" may focus on buying out-of-favor stocks that are trading at a discount to the market. That's fine so far as it goes. The risk is that the funds you are investing in may advertise one sort of discipline and practice another that's completely different.

For example, in roaring bull markets it becomes hard for some funds to avoid buying into the hottest, riskiest stocks because these may be offering the best return at the moment. That is why you may find your conservative value fund buying some high-flying "momentum" stocks—basically, the riskiest, most speculative issues. The problem is that the investments made are ultimately out of your hands; they are decided by the experts to whom you have given your money. If you don't check up on those experts, you're buying mystery meat when you buy a fund.

The best precaution is to scrutinize the fund prospectus and see what investment the fund manager has actually made to get a sense of whether the fund practices what it preaches before handing over your money.

The other risk inherent in handing over your money to someone is the possibility that the mutual fund firm will go belly up. As with any institution, there's always the prospect of credit risk. If a fund defaults, it may not be able to repay its obligation to you, the shareholder. In general, troubled funds won't stick around for very long, any more so than other troubled institutions. But it's a good precaution to find out how long the company offering a particular fund has been in the business, how long the particular fund has been offered, and whether the fund has steadily delivered a good performance to shareholders over the years.

Trading Mutual Funds

Mutual fund and bond trading is an automatic part of any brokerage account. You can start trading both as soon as you are cleared for trading. In some cases, however, you may be required to maintain a minimum balance in order to trade mutual funds. A required balance of $1,000 is not uncommon.

Buying Mutual Funds

Buying mutual funds online from your broker is very similar to purchasing shares of stocks online. The basic steps are as follows:

- There is usually a special section of the Web site where you trade mutual funds. Go there first.

- There will be a form where you can enter the ticker symbol for the fund (or look up the symbol using the name of the fund family; for example, Fidelity).

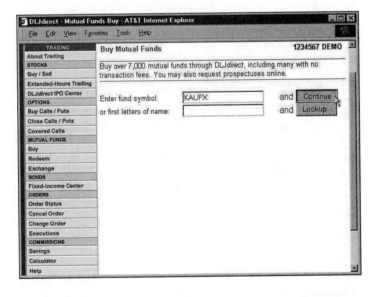

The mutual fund lookup screen.

- Next you'll see a screen listing the fund name and details. If this information is correct, you can proceed to the ordering screen.

• You'll then be taken to the main order form, where you'll have to enter the amount in dollars you want to place in the fund.

The fund order form.

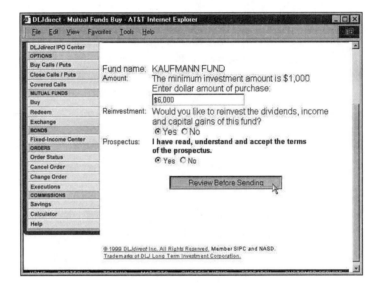

• This is where you can specify if you'd like dividends from the fund to be reinvested automatically by your broker.

• When you press the Submit button, you'll receive the standard review screen, asking you to check your order.

The order review screen.

• Lastly, you'll see the standard confirmation screen.

The confirmation screen.

Selling Shares of Mutual Funds

Selling the mutual fund holdings in your portfolio, also known as *redemption* (but separate from bond redemption), is, again, similar to selling shares of stock. There will most likely be a section of your broker's Web site for selling shares from your holdings. You'll be shown a list of the funds you hold, at which time you can select which ones to sell and go through the usual confirmation process.

Unique Aspects of Buying and Selling Bonds

As mentioned back in Chapter 6, a bond represents ownership of a company or another institution's debt. All kinds of entities issue debt, including major corporations listed on the stock exchanges as well as municipal governments. The appeal of the latter, of course, is that in most cases the profit on "muni's," as they're called, is tax-free.

By purchasing a bond, you are essentially purchasing an IOU. The appeal of a bond is that it offers a fixed return on investment. Unlike with shares of common stock, or even with a mutual fund, you know exactly what you'll get back if you hold the bond until the lender pays you back.

Profit on municipal bonds is tax-free.

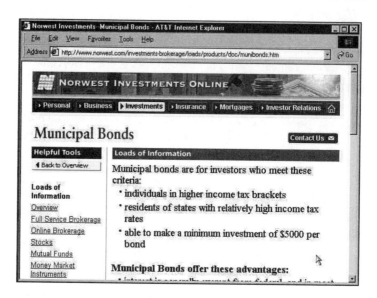

The following explains what principal and return mean in the case of a bond:

- Unlike common shares of stock, which are priced based on whatever the going rate is in the market, bonds are issued by a lender with a fixed price initially. This price is known as the *par value*, also referred to as *face value*.

  Par value is the price at which a bond is issued. The term is synonymous with *face value*, and you will see both terms in current usage.

- Because bonds represent debt, they have an expected "life-span" unlike equity such as shares of common stock or shares in a fund. That means that there is a specified time frame in which they are to be held, ranging from 2 to 30 years, and a date at which they *mature* or are repaid by the borrower.

  Maturity means the time at which the principal invested in a bond must be repaid to the bond holder. If you are investing in bonds, you want to know how long it will take until the bond reaches maturity and you get your money back. For example, a five-year bond means the principal will be repaid five years from the issue date. If you buy a bond later in its life, say, two years after it has been issued, the bond will be closer to maturity, in this case only three years away.

- Chapter 6 talked a little bit about dividends, which are annual or semi-annual interest payments that come with certain securities. Although interest in dividends fluctuates in the common stock market, they are a very important part of bonds. When calculating the total return from a bond, you add up both the repayment of the principal and the interest paid out. The stated rate of interest paid on a bond is called the *coupon*.

  The *coupon* is the annual or semi-annual interest paid on a bond. When you hear the rate of interest discussed for a given bond, you will sometimes hear the term *coupon rate* used.

In essence, the return on a bond is simply the principal plus the amount of interest accrued over the life of the bond, or until maturity. Here's an example:

1. You purchase a bond with a $10,000 par value and an interest rate, or coupon rate, of 6% and a lifespan or maturity of 10 years.

   ▼ **Try It Yourself**

2. You receive annual interest payments of $600, or 6% of $10,000.

3. When the bond comes to maturity, the $10,000 is paid to you and you have collected $600 in 10 annual payments, which means you have $6,000 in interest. Your total return is the interest plus principal, or $16,000.

The following table sets forth the preceding example.

Figuring Total Return on a Bond

Steps to Compute	Amount
1. Compute annual interest. The par value multiplied by the interest rate is the annual interest.	$10,000.00 ×6% $600.00
2. Compute total interest at maturity. Multiply the annual interest by the number of years to maturity to get the total interest at maturity.	$600.00 ×10 $6,000.00
3. Add interest to principal at maturity. Add to the total interest the par value or principal of the bond to get the total return.	$ 6,000.00 +$10,000.00 $16,000.00

Of course, that's not the whole story. Although $16,000 is indeed the total return, what you really want to know is what percentage return you will enjoy on the money you are investing in the bond. This requires you to understand a couple of other things about bonds:

- Although bonds have a par value at the time they are issued, in the markets the price of bonds fluctuate moment-to-moment just as other securities do. A bond will therefore trade at any moment in time in some range of prices surrounding its par value. That means you will usually pay more or less than the par value for a bond.

- Because the interest paid with a bond is computed as a percentage of the par value of the bond, unless you actually pay par value for a bond, the percentage return you enjoy will be different. This measure of return is known as the bond's *yield*.

  Yield is the return on a bond expressed as a percentage of the actual price paid for the bond. The yield will be a different interest rate, or coupon rate, of the bond if the bond is purchased at a price that is different from the par value of the bond.

- In the bond world, you have to keep track of not one, but two types of yield: *current yield* and *yield to maturity*.

  Current yield is the amount of return you'll receive each year in the form of interest payments.

  Yield to maturity is the total return on investment you'll receive when the bond reaches maturity, which includes compounded interest over the life of the bond, but also the difference between how much you paid for the bond—its price—and the face or par value of the bond.

Calculating Yields

Let's take a look at how to calculate current yield and yield to maturity. Remember that current yield is how much interest you earn each year on a bond. Current yield is calculated in the following manner:

1. First, multiply the face value of the bond by the interest rate. The result is the current yield, or the amount you'd earn each year if you purchased a bond at face value. For example, a bond purchased at $10,000 with an interest rate of 6% would yield $600 per year.

2. Remember that you will probably buy a bond for more or less than the par value depending on how the bond is trading in the market. For that reason, the way you figure the *actual* current yield is to divide the yield computed in the first step—that is, the yield based on par value—by the actual price you paid for the stock.

▼ **Try It Yourself**

▲

The following table illustrates both steps.

Figuring Current Yield

Steps to Compute	Amount
1. Interest earned at par value: Take the bond's par value and multiply by the interest rate to get the current yield or par yield.	$10,000.00 ×6% $600.00
2. Interest as a percentage of the price paid: Take the amount you actually paid for the bond (as opposed to the par value). Then take the par yield, as calculated above and divide it by the price you paid. The result is the current yield of the bond.	 $9,000.00 $600/$9,000.00 6.6%

What does this mean? Even though the interest paid out each year stays the same, namely $600, the total return you enjoy is more than if you had purchased the bond at par value.

This brings us to the main point to keep in mind about current yield: Your current yield on a bond each year is inversely proportional to movement in the price you pay for the bond above or below the face value. It's easy to see why. When the price is below par, you are effectively paying less money for the same interest income. Likewise, if you were to pay $10,500 in the preceding example—in other words, more than the face value—you would still earn $600 per year, but the total return you would enjoy on a percentage basis would be $600 divided by $10,500, or 5.71%. You would receive less of a return because you paid more money for the same amount of interest.

Yield to Maturity: The Power of Compounding

Current yield will tell you what kind of return you're getting based on the coupon and the price you pay for a bond. But it won't tell you the total return on investment you can expect when you collect the bond's principal on the date of maturity. To get a handle on the total rate of return, bond experts use something called the *yield to maturity*.

Yield to maturity is the yield on a bond that would make the current price equal to the total payout at maturity, including capital gains and dividend reinvestment.

Specifically, yield-to-maturity models try to calculate the percentage yield of a bond when factoring in that investors who buy a bond below or above par will experience a capital gain or loss when they collect the par value of a bond at maturity. It also assumes that the total amount of interest collected at maturity will be more than the total of all the coupon payments. Instead, the yield-to-maturity model assumes that as each coupon payment is made to the investor, it will be reinvested in the bond at a consistent rate. The result is compound interest. Compound interest leads to a greater total interest payment.

Consider how compound interest increases total return. Say a 5-year 10% coupon bond is selling at par for $100. Using the simple model of interest, which we've been using in all of our examples, the bond pays $10 each year. At the end of ten years, the total interest paid is $100.

But suppose that the $10 is not simply collected by the investor as interest, but is instead reinvested in the bond at the same coupon rate of 10%. In the first year, the interest payment will be $10. In the second year, the interest payment will be 10% of $110, the amount of the new principal when the first year's $10 payment is reinvested to buy more of the bond. Ten percent of $110 yields a larger dividend, specifically $11. If that $11 is reinvested, the third year's payout will be 10% of $121, or $12.10. And so on. The final interest haul over ten years will be not $100, but roughly $159.

The yield-to-maturity model, then, attempts to calculate what the annual interest rate, or yield, would be for a bond trading at a given price if dividends were invested in this kind of compounded fashion. How does it work? Consider first how you would figure the yield on a bond trading at a certain price based on your return with simple interest. The steps would be as follows:

1. First, compute the annual interest payment, or dividend, based on the par value multiplied by the coupon rate for the bond. As in the previous example, a bond with a par of $10,000 and 6% interest will have a par yield of $600.

▼ **Try It Yourself**

2. Next, figure the total interest paid over the life of the bond. You do so by multiplying the annual interest by the number of years till maturity. If the annual interest is $600 and the bond is a 10-year bond, the interest returned at maturity will be $6,000.

3. Remember that when the bond is repaid at maturity, you'll be given the principal or par value of the bond. So your total return is the combination of the interest earned at maturity, in this case $6,000, and the par value of the bond, in this case $10,000, for a total of $16,000.

4. Next, subtract the total purchase price, in this case $9,000, to figure the total interest plus the capital gain. In this case it would be $7,000.

5. Next, divide the total interest plus capital gain, $7,000, by the number of years in the bond. The result, $700, must then be divided by the original purchase price, $9,000. The result is the percentage yield. In this case, it would be 7.8%.

▲

The steps are laid out in the following table.

Computing the Yield Based on a Bond Payout

Steps to Compute	Amount
1. Derive the total gain. Subtract from the total return the price of the bond to get the interest plus capital gain (or loss).	$16,000 -$ 9,000 $ 7,000
2. Figure the total yield. Divide the capital gain just calculated by the number of years to maturity to get the annual interest. Then divide the interest by the price to get the yield to maturity.	$7,000 10 $700 $700/$9,000 7.8%

However, this model is simplistic. We haven't actually factored in the result of reinvesting the annual dividends back into the bond, a factor that will make the total payout at maturity greater than $16,000, and the yield different as well. How do we factor in compounding to arrive at the yield to maturity? In truth, you can't do the math that easily on paper, because the reinvestment of dividends in the yield-to-maturity model involves computing a mathematical model that is itself based on the very interest figure you are trying to find!

For that reason, bond traders use computer models to calculate the yield to maturity, rather than computing it by hand. For a bond trading at 90 with a par value of $100 and a coupon of 6%, a table of yields will give the yield to maturity that will satisfy the equation. In fact, in the preceding example, the yield to maturity required to satisfy the total return is not 7.8%, but rather 7.4%. A bond calculator or a table of bond interest rates could give you this figure.

When you go to buy bonds, you won't actually need to calculate yield yourself. Instead, you'll be presented with a selection of bonds with different current yields and yields to maturity listed. Your job is simply to select one whose yield to maturity matches the kind of return you're seeking.

A table of bonds with different yields.

Ladder	Order	Qty Available	Issue	Coupon	Maturity	Price	Yield	Moody/ S&P
☐	Buy	696	Worldcom Inc Ga Callable 02/00@ Greater of 100 or Make Whole	6.400	08/15/2005	95.279	7.448	A3/ A-
☐	Sell/Buy	1000/1000	Worldcom Inc Ga Callable 02/00@ Greater of 100 or Make Whole	6.400	08/15/2005	94.998/95.279	7.513/7.448	A3/ A-
☐	Buy	950	Worldcom Inc Ga Callable 02/00@ Greater of 100 or Make Whole	6.400	08/15/2005	95.367	7.428	A3/ A-
☐	Buy	20	Worldcom Inc Ga Callable 02/00@ Greater of 100 or Make Whole	6.400	08/15/2005	95.542	7.388	A3/ A-
☐	Buy	600	Worldcom Inc Ga Callable 02/00@ Greater of 100 or Make Whole	7.750	04/01/2007	99.996	7.556(c)	A3/ A-

If you do need to calculate yields at some point, there are numerous tools on the Web to help you calculate the yield to maturity of a bond. Again, if you know the price listed for the bond and the total return at maturity, you can plug those numbers into a bond calculator and compute the yield to maturity.

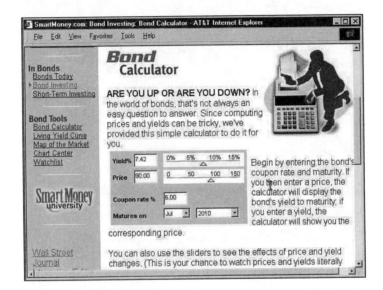

A bond calculator can help you figure a bond's yield to maturity.

The Yield Curve

By now it should be clear that yield is an important concept because it helps you to understand how your invested principal is appreciating on a percentage basis. However, it's also important to understand why yield is what it is in any given circumstance. Consider the fact that the coupon rate of a bond is determined by the prevailing interest rates at the time the bond is issued. What happens when interest rates change? The coupon rate on a bond never changes, so what has to happen is that the price of the bond gets revalued. Because yield is a factor of the price paid, the price of a bond is changed each time it is sold so that the resulting yield will more accurately reflect interest rates.

In fact, yield is so closely tied to what interest rates are doing that the yield on bonds has become a sort of economic indicator for the economy as a whole. Thus, economists talk of the yield curve. The yield curve is usually depicted as a graph with a steadily rising yield moving from left to right as the number of years to maturity increases. Financial Web sites such as SmartMoney.com often use the living yield curve to discuss the overall health of the economy.

Sites such as SmartMoney.com can familiarize you with the "living yield curve."

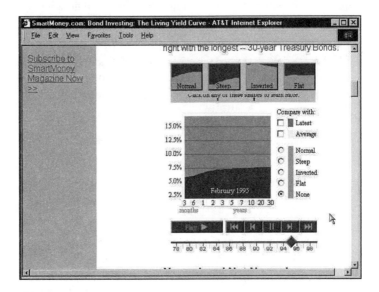

Why is the yield curve important to understand? Because the yield curve expresses a fundamental fact about bonds: Yields tend to increase with the maturity of the bond to compensate the investor against the risk of inflation. That means that a bond with a maturity of two years will normally have a far lower yield than a bond with a maturity of 10 years. The buyer of the 10-year bond is being compensated for the fact that there is a far greater risk that interest rates will rise in the time that the bond is being held, which would reduce the value of investment at cashout time.

The yield curve expresses the fact that bonds are essentially a precaution against a weak economy. In a weak economy, interest rates will tend to decline as a result of slowing economic growth. Following the yield curve, declining interest rates will tend to raise the face value, or par value, of the bond. For that reason, bonds tend be considered a hedge against the risk of slowing economic growth. You're likely to see the bond market cheer at dismal economic news and pull a long face when the economic outlook is rosy. According to the yield curve, the former makes bond prices rise, the latter situation makes them drop.

Risks of Bonds

Although bonds are considered a relatively safe investment, they are not without risk. A few of the main risks include the following:

- The risk of inflation. This pertains to the discussion of the yield curve. With any bond, no matter what the return, you are gambling that interest rates will not rise to a level where they will render your yield from the bond worthless. If interest rates do rise, your yield at maturity may not be worth much.

- Again, if interest rates do rise, the price that the bond commands in the market will fall. If you are holding the bond at that time, you may find that the price you can get for selling the bond on the open market is far less than what you paid for it. You would then have a capital loss, and one which might be enough to offset any interest earned on the bond.

- Finally, because a bond is essentially a loan, there is always a credit risk that the institution that issued the loan will default on its obligation and you will not be able to collect at maturity.

Bond Ratings

The risk of default leads us to our next point, credit ratings of bonds. Unlike the world of common stock, where you'll go by the reputation of individual companies, bond sales involve a fairly sophisticated evaluation process by which bonds are graded on the fundamental soundness of the issuing institution. Two major independent organizations, Standard & Poor's and Moody's, are generally recognized for their unbiased reviews of bond issuers. Issuers are rated for their creditworthiness on a scale ranging from "CCC" (really poor) to "AAA" (excellent).

*Moody's can give
you credit ratings
for bond issuers.*

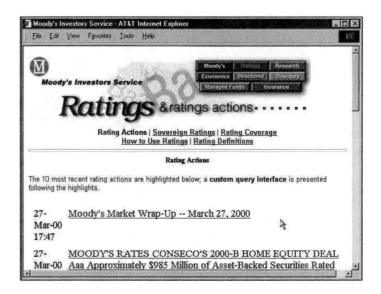

Ladder Investing

The importance of diversifying your portfolio so as to reduce your exposure to risk from any one investment has been mentioned a couple of times in this book. Mutual funds are a way of reducing your risk from any one security by investing in multiple securities simultaneously. Dollar-cost averaging, mentioned previously, is a way to reduce your risk over time by investing in the market on a regular basis, both in good times and bad.

Similarly, you can mitigate the risk of interest rate rise by buying bonds with different yields and creating a *ladder*.

Laddering is when you buy bonds with different maturities.

The ladder balances risk and reward because

- Short-term bonds have a shorter lifespan, so there are few chances that interest rates will rise while you're holding the bond.

- Long-term bonds, while riskier, offer you greater yield.

Ideally, you get the benefits of each kind of bond and the negatives cancel each other out. You can either put together your own ladder strategy or you can use tools provided at your broker's site.

Redemption

Although you may hold a bond until it matures, when you are scheduled to be paid back you may find yourself with an early cashout of sorts. This is generally referred to as *redemption*.

Redemption is when either your principal is returned to you by the issuer of a bond before the formal maturity date or you request that the issuer pay back your principal early. The former is called a "call," the latter a "put," as discussed in Chapter 14, "Getting Into Options Trading."

Most advisers caution you to avoid bonds that have an option for the borrower to call the bond. The call option may be exercised if interest rates fall below a certain amount. The reason this is bad for you goes straight back to the yield curve: If you are holding the bond when interest rates decline, the face value of the bond will increase, leaving you with a potential profit. By having to turn over the bond and collect your principal, you are potentially leaving capital gains on the table.

For this reason, bonds that are callable will sometimes contain a provision for you to collect a higher yield in the event that they are called.

A put option, on the other hand, may protect you from rising interest rates. A put option will allow you to cash out the bond early if you see interest rates rising. This saves you from holding the bond as it grows less valuable (remember the yield curve, which moves inversely to price). You can then reinvest the principal at the higher interest rate.

Bond Trading

Before we get into the details of placing buy and sell orders for bonds, there are a few important points to keep in mind that make the actual trading of a bond different from trading shares of stock or mutual funds:

- For one thing, there are obviously many more variables to consider. Bonds are complex instruments in that you're not simply looking at the price, you're looking at the yield or fixed return you can expect at the end of the bond's lifetime. In addition, you're looking at when the bond will mature and

when your principal will be repaid. You can search for bonds
under all of these criteria at your broker's Web site or using
third-party Web sites.

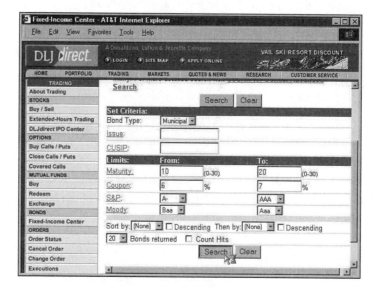

- Similar to mutual funds, there can be several different bonds
  attached to or originating from one entity. For example, in the
  case of corporate bonds, a company may issue several bonds
  with different expiration periods, different yields, and so on.
  For this reason, you may want to search for bonds by *issue*.

  The *issue* of a bond tells you which entity (company, municipal government, and so on) has issued the bond.

- As mentioned earlier, bonds are sold individually rather than
  in shares. You can buy as few as one single bond and as many
  as the amount on offer from the issuer.(This amount will usually be listed as the total offering when you go to purchase
  the bond online.) The bond has a par value, which is the price
  it is trading for currently. However, you'll end up paying
  some multiple of the par value for the bonds you purchase.

- Pricing for bonds is different than pricing for shares of stock
  or shares of mutual funds. When you go to place a buy or sell
  order, you'll have a choice of purchasing the bond at whatever the current price in the market is, at a limit price, or at a
  yield that you specify, whatever the resulting price will be.

Ordering the Bond

You'll usually find bond trading in a special section labeled either Bonds or Fixed Income.

The steps to place orders for bonds involve the following:

- First, find the bond you're looking for using the search tools on your broker's site. Your broker may offer a special section listing bonds available for purchase immediately. If so, that should be your starting place.

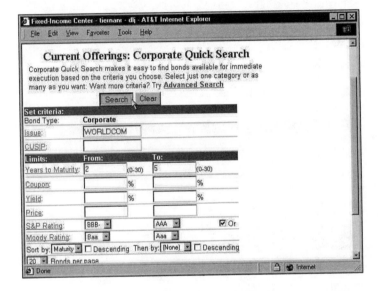

You should first look for bonds in current offerings.

- You'll get a page of results, from which you can select to buy bonds.

- Once you click on the buy button for the bond you want, you'll be given a screen in which to select the particulars of your purchase. Unlike typical stock orders, discussed in Chapter 8, "Placing Your First Trade," you have the option to specify the yield at which you want to buy the bond, rather than the price, so that you can lock in the yield to maturity that you are seeking.

*Your search
should bring up
a series of bonds
you can pick from.*

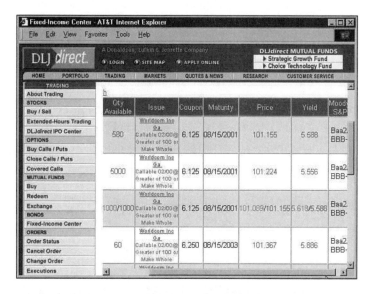

*You'll be asked to
enter the particu-
lars of your order.*

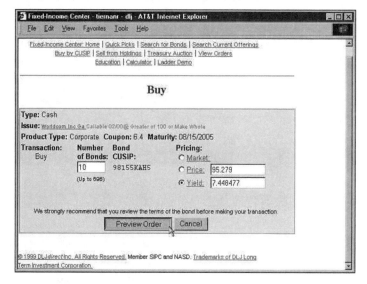

- You'll then be asked to review the terms of your order and click the submit button.

- Finally, you'll see the confirmation screen showing that your order has been received.

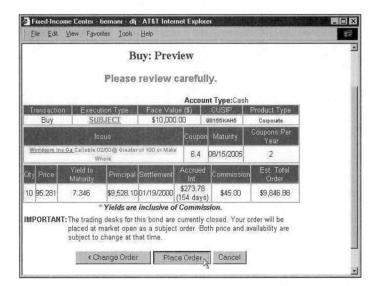

You'll be asked to review the details of your order.

You should see the confirmation screen after submitting your order.

- If you want to cancel your order, you may be required to do so within a separate fixed-income order status window. If so, you should be able to find this link from the usual order status page where you go to check the status of other orders you've placed.

*You can cancel
your orders from
the bond status
screen.*

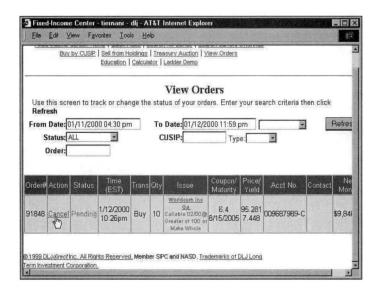

Selling Bonds from Your Account

Selling bonds is similar to selling other securities in your account.
You'll see a screen listing the bonds you hold and asking you to
specify how many of the bonds you want to sell. The tricky part is
that unlike stocks, you can either choose to sell bonds at whatever
the best market price offered currently is, or you can choose to
specify either a specific price you want to attach to the bond or a
yield at which you are offering the bond. Obviously, if you intend
to sell the bond at a profit and you want to specify the price or the
yield of the bond, you will have to review what you paid for the
bond and what yield you are presently enjoying in order to figure
out what numbers will allow you a profit when you sell the bond.

Tax Considerations with Bonds and Mutual Funds

Taxes on bonds and mutual funds are fairly straightforward, and
as mentioned at the beginning of the chapter, mutual funds can
ultimately simplify some of your bookkeeping for tax purposes.
But there are a few details that you will have to keep track of that
are different from the way you calculate and report taxes on sales
of stock:

- You'll have to keep track of both dividends and mutual fund
  distributions. Dividends from bonds and mutual funds will be

reported in the same part of your tax form as short-term capital gains from stock sales. Distributions are the same as long-term capital gains on stock sales and should be reported in the same way.

- You have to keep in mind that some bonds, such as corporate bonds, will be taxable. Others, such as Treasuries, will not. Likewise, you should not have to pay taxes on distributions and dividends from funds you are invested in that hold non-taxable bonds.

- In addition to paying taxes on distributions and dividends, you will pay normal capital gains taxes—either short-term or long-term—on profit you make from selling shares of mutual funds or bonds.

- When you calculate your basis, as discussed in Chapter 10, you will factor in the fees paid to your broker to purchase bonds and shares. However, you will also need to factor in any dividends reinvested in mutual fund shares. These reinvested dividends count as an expense, and they should be deducted from your profits on the mutual fund.

Beyond these points, you'll find that some situations have more subtleties. For example, there are bonds sold called "zero coupon" bonds. These are bonds that pay no dividend, but that trade at a substantial discount to their par value. While the result seems like a big capital gain, in fact the difference between the price and the par value is actually calculated as interest income. For that reason, it should be figured into your tax basis as dividends reinvested that form part of your tax basis, just as with normal bonds that have dividends reinvested. In special situations such as this, check with your accountant on the details.

What You've Learned

Mutual funds, but more so bonds, can be tricky instruments to figure out. Unlike the thrill of trading stocks all day, they involve some complex measures of success. Just thinking about things like the yield curve can make your head hurt. The good thing about both, however, is that they are widely recommended for adding stability and safety to your portfolio. Hopefully this chapter has helped you to appreciate that fact. You should have a basic feel for what trading mutual funds and bonds will require.

- You should have learned how bonds and mutual funds differ from stocks in their return on investment.

- You should understand the intricacies of how bonds and mutual funds generate a return on investment.

- You should have a sense of how you would trade these securities from your own account.

PART V

The Future of
Online Trading

CHAPTER 16

Day Trading Online

Chances are you know someone who's recently quit his or her job to "sit at home and trade stocks," as they put it. Even if you're only mildly interested in following the market day-to-day, you've probably had your curiosity piqued by the thought of rogue individuals trading thousands of shares a day, making enormous fortunes in millisecond time frames between nine and five, and losing even greater amounts of money.

Enter the world of the bandits. This chapter is for anyone who's wondered what day trading is all about, and how you might explore it on your own. In this chapter, you'll get a taste of some of the tools used and the implications of the fast-paced environment of day trading. If you're a beginning investor, day trading is probably more complexity than you want to deal with; it can also be quite a dangerous pursuit for the average investor. Nonetheless, understanding how day trading works can give you perspective on the investment world in general.

What You'll Learn in This Chapter:

▶ An overview of day trading.

▶ How you can day trade with your e-trading account.

▶ Using a professional day trading firm.

▶ What you could get from a boutique day trading firm.

▶ Some day trading risks.

▶ The next generation: Internet-based day trading.

What Is a Day Trader?

Day trading is analogous to online trading. Just as you can dump your broker by entering stock trades on the Web, you can go even further with day trading and dump the trader who places your order with the securities exchange. A day trader can directly place a bid or ask for a certain security in the markets where that security trades without the intervention of a professional securities trader.

How does this work? Let's go back to what was discussed in Chapter 6, "Understanding the Basics of Stock Trading." In a typical trading situation:

Try It Yourself ▼

1. You enter the order on the Web.

2. Your order is reviewed for compliance with your account privileges.

3. Your order is entered into the brokerage's trade processing system and passed to a trader.

4. The trader looks through the prices asked and offered for a given security displayed on a computer screen, to try and get you the best price if you've entered a market order, or to get you a more specific price if you've entered a limit or stop order.

As you can see, there are a lot of layers of intermediaries between your Web browser and the actual purchase of a stock: The Internet itself, the traders who enter orders, possibly the floor brokers on the exchange who have to negotiate for prices, as well as all the order-processing computer systems that sit at your e-broker's facility and process the trade.

In day trading, you use special software tools to send your bid or ask price to the exchange where the stock is trading. Rather than going through a trader, your electronic request is sent directly from your computer to the exchange—or at least with greatly diminished intermediation—and your purchase or sale of the security is executed almost instantaneously.

Day trading firms such as Tradescape offer really fast direct connections to the securities exchanges.

‍

What Day Traders Do

The point of sending orders directly is that day traders can quickly execute dozens or hundreds of trades a day.

Why do they do this? Day trading has changed a bit over the years, and there are some lingering misconceptions about how day traders conduct their business. Let's talk for a moment about what day trading is not.

Once upon a time, the day trader's goal was solely to make money off of what is called the *spread* between prices.

The *spread* is the difference between the price at which a share of a stock or a bond is offered for sale and the price at which someone offers to purchase it—the ask and the bid, respectively.

As mentioned in Chapter 6, there is usually a difference between the ask and the bid of at least a sixteenth of a point. Sometimes the difference will be an eighth of a point, a half a point, or larger. It used to be the case that all a day trader would do was buy securities all day long at one price and turn around a moment later and sell at another price a fraction of a point more. For example, shares purchased at 50 5/8 and sold a moment later for 50 and 11/16 will net a profit of 1/16. A sixteenth of a point, when you are gambling tens of thousands of dollars, can actually be a lot of money.

In days of old, day traders manipulated the spread using something called the SOES, an acronym for Small Order Execution System. The SOES was established by the Nasdaq under a mandate from the SEC in 1987, following the stock market crash of that year. Since SOES allowed individuals to enter orders directly, day traders, dubbed "SOES bandits," used the SOES to make point spreads of 1/8 or 1/4 or more. Nasdaq eventually cracked down on the practice.

Today, day trading is a more sober exercise—relatively speaking. Rather than simply trying to ride point spreads, day traders take gambles that stocks will move in certain directions based on news, based on rumor, based on tips. In other words, day traders make money not by investing in the long-term potential of a security, but by gambling on short-term movements in price.

Speculation is the pursuit of profit from short-term movements in the price of a security.

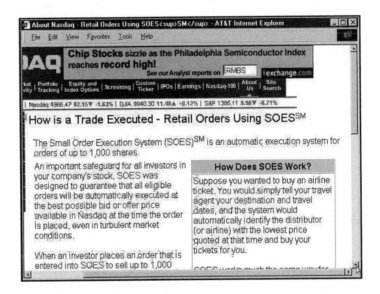

Nasdaq's SOES system is an important part of day trading lore.

Narrowing the Spread

Day traders are not the only members of the market who speculate, and they're not the only ones who make money on the spread between prices. In fact, the Nasdaq has traditionally functioned by allowing market makers to pocket a profit from the spread between buy and sell orders that they fill simultaneously. Market makers have an important responsibility in that they ensure that offers to buy and sell will be met. But a 1994 study by two academics led to charges of price manipulation by Nasdaq market makers. It was alleged that major brokers on the Nasdaq would not quote "odd eighths," meaning 1/8, 3/8 instead of 2/8, 4/8, and so on, thereby increasing the spread they quoted to 1/4 point, 1/2 point, and so on. This practice reduced the average investor's ability to get a good price for his or her trade. The paper led to an investigation by the SEC, fines, and, ultimately, a change in the way prices were quoted: Nasdaq market makers were forced to quote prices in sixteenths, narrowing their potential spread.

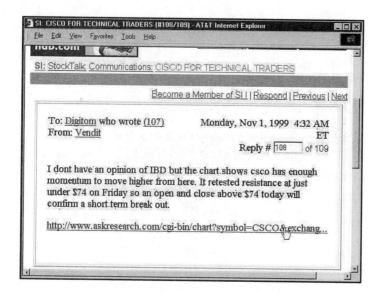

Surfing rumor and gossip on Internet message boards is one way day traders get tips about short-term movements in securities prices.

What Makes It All Possible

Day traders make upwards of 300 trades a day in order to specu-late on their hunches about stocks. In order to do so, they must strip away the layers of intermediation. They do so by making use of certain innovations in trading developed in the last two decades, including the following:

- The conversion of trading from an auction on the floor of the exchange to an electronic market, where traders sitting at terminals can enter buy and sell offers. The advent of the Nasdaq's virtual trading room opened up the possibility of traders in far-flung parts of the world placing orders with the electronic exchange directly from their computer, rather than having to work with a professional trader.

- The streamlining of the various computer systems used by brokerages. Technical types call these the "back office" sys-tems. They are the computers that verify your account privi-leges when you send an order through your online brokerage account and that send your order onto the exchange. Without really fast systems behind the trading screen, day traders could not achieve the kind of hair-trigger timing that makes their business possible.

- New electronic markets. SOES is only one way to get an advantage on the markets. As you'll see in the next chapter, the Nasdaq is not the only market where traders can sit at a terminal and exchange orders with other traders around the world. The advent of the Instinet, a 24-hour broker matching buyers and sellers across various global securities markets, in the late '60s moved trading beyond the realm of the established, clubby world of the Nasdaq and the NYSE. Suddenly, non-Nasdaq traders can be matched to the Nasdaq, as well as to other traders around the world. The advent of electronic communications networks (ECNs), which we'll also examine in the next chapter, further raises the prospect that traders outside of the Nasdaq and the NYSE can trade among themselves around the globe.

ECNs such as Island, Inc. are an increasingly important part of day trading.

- Affordable computing power. Certainly, day trading would not be possible without the same computer infrastructure that makes online trading possible. A desktop PC with a fast connection to the Internet may be all you need in most cases to start day trading. The standard PC will set you back as little as a few hundred dollars today versus the thousands of dollars required traditionally to outfit a trading desk with multiple professional computer workstations. The advent of low-cost desktop computing in the last two decades has spread the ability to trade on a virtual trading floor.

From Wall Street to Main Street

Day trading is the latest in a long process of getting investors closer to the action. For decades, the financial world has tried to draw consumers into the securities business to increase the retail market for buying and selling stocks, bonds, and mutual funds. Retail brokerage services have expanded in the last 40 years thanks to the efforts of large Wall Street firms such as Merrill Lynch, which single-handedly pioneered Main Street investing. Starting in the late '70s and continuing into the '80s and '90s, Charles Schwab and Co. spread the discount brokerage religion throughout America with cheaper rates on trading fees and commissions, and an army of retail brokers at more than 300 branches throughout the country. Online trading, and now day trading, are making individuals more intimately involved with the day-to-day activity of buying and selling securities. In a recent sign that day trading is becoming more of a mainstream occupation, Schwab purchased a fairly prominent day trading firm, CyberCorp., in early 2000.

Means of Day Trading

How exactly do day traders enter the trades they use to flip stocks all day long? There are a few different ways it can be done. For the purposes of this book, we'll break down the day trading market into three classes of investing that you could attempt, varying from effortless to complex:

- Fake day trading. You could sit at your computer and trade stocks all day with little more than what we discussed in Chapter 4, "Tools of the Trade: Hardware and Software Considerations." You could add in some slightly more sophisticated tools that let you obtain real-time prices and see who is making markets in a particular stock. And you could make sure your broker is connected directly to the transaction clearing system of the markets. That way you could speculate on short-term gains in stocks. This is not really day trading, but it is certainly one way to emulate some of the excitement of it.

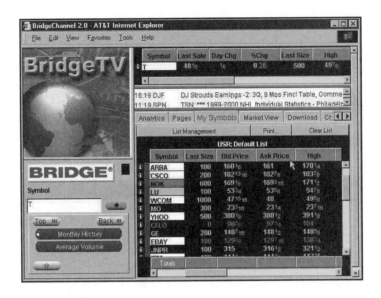

You could get some fancy real-time quote software, like a bridge terminal, and feel like you're day trading when using your normal e-trading account.

- Internet-based day trading. This is a bit more sophisticated than trading stocks through your current brokerage account. It's possible to get hold of some sophisticated software, find a day trading brokerage, and practice day trading from your computer at home. Given a fast, reliable Internet connection, a back office computer system at your broker that's super-efficient, and the right tools on the desktop, it is possible to practice something more like true day trading from home.

- The nirvana of day trading is a whole 'nother thing. Hard-core day traders go to special brokerage houses that focus on day trading. They are assigned their own super-fast work-station computer with all the necessary software tools. The brokerage has its own super-fast connection to the securities exchange. Using this special environment, it's possible to get the fast response times critical for day trading.

Let's take a look at each of these day trading arrangements in turn.

Day Trading Through Your Existing Account

Trading online as we've been discussing it in this book is extremely different from day trading per se. The fundamental reason is time: If you are trying to make a profit by racking up the spread between stock prices over several trades, the response time you get with normal e-trading may simply not be fast enough. Instead, you need:

- Real-time information. Most brokerages are just getting around to offering you real-time quotes of stock prices. But the first thing you need to day trade is a palette of real-time information about how many shares are trading hands, what the current price is, and who's currently offering how many shares for sale or who's buying. It's this timely information that you have to act on.

- Quick processing of your order. If your brokerage has to take time to verify that you are approved to make the kind of trade you are making, and if your order has to wait in a queue with other orders that also need to be filled, then you may miss the window of opportunity in which to pick up the stock at the price that's right.

- Quick confirmation that your trade has been placed. It's not sufficient to find out by email later in the day that a trade has gone through, certainly not if you intend to turn around and "flip" that stock, meaning sell it at a profit. You need to know instantaneously if your trade has been successful.

These factors make it virtually impossible to really day trade with a normal online account. In addition, there are quite a few other differences between speculating online and real day trading:

- Margin privileges are extremely important. As mentioned in Chapter 13, "Trading on Margin and Trading Options," margin lending allows you to increase your buying power. That's important because a large part of the strategy with day trading is to move money around quickly throughout the day— more money than your up-front, invested capital. Being able to buy on margin is key.

- Aside from margin lending, it takes a lot of capital to start with to be in the day trading game. It's not uncommon for day traders to start their trading in the morning with $50,000 or more, prepared to lose all of it if necessary, to make the large bets that day trading requires. Since profiting off short-term moves in prices is a game of aggregate successes, day traders need plenty of cash so they can make the largest number of bets, so that their wins will balance out or exceed their losing bets.

- Day traders often (but not always) close out their positions at the end of the day. What this means is that day traders end their day with no stocks in their account, but rather the cash profit or loss from trading. That way, traders make sure that the only investment question they face is how great their gain or their loss will be during the day, not how well or how poorly their stocks will do over the longer term. Few normal investors would expect to buy tons of securities all day long and end up owning nothing at the end of the day!

You're unlikely to approach investing in this manner on a day-to-day basis. Still, even if you can't day trade like a pro, you can use your existing online account as a means of speculation. What are the ingredients of a more fast-paced online trading experience? At a minimum, you should consider the following:

- Fast gear. This is a time to review the basic building blocks discussed in Chapter 4 and make sure you've got fast gear. Having a fast connection to the Internet is part of it, but so is having a computer fast enough to run more sophisticated market-tracking software that will be digesting real-time quotes and helping you form models of how trading is proceeding. At the very least, you should consider upgrading to the latest Power Macintosh G3 or G4 computer or Intel Pentium III system from the PC vendors. You want to make sure you have at least 64 megabytes of DRAM for running big applications, though 128 megabytes is a lot better. Consider, too, obtaining one of the fast cable modem connections or digital subscriber line modems mentioned in Chapter 4.

- A broker with a clearinghouse relationship. Not all brokerages are created equal. Some brokerages maintain a privileged position in that they are subsidiaries or divisions of larger firms whose business is to perform the *clearing* of securities transactions.

Clearing is the actual settlement of buy and sell orders. It involves the transfer of funds between the buying and selling parties, and the recording of the transaction in multiple electronic databases. Clearing firms specialize in handling large volumes of transactions, with multiple steps involved. They play a crucial role in coordinating the various parties involved in the transaction, and often they may put up the securities to satisfy a sale so that the buyer does not have to wait for the actual stock certificates to be transferred from a seller's account.

Why is it important to have a relationship with a clearinghouse brokerage? By their nature, clearinghouses are closer to the action in certain areas of the business. The computers of the clearinghouse know first when a trade is confirmed. As a result, brokerages with ties to clearing firms may enjoy a faster response time when confirming your trade. Some established brokerages with online offerings advertise their relationship to clearinghouse firms. They include Suretrade and Quick & Reilly, both of which are subsidiaries of FleetBoston, which in turn owns U.S. Clearing, a clearinghouse that processes trades executed on the Nasdaq.

If your broker has a securities clearing relationship, such as that between Quick & Reilly and U.S. Clearing, it may offer you an edge in response time on trades.

- Perhaps more important than finding which brokers have clearing relationships is finding which brokers have the top marks for overall performance. Some online financial publications periodically do their own reviews. You can also check with special firms such as Keynote Systems, which provides additional broker reviews using special equipment that can, for example, test the actual response time of a connection to any online broker's Web site.

- Another thing to look for in a broker is which of the new electronic markets they support. We'll talk in the next chapter about electronic trading venues such as Instinet and Island. These are basically big brokerages that send your order to a variety of markets around the world to get the best offer. They compete with each other by deploying cutting-edge technology to get the best prices and the best response time. Your broker may already have an arrangement to use the services of one of these firms. If so, you may want to check with your broker to find out which service he or she is using and, if you're not satisfied, find a broker who uses a different service.

- Lastly, you can get yourself some special software packages that will give you the kind of real-time information that is used by professional traders to see what prices are being offered for a stock at any moment in time and who is buying and selling. Software in this area is in the dozens. There are tons of tiny firms providing various packages. For example, Data Broadcasting Corporation offers something called eSignal. eSignal provides quotes in real-time for any number of stock symbols, updated continuously throughout the day. The program can also give you what's called *Nasdaq Level II data.*

Nasdaq Level II data refers to the display of data about the Nasdaq market on a trader's screen. Specifically, Nasdaq Level II reports which brokerage firms are offering what prices for a security, and for how many shares, at any given moment in time. Traders use Level II data to gauge the interest in a stock among major brokerages.

The big advantage of a program like eSignal is not only that it can display a lot of continuously updated market data, but that you can use that data as a way to organize trading. If your broker has a deal with Data Broadcasting Corporation, you can click on the ticker of a stock that comes to your attention and automatically enter a trade right from the Nasdaq Level II screen.

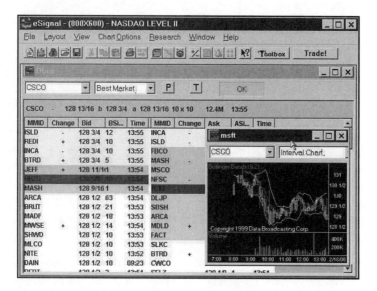

Programs such as Data Broadcasting's eSignal can give you the real-time information that's critical in day trading.

Brokerage-Based Day Trading

When most people talk about day trading, they don't mean trading with a standard brokerage account. Nor are they referring to using a fast Web-based trading system. Most day trading takes place at the offices of special boutique brokerage firms set up exclusively for that purpose. The nirvana of the day trader is to have the largest selection of markets in which to place an order, an ultra-fast execution system to process orders rapidly, and a sophisticated suite of tools. Day trading firms specialize in these things.

There are literally dozens of these firms in the U.S. You can find a complete listing of day trading firms at The North American Securities Administrators Association Web site, *www.nasaa.org/firms.pdf.*

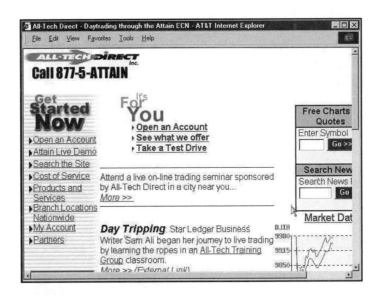

Myths About Day Traders

Before we go any further, let's clear up a few myths about day traders. Contrary to popular belief

- Day traders do not make their money purely by trading spreads of a sixteenth of a point or an eighth of a point. Often, traders are taking more calculated bets that stocks will move dramatically based on news. In fact, in today's rocketing stock market, it's increasingly common for hot stocks—and not-so-hot stocks—to have violent swings day to day, or during the trading day. The 20 point change is what a trader is looking for.

- Not all traders close out their positions at the end of the day. Though this is common practice, some traders do in fact hold a position if they think it will move in their favor overnight or over the course of a few days.

- Traders do not make huge sums of money every day. On average, a day trader will lose money four days out of five. Day trading is all a game of averages. If a day trader wins really big one day of the week, it may make the rest of his or her week worthwhile.

- Nor do traders play by losing endless sums of money on crazy bets. In fact, most day traders set a limit of how much they are willing to lose in a day before calling it quits for the day to cut their losses.

We can say a few things that *are* true about the general traits of a successful day trader:

- Day traders are competitive, but not without a sense of the good luck/bad luck nature of the pursuit. It's natural for day traders to revel in a good day when they can walk away with tens of thousands of dollars in profit after trading only a few hours—and good traders have many such successful days. However, professional traders are equally adept at losing tens of thousands of dollars and putting the matter behind them to begin afresh the next day. Successful day traders, in other words, are able to put both the good and bad trades in perspective.

- Day traders are used to putting up a lot of capital. Many day traders start the trading day with $250,000 or more to play with. To have that amount of money at one's discretion is mind-boggling to most people. To be gambling based on your wits and your hunches with that much money on a daily basis is probably more than the average investor can handle.

- Day traders are able to discipline themselves. They tend to set goals for themselves both for the amounts they are willing to win and the amounts they are willing to lose. Just like being disciplined at the craps table, successful day traders are able to walk away from the action when they've reached either their goal on the upside or they've broken through their maximum loss level. Most serious day trading firms do not encourage a "cowboy" attitude of losing big and going for unreasonable wins; these types of traders are usually viewed by other traders as potential flameouts down the road.

- Certainly day traders have to be able to react quickly. Traders make 300 orders to buy and sell per day, on average. Most of that time they are pressing the trade button based on a quick assessment of a company press release, or some change in a stock's rating by one of the Wall Street firms. Acting on instinct and going with a gut feeling are part of the game. But so is being able to move on from one bad trade to the next trade without getting slowed down. Reflexes are part of all this, but so is an ability to start over.

• Day traders follow some counter-intuitive rules that are part of the toolkit of the professional day trader, but that you might not be comfortable with on a day-to-day basis. For example, day traders usually don't use limit orders and other risk-reducing strategies. Unlike with traditional brokerages, where you will be encouraged to use limit orders with volatile markets or at certain volatile periods of the day to limit your exposure to wild price swings, brokerages for day traders tend to eschew these order specifications because they can make it impossible to get an order processed in time. Limit orders, for example, will be put in a queue, which could force the day trader to miss the small window of time in which the trade must be placed. This is a kind of "flying without a parachute" aspect of day trading that makes the pursuit so nerve-wracking.

• Day traders are a dressed-down crowd. Whereas bankers may have a tendency to wear pin-striped suits and flaunt their Jaguars, it's common to see traders who are making hundreds of thousands of dollars in a week coming to the firm in sweat pants and T-shirts. There is a kind of informal ethic among day traders of not flaunting one's wealth with the usual Wall Street status items.

What the Day Trading Boutique Offers

True day traders spend as much as 12 hours, from 8 a.m. to 8 p.m., at small boutique brokerages that cater to them. These brokerages offer the day trader things they won't find elsewhere. They include

• Super-fast connections to the trading systems. One of the problems of trading either through your typical online account or even through Web-based day trading software is that you will always be limited by the speed of your connection to the Internet, which for most people tops out at 56 kilobits per second, the speed of today's best analog modems. When you go to a day trading firm, you share a direct connection to the securities exchange that will probably be at least 20 times that speed, if not faster. With a day trading firm you get a fast, direct connection to the electronic trading floor and your order goes over a private network, not the public Internet.

- Sophisticated tools. Day trading firms will outfit you with the latest and greatest software running on a spiffy new computer. You'll have fast response time from the computer, Nasdaq Level II trading information, and other applications, some designed in-house, to help you analyze movements in stock prices.

- Incredible margin capabilities. We talked a little bit in Chapter 13 about margin privileges. As we mentioned then, most online brokers will give you 2x margin capabilities, meaning you will have as much again in borrowed money to spend buying securities as you have in securities in your account. With a day trading firm, you'll get far more to play with. It's not unusual for a day trading firm to give you 10 times your money. So if you come in the door with $100,000 cash, you'll actually have $1 million to gamble. What kind of margin privileges you will enjoy is at the discretion of the firm.

- Arbitration of complaints. If traders feel that the other party with whom they're trading has not kept his or her end of a trade, they can get instant and effective arbitration. By making a complaint to the officials of the day trading firm, the trader can get a judgment from the Nasdaq within half an hour as to whether the actions of the other party are fraudulent.

- Access to more markets. Some alternative electronic trading venues, such as SOES and Instinet, were mentioned earlier in the chapter. While some electronic brokerages will give you access to Instinet or another system through your normal account, day trading firms actually let you connect to several of these trading networks simultaneously. You can have your pick of a vastly expanded field of potential trading partners, which can dramatically improve the kinds of prices you get for stock.

- Professional advice. While most firms expect day traders to more or less know what they're doing, there's always a benefit to sitting in a room filled with experienced traders. In some cases, seasoned day traders can help a neophyte to put the experience into context. While most traders don't expect to offer extensive advice, and most firms frown on their doing so, working side-by-side with pros may rub off on a beginning day trader and provide a healthy example.

- More marginable securities. While the SEC sets some guidelines for which securities are marginable, meaning able to be bought with borrowed money as mentioned in Chapter 13, the list of securities that can be traded on margin is ultimately at the discretion of the brokerage firm. And so in keeping with the policy of allowing their customers greater trading power, many day trading firms will make marginable risky stocks that would not be marginable at other firms.

- Better fee schedule. Unlike typical online trading accounts, where fees increase the more shares you buy, day trading firms actually lower the fee you pay per trade the more shares you trade with each order.

- Insurance. When you're playing with large amounts of money, you might want to have a little coverage. As mentioned in Chapter 11, "Troubleshooting and Ending Your Online Trading Relationship," most brokerage houses are aligned with SIPC for insurance up to $500,000. However, given the large amounts of money day traders move, most day trading firms offer insurance in the millions. It's not unheard of for a firm to have as much as $100 million to cover all its traders' accounts.

Requirements of the Day Trading Firms

To get all these benefits, there are certain rules of the day trading firm:

- Reputable day trading firms screen their applicants thoroughly. Some of this might be familiar to you from setting up an online account. You may be asked about your trading experience, your net worth, how much you own in securities, your marital status, whether you own a home, how often you trade each year, and how often you trade on margin. Acceptance into a day trading firm is at the firm's discretion, and so you can be rejected based on your answers to any one of these questions. Basically, the brokerage firm is looking for experienced, professional traders. They will be looking for evidence that you've traded often, and perhaps that this is not your first time trading large amounts of money.

  You should check out the broker as well. As mentioned in Chapter 11, you can use the NASD's database, at *http://pdpi. nasdr.com*, to check out most brokerages. It's especially important to check out whether your broker has any black marks when putting more capital at risk than usual. Also, it's worth checking the SEC's suggested list of questions again, posted on the SEC Web site at *www.sec.gov/consumer/ jchkout.htm*.

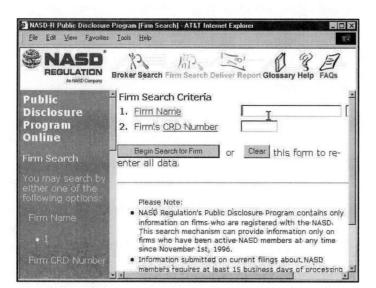

Remember that the NASD database of broker records can help you check up on day trading firms.

- If your application is accepted, the brokerage will likely ask for a substantial minimum deposit on the order of $25,000— far more, in other words, than the $2,000 to $5,000 typical of most e-trading accounts.

- A supervisor at the brokerage firm, dubbed a "risk manager," surveys the traders in the room. If the supervisor judges that you're losing too much money too fast, or that you've lost control of the trading situation, he may suspend your trading and ask you to take a breather or even to go home.

The Risks of Day Trading

It probably can't be emphasized enough how risky day trading is. It is quite possible to lose the shirt off your back by day trading. And it's no joke to say that you could even wind up dead from day trading. Enraged day traders have been the stuff of front page news in recent years, and with more amateur traders flirting with the day-trading world, there's bound to be a lot more upset in this corner of the investing community.

Perhaps the biggest reason investors may end up disappointed with day trading is that so many individuals think that because they've had some mild success with their online trading accounts, they can simply replicate that success in the very different world of day trading. Too many amateur traders learn the hard way that day trading can be a losing proposition most of the time.

The SEC has posted several important points about the risks inherent in day trading on its Web site at *www.sec.gov/consumer/daytips.htm*. It's also not a bad idea to check out what SEC Chairman Arthur Leavitt has to say about the practice of day trading. You can read his testimony at *www.sec.gov/news/testmony/tsty2199.htm*.

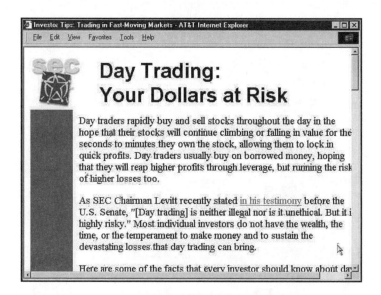

*Check out the
SEC's comments
regarding day
trading.*

Let's look at the some of the serious risks of day trading:

- Substantial capital at risk. Day traders are encouraged to place
  large amounts of capital into their day trading accounts to get
  the most leverage from margin loans. Gambling this much
  money is as risky as taking down payments on your mortgage
  to the race track. You should be aware of how much money
  you are placing at risk.

- Large margin exposure. Remember that day trading firms are
  all too eager to help you put even more of your capital at risk.
  The leverage that comes from margin loans can quickly turn
  into an inescapable pit of debt if the market turns against
  your margined gambles.

- The no-limit-order trade. As mentioned earlier, day traders
  focus on use of the market order. But using the market order
  exclusively means going without the protection of the limit
  order. That means an overall increase in your exposure to
  volatile price swings.

- No checks on illegal trades. When you trade through your
  existing online account, you are prevented from making trades
  not allowed by your broker. Because the software used by
  day trading firms is designed to execute trades as quickly as

possible, the software will not prevent trades from going through that shouldn't be executed. For example, as noted in Chapter 12, "Getting Into IPOs Online," it's against the law to sell short initial public offerings of stock because of the tremendous price swings of these stocks. However, you can do so using software at a day trading firm. And that could result in your breaking the law and even going to jail.

Internet Day Trading

If you can't or don't want to trade at a boutique firm, the next level down is to trade "remotely," as is the term in the industry.

Some online brokers specialize in so-called "remote" day trading.

This means using some slick day trading software and an Internet day trading account to trade from home. It's a far cry from the trading room of the brokerage house, but it offers some advantages over trying to day trade with your normal e-trading account.

Many of the brokerage firms that will let you day trade at their facilities will also let you trade remotely from home, although they will discourage the process. In general, the process offers

- A fairly sophisticated software package offering Nasdaq Level II data, as well as sophisticated stock charting and analysis.

- The ability to work on your own computer at your home or office, and to send trades to the broker's computers just the way you would with your regular broker.

- Fast computer processing of your order. In many cases, these firms have stripped-down computer systems to handle your trading request that are designed to throw the least amount of interference into your trade. For example, they will have short-cuts for checking account privileges so that your trade is not delayed during a lengthy approval process.

- Routing your order not only to the stock market, but also to the SOES and to several ECNs. Again, this gets your order in front of more market participants, which means you stand to garner a better price, on average.

- Fees that are usually as cheap if not cheaper than a standard online trading account, although you will likely have to submit the higher minimum deposit associated with the day trading brokerage.

There are obvious advantages and disadvantages of the online day trading arrangement. The advantages are

- Faster processing of your order.

- Potentially much better prices as a result of processing in several markets.

- Far more information than you would have during normal online trading.

Some obvious disadvantages of the Internet day trading approach are

- You are still limited by how fast your order can travel over the Web to the brokerage's computers.

- You receive minimal supervision as far as what securities to buy or sell. Where a traditional broker may decide some stocks are not marginable, the Internet day trading operation may have drastically more relaxed conditions for marginability, sometimes too relaxed.

- Obviously, there's a risk in that you are being encouraged to place orders frequently and with little premeditation. If you don't build a concerted plan beforehand, you may start losing lots of money without anyone to intervene and tell you to stop trading for awhile, to take a breather, and so on. Remember that, unlike being in the day trading boutique, you won't have support or consultation from other day traders, at least not face-to-face.

What You've Learned

The risk analysis in the last section should give you pause when considering day trading. On the whole, it's an extremely high-pressure pursuit with potential for tremendous losses. Day trading truly takes nerves of steel, and plenty of disposable cash.

If you're still interested, this chapter has hopefully given you the basics.

- You should understand what it is that day traders do, and the profile of the day trader.

- You should have some rough idea of the different ways in which you can day trade.

- Hopefully, you have a sense of the enormous risks inherent in day trading

CHAPTER 17

After-Hours Trading and Electronic Communications Networks

Perhaps you can't get to the market in time. Perhaps you can't get enough of stock trading, and trading stocks all day long while sitting in front of your computer is just a warm-up for you. Perhaps, like many rogue traders, you find the safe, regulated environment of daily trading just plain dull. You're ready to move up to the world of after-hours trading and Electronic Communications Networks.

Over the past few decades, the process of securities trading has become more and more accessible to the average individual. Chapter 1, "The Pros and Cons of Online Trading," talked about how the buildout of the electronic trading systems at the end of the 1960s, in the form of the Nasdaq National Market, laid the groundwork for the retail brokerage movement that was to follow. That gave customers the ability to simply phone in an order to buy or sell securities for a low fee. The Web has taken that system into every home and office. But the market is primed now to go 'round-the-clock. Trading already goes on in markets around the world throughout the night—you just can't get in on it, in most cases. However, with the ability to trade anywhere there's an Internet account, and with the ferocious interest in stock trading by the average investor, why, some have asked, shouldn't the markets operate 24 hours a day? After-hours trading is your first taste of what may eventually be an all-day e-trading world.

What You'll Learn in This Chapter:

- ▶ What is after-hours trading?
- ▶ What is the Instinet system?
- ▶ The rise of Electronic Communications Networks.
- ▶ How you can trade after hours from your existing account.

Understanding After-Hours Trading

As you may know, financial markets on the East Coast of the U.S. open trading at 9:35 in the morning and close at 4:00 in the afternoon. For most people, this is the stock market.

But obviously that's not true for much of the world. In Europe, in Asia, in India, and everywhere else in the world where there are securities exchanges, trading is going on while you're sleeping. The question arises, "Can you keep trading after the floor clears out in New York?"

Overseas exchanges such as the Bombay Stock Exchange are an indication of the global, 24-hour nature of securities trading.

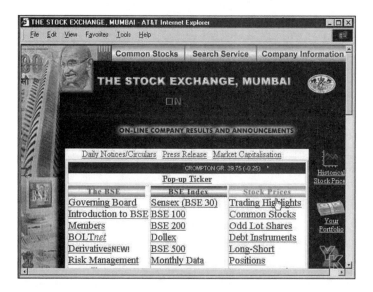

The answer is yes, in a couple of ways. Although stocks and other securities are listed on the various exchanges throughout the world, there is a long tradition of investors placing orders for those securities through channels other than the exchanges themselves. In fact, today's sophisticated Nasdaq electronic trading system evolved from a network of brokers at various houses trading over the telephone to get better deals on exchange-listed securities.

Today, there are three primary forums in which to place orders for stock to be settled outside the traditional structure of the major exchanges:

- Nasdaq and the other major markets, which are extending their hours to accommodate the demand for after-hours trading.

- Instinet, a subsidiary of the financial news firm Reuters, PLC.

- Electronic Communications Networks (ECNs), which are networks owned by the major brokerage houses and investment banks.

The most obvious way for the average investor to keep investing after 4 p.m. (or before 9:30 a.m.) is for the exchanges to open earlier and stay open longer. This is happening. The various exchanges are following their own individual courses for extending trading hours incrementally. For example, in October of 1999 the Nasdaq created an after-hours session between 4:00 p.m. and 6:30 p.m. There are efforts underway to extend hours even further, and it's quite possible that the exchanges will move to 24-hour order processing at some point in time.

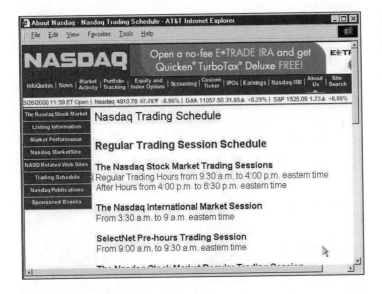

Nasdaq and other exchanges are steadily increasing their trading hours.

Outside of extended hours, Instinet and the ECNs form a way to create markets between subscribers and exchanges around the world where stocks continue to trade given the time difference. Both systems (Instinet is really a pre-ECN type of ECN, when you come down to it) fall short of exchange status. They are really big brokers that match orders between clients and that send orders to the actual exchanges. Instinet and the various ECNs have applied for exchange status so that they may directly list stocks for trading and, perhaps someday, move away from a dependence on the exchanges for stock listings.

Catching Up with the Coast

After-hours trading is also important if you live west of the New York stock markets. The trading day ends at 4 p.m. eastern standard time, which is only 1 p.m. on the West Coast. If you're a busy individual, having to trade before lunch hour is over may not fit with your schedule. After-hours trading is a way to get an extra two or three hours to enter your trades.

Neither Instinet nor the ECNs are a complete solution to after-hours trading. Some equities cannot be traded on these networks at all. But more stocks are being cleared for trading all the time. For example, the NYSE recently revoked Rule 390, which said that some stocks listed on the exchange could not be traded outside of the floor of the NYSE. That meant that clients who used Instinet or the ECNs could not place orders to trade NYSE stocks. The revocation of Rule 390 is a major coup for the ECNs because it extends their trading to some of the most broadly held stock in America, such as that of General Electric.

Next we'll take a look at the two systems.

Instinet

Instinet is really just a large brokerage house handling the sale of securities listed on the various exchanges, including the Nasdaq and the New York Stock Exchange. The firm was founded in 1969 and is a subsidiary of Reuters, the financial news firm. Instinet places trading orders throughout the day and night for client firms, which include brokerage houses, and also many of the most prominent mutual funds. Instinet matches up offers between clients and also sends these orders to the various global stock exchanges to be matched with orders there.

Instinet was the first after-hours trading network.

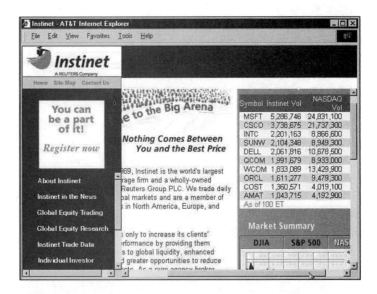

Individual retail investors do not trade directly as clients of Instinet. Instead, you will use Instinet if your broker uses the service to provide after-hours trading. E*Trade, for one, is among the online brokerages using Instinet to provide after-hours trading to its retail clients. However, Instinet is in the process of setting up its own online discount retail brokerage operation. By the time you read this, you may be able to sign up to use Instinet's brokerage services.

After-hours trading has a somewhat shadowy air to it, mainly because a firm such as Instinet is a brokerage, not a genuine securities exchange in its own right. Therefore, its conduct is not regulated in the same strict way that the SEC regulates the conduct of, say, the NYSE. Consider how Instinet trading differs from the established exchanges:

- Chapter 6, "Understanding the Basics of Stock Trading," discussed the concept of liquidity. To review, a liquid market means there is relative certainty that there will be buyers and sellers available to meet your buy or sell order.

  In many traditional markets, there is tight control of who can be a market maker, meaning the party that simultaneously presents buy and sell orders to the exchange to create a liquid market for securities. This is to ensure liquidity. On Instinet, by contrast, any number of parties can be buying and selling stocks simultaneously. That could mean excess liquidity or, if no one is fulfilling both buying and selling functions, it could mean less liquidity than usual. (We'll return to this point in more depth in the section "After-Hours Trading in Your Existing Account" later in the chapter.)

- Whereas traders in the Nasdaq or the NYSE have full information about who is making offers to buy or sell stock, all offers on the electronic trading screens of Instinet are entered anonymously. You won't know whether the 1,000 shares of a stock that were just dumped on the market came from a large institution or from a single individual.

The anonymous order book at Instinet is one of the staples of after-hours trading.

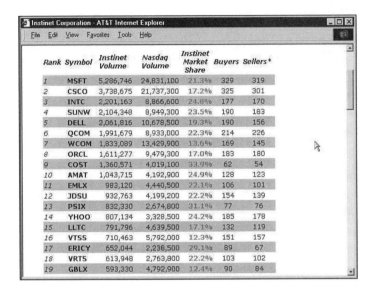

Rank	Symbol	Instinet Volume	Nasdaq Volume	Instinet Market Share	Buyers	Sellers*
1	MSFT	5,286,746	24,831,100	21.3%	329	319
2	CSCO	3,738,675	21,737,300	17.2%	325	301
3	INTC	2,201,163	8,866,600	24.8%	177	170
4	SUNW	2,104,348	8,949,300	23.5%	190	183
5	DELL	2,061,816	10,678,500	19.3%	190	156
6	QCOM	1,991,679	8,933,000	22.3%	214	226
7	WCOM	1,833,089	13,429,900	13.6%	169	145
8	ORCL	1,611,277	9,479,300	17.0%	183	180
9	COST	1,360,571	4,019,100	33.9%	62	54
10	AMAT	1,043,715	4,192,900	24.9%	128	123
11	EMLX	983,120	4,440,500	22.1%	106	101
12	JDSU	932,763	4,199,200	22.2%	154	139
13	PSIX	832,330	2,674,800	31.1%	77	76
14	YHOO	807,134	3,328,500	24.2%	185	178
15	LLTC	791,796	4,639,500	17.1%	132	119
16	VTSS	710,463	5,792,000	12.3%	151	157
17	ERICY	652,044	2,238,500	29.1%	89	67
18	VRTS	613,948	2,763,800	22.2%	103	102
19	GBLX	593,330	4,792,900	12.4%	90	84

There are a variety of other rules of conduct that a formal exchange must observe but that don't apply to a simple "order-matching" system such as Instinet. What are the benefits of such a system?

- One of the main benefits is simply that Instinet is open around the clock. The firm offers clients the potential to trade on exchanges around the world 24 hours a day.

- Unlike with traditional exchange-based trading, clients can request that buy or sell orders be routed to particular exchanges in the U.S. and around the world to obtain the best price. This may offer a greater level of control over the actual trading process than most investors need, but it may have its appeal for Instinet's large institutional clients.

- Global liquidity. Although Instinet may not have the same stringent requirements for setting market makers, the firm argues that traders on Instinet ultimately enjoy greater liquidity because their trades may be sent to 40 different live exchanges around the world.

- Instinet officials argue that the anonymity of who is buying and placing orders makes for a less lopsided market. No single institution can send shockwaves through the after-hours market, based on its reputation, simply because it is buying or selling shares.

- Another claim made by Instinet is that it can secure better prices for clients because it acts as an impartial broker. What this means is that because Instinet does not own any positions in securities, it is not conflicted or biased when it comes time to find prices in the market on behalf of clients. In particular, Instinet makes money off of fees for executing trades. The company doesn't make money on the spread between bid and ask prices it can transact simultaneously, which should make its trades impartial.

- With its electronic display of bid and ask prices on each trade, Instinet offers investors the ability to know in real-time the cost of a particular trade, rather than waiting hours for a confirmation of the price paid (in the case of a market order).

Currently, Instinet is limited to trading of equities. The firm plans to introduce trading of bonds in the near future.

Here Come Electronic Communications Networks

Instinet is already getting some competition. Other firms have registered themselves as broker dealers and enjoy the financial backing of some of the most powerful brokerage firms and investment banks. Like Instinet, these newcomers are essentially "order matching" systems that are designed to pair buyers with sellers using a computer system. The ECN takes no cut of the profit or loss on stock trades, but simply collects a fee for each transaction.

The ECNs are not just for after-hours trading. They are already becoming part of the fabric of how most traders obtain the best pricing on deals. It's estimated, in fact, that one-third of the Nasdaq's total volume is settled on ECNs.

For our purposes, we'll consider these brokers merely as after-hours trading systems. The most prominent ECNs are

- REDIBook

- Island

- Archipelago

Let's take a look at each.

REDIBook

REDIBook is a joint venture between stock clearinghouse Spear, Leeds & Kellogg, mutual fund giant Fidelity Investments, discount broker Charles Schwab, and investment banker Donaldson, Lufkin & Jenrette. REDIBook maintains after-hours trading from 4 p.m. until 10 p.m., which is substantially later than some of the other ECNs.

The REDIBook ECN is backed by Schwab and Fidelity, among others.

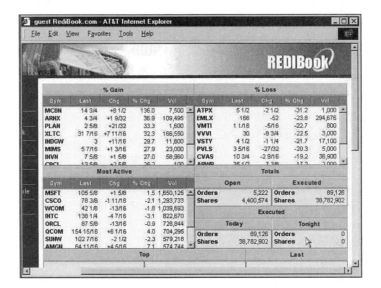

Island

Island accepts orders between 8 a.m. and 8 p.m. Island clears an estimated 180 million shares per day, representing $11 to $15 billion in trades daily. Island has an application with the SEC to become a genuine stock exchange, which would allow the network to list its own securities, rather than simply trading shares of securities listed on the Nasdaq, the American Stock Exchange, and other exchanges. As of this writing, approximately 200 brokerage firms are signed up to use Island's services. (Bear in mind that trades can be sent to the exchanges during the time the exchanges are open, so the actual list of trading partners is much larger than 200 when an order is processed on Island.)

Island ECN was early to market and has earned a broad following among traders.

Archipelago

Archipelago is backed by E*Trade, J. P. Morgan, Goldman Sachs, Instinet, and Merrill Lynch. Archipelago boasts its unique ability to connect to other ECNs and all the national stock exchanges. That means that when you go to the Archipelago "book" of buy and sell orders, you see prices listed not just from the participants in Archipelago, but also those on Island, Instinet, and so on. The company can also route orders directly to the Nasdaq for processing, rather than into its general pool of orders. Archipelago's volume falls short of that on Island, with roughly 50 million shares traded each day. However, the company has embarked on a new tactic to increase its dominance in electronic trading. Working with the Pacific Stock Exchange, a traditional securities exchange, Archipelago will become the equities trading arm of that market, allowing it to list securities for trading rather than simply processing orders. While Archipelago has an application before the SEC for exchange status, its arrangement with Pacific Stock Exchange would be a quicker route to true market status. Archipelago's hours are from 8 a.m. to 8 p.m.

Archipelago
receives orders
from online
traders through
arrangements
with E*Trade.

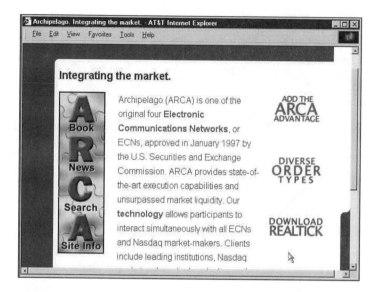

The Nasdaq lists
which ECNs and
regular brokers
trade the most in
a given security.

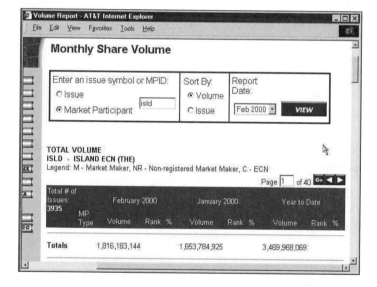

Ranking the ECNs

Curious about which is the most liquid market for a particular stock you're interested in? Check out the Nasdaq's monthly rating of market partici-pants. Each ECN has a Nasdaq market participant ID. For example, Island's is ISLD. You can enter this ID on the Nasdaq site and find out what per-centage of the entire trading volume for any given stock passed through that ECN. Because the ECNs are brokers just like other banks, you can also see a breakdown of how the ECNs rank among the other brokers in trading volume of a given stock. The rankings are at *www.nasdaqtrader.com/static/tdhome.stm*. A recent check, for example, indicated that in February of 2000 Island ECN was the largest market maker in stock of Cisco Systems, clearing 46.4 million shares, or 7% of the stock's trading volume, in the month of February.

What are the benefits of the ECNs? Broadly speaking, they are

- Finer point spread. While listed exchanges may offer fractions of a 32nd or greater as the point spread between bid and ask prices, the ECNs may offer fractions as small as 1/256. For large trades, that could result in a real savings for buyers of securities. Some ECNs are also planning to offer decimal quotations for prices.

  Because the ECN does not take a profit from the point spread between buy and sell orders, and because there is sufficient competition between ECNs to deliver the best offer to clients, the ECNs should be able to deliver a better price on average than traditional exchange trading.

- Greater liquidity. Theoretically, because the ECN is interconnecting different exchanges and market makers throughout the world, there may be greater liquidity for offers placed through the ECN than if they are simply sent to the exchange. Bear in mind, however, that in after-hours trading some of this liquidity may decline because volume ceases on the conventional exchanges. After 6:30 (the end of extended hours on the Nasdaq), for example, orders cannot be sent to the Nasdaq to be filled at all. (Again, we'll talk more about this factor in the next section.)

- Access to the trading "book." With some brokers that make use of the ECN services, you may be able to see the ECN's "book," meaning its list of buy and sell offers for a stock, with prices in real-time. Not every brokerage offers this service. Individual brokers, however, such as MB Trading, may offer you direct access to the ECN book in real-time. This is yet another tool you can use.

> ### Back Pages of the ECN "Book"
>
> Even if you can't get direct access to the ECN book of orders from your
> online broker's account, you may be able to view the book directly from
> the ECN's Web site. Island, for one, offers browsers the opportunity to
> view its book of buy and sell orders in real-time. Check it out at *www.
> island.com/BookViewer/index.html*. REDIBook also lets you surf its order
> book for quotes.
>
> In addition, Island recently introduced a program for the Palm VII wire-
> less handheld computer that can display its order book for any stock
> ticker entered.

Viewing the Island
book of trades.

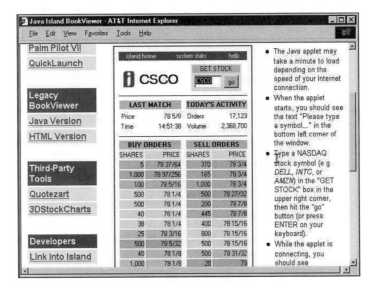

Keep in mind these points about the ECNs:

- You cannot send your order directly to any of the ECNs. The
  ECNs act as traders for your brokerage, so your brokerage
  must be a client of a particular ECN for you to use that
  ECN's services.

- The ECNs do not generally disclose who their clients are. If
  you want to know whether your broker uses the ECN, you
  will have to ask your broker directly.

- There is a broad effort underway to form greater linkages
  between ECNs. In particular, Archipelago is positioning itself
  as an electronic link between the exchanges, its clients, and

the other ECNs. It's conceivable that at some point the various ECNs will fuse into one entity, or at least consolidate to some extent.

After-Hours Trading in Your Existing Account

With most brokerage accounts, after-hours trading is a standard feature. Brokerages generally offer a set period of time before the opening of the New York exchanges and after the closing that are designated as the "extended hours" trading period. For example, your broker may offer extended hours trading from 8 a.m. until 9:15 a.m. (just before the national exchanges open), and then from 4:15 p.m. (just after the close of the NYSE and the Nasdaq) until 7 p.m.

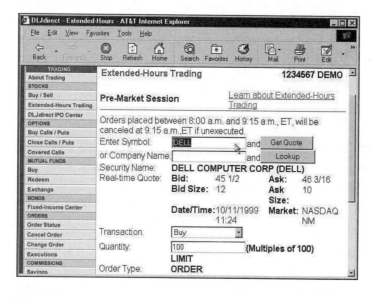

An after-hours/extended hours trading screen.

There are a few simple things you need to be aware of before you can make use of these after-hours trading privileges:

- Most brokers charge no extra fees for trading after hours.

- You may be asked to read an online form concerning the conditions for after-hours trading and to indicate your assent to the terms.

- Your broker will post the hours you can trade before the market opens and after the market closes.

- In most cases, brokerages will require that you enter only limit orders. That is because in the highly volatile after-hours trading systems, dramatic point changes can happen quickly and a market order could expose you to unusually high risk.

- Chapter 8, "Placing Your First Trade," talked about so-called "good 'til canceled" orders, which may remain in effect until the market conditions meet the requirements of your order or until you cancel the order. In most cases, your broker will not accept good 'til canceled orders. Instead, all orders are canceled if they have not been executed by the end of the after-hours trading period.

- Not all securities can be bought and sold after hours. Nasdaq-listed securities can all be traded, in most cases, and there is limited trading of stock on other exchanges as well as so-called "over the counter" stocks. NYSE shares cannot be traded. In most cases, your broker should have details posted about which stocks can or cannot be traded using the system.

- Short selling is generally permitted during after-hours trading, although you should consult your broker's terms on the matter.

- All your margin privileges should be good after-hours, if you want to trade on margin. In most cases, your broker will refer to a security's marginability as of the close of the last regular trading session (meaning during the day).

- An after-hours order is just like any other order that day for clearing purposes, meaning that you still must have funds in your account within the following three days to cover the order, per Regulation T.

In addition to basic equities trading, trading of initial public offerings for new stock may become part of the after-hours scene in the near future. Instinet has an investment in WR Hambrecht & Co., which was mentioned in Chapter 12, "Getting Into IPOs Online." Hambrecht is trying to create an informal auction market for IPOs.

It's important to remember, of course, that after-hours trading and the ECNs are an evolving phenomenon. There is one very big problem with ECNs that stems directly from their immaturity. Although ECNs add to the volume of offers for securities during the day, which is a good thing, during after-hours trading an ECN may be the only collection of buyers and sellers around for a particular security. As mentioned earlier, that means decreased liquidity and, consequently, a less desirable pricing environment for buyers and sellers.

You can easily see this by surfing to the Nasdaq's trading data site at NasdaqTrader.com. Under the section Trading Data, the Nasdaq displays share volume during its after-hours sessions. As you can see if you check the site, the volume starts to dry up as it gets later in the evening. By the 5 p.m.-to-6 p.m. session, trading has dried up from say, 20 million or more shares changing hands to only several hundred thousand shares—most likely because other exchanges around the world are shutting down, brokers are going home, and normal investors are heading for the dinner table.

Nasdaq's data show that volume starts to dry up in after-hours sessions.

What that means is that order systems such as REDIBook and Island that stay open later run the risk of seeing orders decline precipitously. REDIBook, for example, allows traders to keep placing orders until 10 p.m. However, as mentioned earlier, the

Hanging on the Line

In the rough-and-tumble atmosphere of after-hours trading, it's especially important to know if you can reach your broker by phone in the event that you require fast response—say, to cancel a trade. You should make sure to find out whether your broker's phone representatives will be available after hours.

Nasdaq National Market closes for good at 6:30 p.m., meaning REDIBook would not have any access to better offers from the Nasdaq. In the future, this problem may be solved by longer and longer trading hours at the exchanges, but for the time being, you should be aware that while using the ECNs may mean increased liquidity during the day, it can mean dramatically decreased liquidity during off-hours.

Untethered After Hours?

As mentioned in Chapter 4, "Tools of the Trade: Hardware and Software Considerations," some brokers are rolling out wireless trading software on handheld computers. As of this writing, these devices do not support after-hours trading.

What You've Learned

If you're ready for even more trading, this chapter has hopefully introduced you to the basic infrastructure for conducting trades outside of the normal hours of the securities exchanges. You should now have a feel for

- What after-hours trading is.

- What differentiates Instinet and the major ECNs.

- How to trade stocks after hours with your online account.

PART VI

Appendix

APPENDIX A

Useful Web Sites for the Investor

Chapter 1: The Pros and Cons of Online Trading

E*Trade
One of the pre-eminent Web brokerages and a pioneer of Web-based securities trading.
www.etrade.com

National Association of Securities Dealers
Official regulatory body for the brokerage industry and parent of the Nasdaq stock market.
www.nasd.com

The New York Stock Exchange
The original downtown stock market of the New World, the New York Stock Exchange was founded 183 years ago.
www.nyse.com

The Nasdaq National Market
The world's first all-electronic trading exchange and home to some of the best-performing tech stocks in America.
www.nasdaq.com

Philadelphia Stock Exchange
One of America's regional stock exchanges, where shares of local businesses change hands, as well as Nasdaq and NYSE stocks.
www.phlx.com

Island ECN
Island is one of the latest Electronic Communications Networks, virtual marketplaces that are increasing the number of places to trade.
www.island.com

Securities Industry Association
The SIA, an industry consortium representing stock brokers, performs original research into the state of the securities market.
www.sia.com

Chapter 2: Is Online Trading Right for You?

The Investing Online Resource Center
Nonprofit group sponsored by the Washington State
Department of Financial Institutions offering free advice about
online investing.
www.investingonline.org

Bill Gates Wealth Clock
An unofficial score card for the financial assets of the world's
richest man.
www.webho.com/WealthClock

NASD Investor Education
The NASD Web site features a step-by-step online guide to
investing.
Go to *www.nasd.org* and follow the link in the sidebar to
Investor Services.

SmartMoney Magazine Asset-Allocation
The Web site of the popular personal finance magazine features
interactive tools for planning how to balance your investments.
www.smartmoney.com/si/tools/oneasset/

North American Securities Administrators Association (NASAA)
The NASAA is a voluntary organization made up of state securities regulators and dedicated to protecting investors. Its investor
education page is a must-read.
www.nasaa.org/investoredu/informedinvestor/ii3.html

The Certified Financial Planner Board
This private, federally registered regulatory body provides certi-
fication of financial planners. Check out their recommendations
on finding financial planners.
*http://natasha.cfp-board.org/internet/consumer/
nd_cons_main.asp*

Other Financial Planning Sites

There are several other sites you should consider in your search
for advice, education, and tools for planning your personal investments. In addition to the following sites, you can consult the list
of brokers in Chapter 5; many of these sites feature original tools
and planning worksheets, as well as investor education materials.

Forbes asset-allocation calculator
Play with different combinations of bond, stock, and cash investments using this interactive tool from *Forbes* Magazine.
www.forbes.com/tool/toolbox/calc/portfoliocalc.asp

Financial Engines
Features a personalized Investment Advisor service that forecasts
how your wealth will grow, assuming certain types of investments.
www.financialengines.com

Financial Plan Auditors
Offers the unique Plan Audit Wizard, which uses historical market
data to tell you how likely a financial plan is to succeed in the
future.
www.fplanauditors.com

Quicken.com retirement guide
Includes tools for planning retirement income, as well as how to
manage your IRA, and links to financial planners.
www.quicken.com/retirement

S&P Personal Wealth
Register to set up an online financial plan with this premier
investment advising service.
Go to *www.personalwealth.com* then follow the link to Plan &
Recommendations at the top of the page.

Vanguard
The prominent mutual fund firm offers an online financial
planner focusing on IRAs.
http://majestic5.vanguard.com/RRC/DA

American Association of Individual Investors
This nonprofit group features memberships for $49 that provide
an annual subscription to its investment journal and suggested
portfolios of stocks, as well as particular advice about online
investing.
www.aaii.com

TeachMeFinance.com
A simple, elegant site featuring articles about basic principles of
investing.
www.teachmefinance.com

The Investment FAQ
A "Frequently Asked Questions" compendium with answers on
basic matters of investing.
www.invest-faq.com

SmartMoney University
Content-rich site for education about investment basics, from
IRAs to stock investing.
http://university.smartmoney.com

National Association of Investors Corporation
This nonprofit association features an emphasis on dividend-
reinvestment and dollar-cost averaging; requires membership.
www.better-investing.org

DirectAdvice.com
Bills itself as a personal online financial advisor. After you answer an online questionnaire about your financial situation, a custom financial plan is generated.
www.directadvice.com

TeamVest
Oriented toward the 401K owner, TeamVest offers a 10-minute online evaluation that prepares a personalized action-plan for investment goals.
www.teamvest.com

Fidelity Portfolio Selector
A questionnaire helps you evaluate how current investments compare to your investment goals. But watch out: you'll be advertised a selection of Fidelity mutual funds at the end of the quiz.
Go to *www.fidelity.com/tools.shtml* then click on the link to Asset Allocation Planner.

The Motley Fool's Fool School
The opinionated investment site features a 13-step plan to learning its idiosyncratic investment approach.
www.fool.com/school.htm

ThirdAge
Investment advice and planning articles for retirement-age investors.
www.thirdage.com/money/

FinanCenter
Basic investor questions answered through a series of interactive calculators.
www.financenter.com

Chapter 3: Selecting the Right Online Broker for Your Needs

Brokerage Resources

There are lots of Web sites that will give you important background information regarding brokers. Check out these links before you consider any broker. Keep in mind that most online financial news sites will have their own reviews of online brokers.

SEC brokerage background
The SEC explains the basic functions and requirements of brokers, online or offline.
www.sec.gov/consumer/pick.htm

NASD Brokerage Records Database Search
A crucial database of public records regarding background of brokerages and individual broker firms; make sure you check here before picking a broker!
http://pdpi.nasdr.com

Gomez Advisors
A professional consultancy featuring a broker "scorecard."
www.gomez.com

Internet Investing
A subjective rating of the differences among individual brokerages.
www.internetinvesting.com

Keynote Web Brokerage Index
A professional rating firm featuring reports on the responsiveness of brokers' Internet connections.
www.keynote.com/measures/brokers

Online Investment Services
A rating of the "best" online brokers, gathered from customer feedback.
www.sonic.net/donaldj/best.html

SmartMoney.com broker ratings
Reports from SmartMoney's regular survey of online brokers that ranks firms according to several criteria.
www.smartmoney.com/si/brokers

SmartMoney.com broker meter
An interactive tool showing the relative performance of different brokers.
www.smartmoney.com/si/brokermeter

Money Magazine broker ratings
Money.com's broker ratings start with an interactive question-naire that lets you screen for brokers meeting certain require-ments.
www.money.com/broker

Brokerages

There are more than 200 online brokers and counting. Here's a selection of some of the most prominent.

E*Trade
www.etrade.com

Charles Schwab & Co.
www.schwab.com

A. B. Watley
www.abwatley.com

Ameritrade
www.ameritrade.com

Datek Online
www.datek.com

J B Oxford & Company
www.jboxford.com

American Express
www.americanexpress.com

Brown & Co.
www.brownco.com

DLJ Direct
www.dljdirect.com

Fidelity PowerStreet
http://personal.fidelity.com

Merrill Lynch Direct
www.mldirect.com

International Trader
www.intltrader.com

Morgan Stanley Dean Witter
www.deanwitter.com

My Discount Broker.com
www.mydiscountbroker.com

National Discount Brokers
www.ndb.com

PaineWebber Edge
www.painewebberedge.com

Prudential Securities Online
www.prudential.com

Quick & Reilly
www.quickwaynet.com

Salomon Smith Barney
www.smithbarney.com

TD Waterhouse
www.waterhouse.com/

Web Street Securities
www.webstreetsecurities.com

Muriel Siebert & Co., Inc.
www.siebertnet.com

T. Rowe Price
www.troweprice.com/

Wingspanbank.com
www.wingspan.com

NetBank
www.netbank.com

SmartVest by H&R Block
www.smartvest.com

Chapter 4: Tools of the Trade: Hardware and Software Considerations

Web-based Stock Quotes

The Web is full of free tools for obtaining basic stock quotes, as well as more extensive profiles of companies. While all sites offer quotes with some time delay (usually 15 minutes), an increasing number of sites offer real-time quotes, meaning you will see the current price in the market at the time you request the quote, albeit with whatever delay it takes for your Web browser to load the data. Make sure you check out these free services before you sign up with a brokerage based on its stock quotes.

411 Stocks
www.411stocks.com

The Motley Fool
http://quote.fool.com

EquityWeb
www.stockfever.com

S&P Comstock
www.spcomstock.com

Bullsession.com
www.bullsession.com

Datalink.com
www.datalink.net

Quote Central
www.quotecentral.com

DBC Online
www.dbc.com

DTN IQ
www.dtniq.com

FreeRealTime.com
www.freerealtime.com

InterQuote
www.interquote.com

JustQuotes
www.justquotes.com

MoneyScope.com
www.moneyscope.com

PC Quote Online
www.pcquote.comquote

Money.net
www.money.net

Island ECN "Book"
www.island.com/BookViewer/index.html

Yahoo! Finance
http://quote.yahoo.com/

CNNfn
http://qs.cnnfn.com/tq/stockquote

CBS Marketwatch
Surf to the Marketwatch site, *http://cbs.marketwatch.com*, then click on the link at the top for Market Data.

TheStreet.com
www.thestreet.com/quote.thestreet.com/cgi-bin/texis/ StockQuotes

Web-based Charting

In addition to obtaining quotes, getting a good chart of stock prices is essential for making investment decisions. Here are some of the more prominent charting tools offered free (or at a minimal cost) over the Web.

Chart Trend
www.charttrend.com

Money.com iWatch
www.money.com/money/depts/investing/

Decision Point
www.decisionpoint.com

ClearStation
www.clearstation.com

Elliot Wave Chart
www.wavechart.com

Equis International
www.equis.com

IQC.com
www.iqc.com

MarketEdge
www.stkwtch.com

MoneyTeq
www.moneyteq.com

Prophet Finance
www.prophetfinance.com

Sixer.com
www.sixer.com

Tradingcharts.com
www.tradingcharts.com

SmartMoney Map of the Market
www.smartmoney.com/marketmap

Smart Portfolio
SmartPortfolio.com

Barchart.com
www.barchart.com

Brokerage Software

Brokers are increasingly offering their own trading software.
You won't be able to use this software with any other brokerage
accounts, however.

DLJ Direct MarketSpeed
Go to *www.dljdirect.com* then follow the link at the bottom
left-hand corner of the page for MarketSpeed.

Schwab & Co. Velocity
Go to *www.schwab.com*, surf to Accounts & Services, then click on the link for Special Services. Follow the link for Signature Services, then follow the link to Schwab Signature Platinum, and finally scroll down the page until you see the link to Velocity Trading Software.

Fidelity Powerstreet Pro
Go to *http://personal400.fidelity.com/accounts/activetrader* then follow the link in the left-hand column for Powerstreet Pro.

Datek Online Streamer
www.datek.com/account_demo/strquotes_rolling.html

Desktop Software

If you want more complex functionality than the basic quotations and graphs found on the Web, download one of the following desktop software applications.

Spredgar 2000
www.spredgar.com

TC2000
www.tc2000.com

SmartMoney Mapstation
www.smartmoney.com/mapstation

LimitUp! futures trading software by VisionQuest
www.jbrub.com/visionquest

Quicken
www.quicken.com

Microsoft Money
www.microsoft.com/money

Kiplinger's Net Wealth by H&R Block
www.net-wealth.com

StockTick
www.naconsulting.com

Medved Quote Tracker
www.medved.net/QuoteTracker/

InvestorLinks directory of software
www.investorlinks.com/software.html

About.com list of day trading software
http://daytrading.about.com/finance/daytrading/msubchartingsoftware.htm

SMOTASS links to futures trading software
www.smotass.net/tselliott+.html

Yahoo! commercial software listings
http://dir.yahoo.com/Business_and_Economy/Companies/
Financial_Services/Investment_Services/Software/

Yahoo! free software listings
http://dir.yahoo.com/Computers_and_Internet/Software/
Shareware/Financial/

Investormap links to charting software
http://investormap.com/quotes-software.htm

Macintosh Software

Users of the Macintosh computer need not be left out. In addition
to the software mentioned here, check the preceding lists of links
for other Macintosh financial packages. Also, some of the more
popular packages, such as Kiplinger's Net Wealth and Intuit's
Quicken, are available for both Windows and Macintosh.

MacChart and Personal Analyst by Trendsetter Software
www.trendsoft.com

ProTA by Beesoft
www.beesoft.net

Wireless Software

There is an increasing constellation of software for trading and
checking quotes wirelessly. The largest platform for this software
is Palm Computing's Palm VII wireless handheld computer. But
other wireless devices, including cell phones with Internet access,
are sure to follow. Be sure also to check the Web sites of individual brokers, as new programs are sure to be released in the coming year.

Palm.net
The official site of the Palm VII wireless handheld. Features a
wide assortment of programs for checking price quotes and
even making trades while away from your computer.
Go to *www.palm.net/apps* then follow the link to Financial
programs.

CyberAlerts
A subscription service that delivers stock quotes to a range of
wireless devices including handhelds, cell phones, and pagers.
www.quotebeep.com

Chapter 5: Researching Stocks, Bonds, and Mutual Funds Online

Standard & Poor's 500 Index of companies
This popular index to the performance of 500 global U.S. companies will give you a starting place in your search for companies in which to invest.
www.spglobal.com/500mainframe.html

Investinginbonds.com list of bond sources
Information-rich site sponsored by the Bond Market Association, a trade group representing securities dealers.
Go to *www.investinginbonds.com* then follow the link to Bondmarket Gateway.

Morningstar.com
Web site for the widely respected third-party mutual fund rating agency. Includes a database of performance ratings for mutual funds.
www.morningstar.com

Moody's Investors Services
Web site for the respected 91-year-old bond creditworthiness rating service. You can look at the most recent credit reviews or perform a limited search for older reviews.
www.moodys.com

Stock Screening Tools

Online stock screens can help you search for companies that match your personal investment criteria. Most of these tools are free with a site registration.

Quicken.com stock screening tool
www.quicken.com/investments

MarketPlayer
www.marketplayer.com

Market Guide
www.marketguide.com

Doh! Stock Picks
www.doh.com

Dogs of the Dow
www.dogsofthedow.com

Money Magazine stock screen
www.pathfinder.com/money/depts/investing/johnneff/

SmartMoney.com Active Investor
www.smartmoney.com/ai/

Wright Research Center
www.wisi.com

InsiderTrader.com
www.insidertrader.com

Great-Picks.com
www.great-picks.com

PeerScape
www.peerscape.com

Telescan
www.telescan.com

NetCurrentAsset.com
www.netcurrentasset.com

Rapid Research
www.rapidresearch.com

StockScreener.com
www.stockscreener.com

DLJDirect Stock Center
www.dljdirect.com/scdisclose.htm

Low Priced Stock Survey
www.lowpricedstocks.com

MPT Review
www.mptreview.com

Hoover's Online
www.hoovers.com

Spear Report
www.spearreport.com

Zacks Advisor
www.zacksadvisor.com

MSN Investment Finder
www.moneycentral.com/investor

Fortune Investor
www.fortuneinvestor.com

EquityTrader
www.equitytrader.com

Where to Find Earnings and Revenue Estimates and Analyst Recommendations

You'll want to have a few data points at hand when considering purchasing common stock in companies. Analyst recommendations will tell you what professional business analysts on Wall Street are thinking about the value and health of a public company. Some of these services are fee- or subscription-based, but you can find basic, no-frills versions of the same at the many free financial Web sites listed in the next section.

Zacks.com
A well-known professional source of earnings reports and historical financial data. This is a subscription service.
www.zacks.com

Bloomberg
Though pricey, Bloomberg is the first name in research information, including earnings estimates.
www.bloomberg.com

Bridge Information Services
Bridge, similar to Bloomberg, offers the ability to receive numerous broker estimates.
www.bridge.com

FirstCall
A well-organized, subscription-based site providing a list of analysts covering stocks and their collective earnings estimates.
www.firstcall.com

Briefing.com
Ex-Wall Street types provide daily breaking coverage of analysts' ratings changes on stocks. This is a subscription service.
www.briefing.com

General Investment News and Information Sites

The Market Reporter
Aside from the usual assortment of news and stock quotes, this site features technical charting to determine price direction.
www.marketreporter.com

Online Investor
A comprehensive survey of online news services, such as Bloomberg and MSNBC, as well as a searchable database of company conference calls and other company-specific resources.
www.onlineinvestor.com

The Motley Fool
Features chat boards and articles on financial news, as well as
investor education.
www.motleyfool.com

Fox Market Wire
The TV network's online site features market stories as well as
a personal portfolio.
www.foxmarketwire.com

News Alert
www.newsalert.com

NewsTraders
www.newstraders.com

Nightly Business Report
www.nightlybusiness.org

Reuters MoneyNet
www.moneynet.com

Radio Wall Street
www.radiowallstreet.com

Kiplinger's
www.kiplinger.com

CNNfn
www.cnnfn.com

CBS Marketwatch
www.marketwatch.com

TheStreet.com
www.thestreet.com

Best Calls
www.bestcalls.com

Street Fusion
www.streetfusion.com

On24
www.on24.com

Earnings Whispers
www.earningswhisper.com

Out There News
www.megastories.com

Cyberinvest.com
www.cyberinvest.com

The BBC's personal finance site
www.bbc.co.uk/yourmoney/

Thomson Investor Network
www.thomsoninvest.com

CNBC.com
www.cnbc.com

Financial Times
A snazzy site for one of the premier business publications.
www.ft.com

Company Sleuth
Design a customized report, sent to you daily, apprising you of
such things as new URLs registered by companies and chat
board discussions mentioning companies.
www.companysleuth.com

Yahoo! Finance
A quick and dirty compendium of basic background information
on stocks and mutual funds.
http://finance.yahoo.com

MSN MoneyCentral
Microsoft's personal investment site, with stock portfolios and
news articles.
www.moneycentral.com

Individual Investor
www.individualinvestor.com

Money.com
Online site for the personal finance magazine *Money*.
www.money.com

Worth.com
Online site for the personal finance magazine *Worth*.
www.worth.com/

The Syndicate
www.syndicate.com

Quote.com
www.quote.com

International Investing Sites

BBC Business News
In addition to a focus on European business and UK companies,
there are good "business basics" primers on the major economic
topics.
www.bbc.co.uk/business

China Online
www.chinaonline.com

Thaistocks.com
www.thaistocks.com

UK Invest
www.uk-invest.com

BusinessDaily
www.businessdaily.com

Public Filings

Public companies must file periodic financial statements, and fortunately they're all open to the public and easy to obtain on the Web. Here are some of the places you can find such information.

Investor Relations Information Network
www.irin.com

Edgar Access
http://edgar.disclosure.com/ea

Federal Filings Online
www.fedfil.com

SEC Edgar database of filings
A searchable repository for all financial filings by public companies.
www.freeedgar.com

Edgar Online
Provides a more sophisticated search form for the SEC database of filings, as well as premium services such as alerts for new filings.
www.edgar-online.com

10K Wizard
Provides a search interface to company SEC filings.
www.10kwizard.com

Stock Detective
www.stockdetective.com

Press Releases

You can always find press releases, which are simply corporate announcements, on an individual company's Web site. But you might also want to peruse sites that aggregate and disseminate press releases from many firms. Two of the more well-known sites are listed.

PR Newswire
www.prnewswire.com

BusinessWire
www.businesswire.com

Brokerage Research

Many brokerages offer their own research as an incentive to get your business. You should check each brokerage you're considering to evaluate its offerings. Following are some of the more prominent proprietary brokerage report listings.

Wall Street Voice
www.wsvoice.com

Merrill Lynch
www.askmerrill.com

Prudential Securities
www.prusec.com/prudadvisor.com

Multex Investor
www.multexinvestor.com

Morgan Stanley Dean Witter
www.msdw.com/institutional/investmentmanagement/

Lists of Links

Aside from the investment sites listed here, there are more "lists of links" and directories of financial sites popping up every day. Here are some of the best.

TradingDay
www.tradingday.com

Lycos Investing
http://investing.lycos.com

FinanceWise
www.financewise.com

Investor Guide
www.investorguide.com

Superstar Investor
www.superstarinvestor.com/

Investorama.com
www.investorama.com

Wall Street City
News articles on breaking financial developments; selection of
technical charts.
www.wallstreetcity.com/

Investing in Stocks
www.investinginstocks.com

Wall Street Directory
Bills itself as a massive book of links to chat rooms.
http://wallstreetdirectory.com/

Chat Sites and Message Boards

Chats and boards are the places to connect with other Web surfers
to share thoughts and tips on investing—or just watch the fray!
Note that some of the forums listed may only be accessible with
memberships and subscription fees.

Silicon Investor
www.siliconinvestor.com

The Motley Fool
www.fool.com

Raging Bull
www.ragingbull.com

Yahoo! message boards
http://messages.yahoo.com

Investorville
www.investorville.com

BrowseMaster
Tool for managing your participation in message boards.
www.browsemaster.com

MarketForum
www.marketforum.com

StockScout
www.stockscout.com

SmartMoney Magazine Forums
www.smartmoney.com/intro/forums/

Wall Street Journal Discussions
http://interactive.wsj.com/documents/voices.html

Stock-Talk
www.stock-talk.com

AOL Market Talk
www.aol.com/community/aimcheck.adp/
url=Market+Watch&Exchange=5

Investorama live chats and message boards
www.investorama.com/community/

Chapter 6: Understanding the Basics of Stock Trading

The following sites provide a mix of market history, economic analysis, and commentary and opinion. They will help start you thinking about the market in a constructive fashion.

Museum of American Financial History
The online site of the New York museum of the same name, the site provides a charming, thoughtful introduction to the various forms finance has taken in America and its role in the nation's history.
www.mafh.org/

Dismal Scientist
A witty, off-beat guide to the basics of investing.
www.dismalscientist.com

National Association of Investors Corporation
A nonprofit corporation offering tutorials and practical advice for beginning investors.
www.better-investing.org

Nasdaq stock market
The sites of the major securities exchanges are full of background information—though some of it is propaganda, it's true.
www.nasdaq.com

New York Stock Exchange
www.nyse.com

American Stock Exchange
www.amex.com

National Securities Clearing Corp.
Major provider of clearing for securities transactions, an important part of the process of securities trading.
www.nscc.com/

Invest-FAQ.com
This site gives you an "FAQ"—Internet-speak for frequently
asked questions—on topics such as bond investing, stocks, and
so on.
http://invest-faq.com/

Emerging Markets Companion
Heavy on quantitative information, this site gives you numbers
on bond rates and foreign benchmark stock indices if you're
interested in learning about overseas markets.
www.emgmkts.com

Chapter 8: Placing Your First Trade

Trading Advice Sites

Many times when you go to make a trade you'll want to consider
different opinions as to whether a stock is likely to go up or down
in the near term, and whether general market trends are favorable
to a particular investment. There are several sites that focus on
trading strategies and can offer advice on timing your trades.

Motley Fool Strategies
www.fool.com/strategies.htm

1010 Wall Street
www.1010wallstreet.com

Investment Wizard
www.ozsoft.com

Worldly Investor
www.worldlyinvestor.com

Buy Sell or Hold
www.buysellorhold.com

Investor-Advice
www.investoradvice.com

Market History
www.markethistory.com

The Financial Center
www.tfc.com

Equis.com
An introduction to the art of technical stock charting.
www.equis.com/free/taaz/index.html

Firstcap
www.firstcap.com

Understanding the Trade

In addition to knowing when to place a market order or limit order, you may want to peruse some refresher material about how these different order types operate.

Invest-FAQ guide to trading basics
http://invest-faq.com/articles/index-trading.html

Money.com guide to placing trades
www.money.com/money/101/lessons/5/placing_trade.html

Individual Investor's guide to stop-loss and stop-limit orders
www.individualinvestor.com/investor_university/article.asp?ID=7547

Chapter 9: Managing Your Portfolio

As mentioned in Chapter 4, there are dozens of online portfolio management tools to choose from. Here's a brief list of some must-see portfolio management sites.

Quicken.com
Go to *www.quicken.com* then click on the link to My Portfolio.

Kiplinger.com
www.kiplinger.com/mn/portfolio.htm

SmartMoney.com
Go to *www.smartmoney.com/intro/tools* then go to the Portfolio section.

MoneyCentral
Go to *http://moneycentral.msn.com* then go to My Portfolio.

Individual Investor
Go to *www.individualinvestor.com* then choose the drop-down option for My Profile.

CNBC.com
Go to *www.cnbc.com* then click on the link along the top for Portfolio.

Chapter 10: Understanding Your Taxes

MSN MoneyCentral
www.moneycentral.com/tax/

Fairmark Press Tax Guide
www.fairmark.com

Deloitte & Touche
www.dtonline.com

Fairmark Press
www.fairmark.com

H&R Block
www.hrblock.com

MSN Money Central Taxes
http://moneycentral.msn.com/tax/home.asp

Quicken.com Taxes
www.quicken.com/taxes

SmartMoney Tax Guide
www.smartmoney.com/ac/tax

The Tax Prophet
www.taxprophet.com

Tax Resources on the Web
http://pages.prodigy.net/agkalman

Chapter 11: Troubleshooting and Ending Your Online Trading Relationship

Internet Fraud Watch
www.fraud.org/ifw.htm

National Association of Securities Dealers
www.nasd.com

NASD guide to investing wisely
www.nasd.com/pg1c.html

NASD Regulation
www.nasdr.com

Securities & Exchange Commission
www.sec.gov

Stock Detective
Tips about various kinds of online scams. This is all unofficial information.
www.stockdetective.com

Federal Reserve Bank of Philadelphia
www.phil.frb.org

StockCop
www.stockcop.com

Chapter 12: Getting Into IPOs Online

CMGI
www.cmgi.com

IPO Central
www.ipocentral.com

IPO Maven
www.ipomaven.com

IPO.com
www.ipo.com

Alert-IPO!
www.ostman.com

IPOHome.com
www.ipohome.com

IPO Syndicate
www.iposyndicate.com

E-Offering
A joint venture of E*Trade and venture capital firms Battery
Ventures and New Enterprise Associates.
www.eoffering.com

FBR.com
www.fbr.com

Direct Stock Market
www.dsm.com

Offroad Capital
www.offroad.com

IPO Data Systems
www.ipodata.com

IPO Monitor
www.ipomonitor.com

IPO Pros
www.ipopros.com

Wit Capital
www.witcapital.com

The SEC's IPO Express
www.freeedgar.com/IPOExpress

Chapter 13: Trading on Margin and Trading Options

Although you will trade on margin from your regular e-trading account, the intricacies and strategies of using margin are unique. For that reason, it's best to visit some sites that offer specialized advice. (Be sure, too, to check the materials about margin at your e-broker's Web site.)

Bankrate.com
www.bankrate.com

The Motley Fool's margin FAQ
www.fool.com/FoolFAQ/FoolFAQ0025.htm

SEC advice about trading on margin
www.sec.gov/consumer/margin.htm

ThinkQuest guide to margin buying power
http://library.thinkquest.org/3298/NoFrames/doc/sbmargin.html

Invest-FAQ.com guide to margin requirements
http://invest-faq.com/articles/regul-margin.html

Chapter 14: Getting Into Options Trading

The following general interest sites cover in detail the ins and outs of puts and calls.

Antix Stock Option Report
www.aantix.com

Chicago Board Options Exchange
www.cboe.com

Chicago Board of Trade
www.cbot.com

Chicago Mercantile Exchange
www.cme.com

Covered Calls
www.coveredcalls.com

Future Source
www.futuresource.com

Futures.Net
www.futures.net

National Futures Association
www.nfa.futures.org

Netpicks Stock Option Advisory System
www.netpicks.com

OEXMaster.com
Informational tools for trading options on the S&P 100 stock
index.
www.oexmaster.com

Option Investor
www.optioninvestor.com

OptionsAnalysis.com
www.optionsanalysis.com

Options Industry Council
www.optionscentral.com

OptionSource
www.optionsource.com

The Pit Master
www.thepitmaster.com

Power Options
www.poweropt.com

1010 Investor options boot camp
www.1010wallstreet.com/seminar.asp?m=on

Chapter 15: Trading Bonds and Mutual Funds Online

Mutual Fund Firms

There are tons of fund firms out there and more are popping up
all the time. What follows is a thoroughly unscientific sampling
of some of the better-known funds.

ValueLine
www.valueline.com

Fidelity Investments
www.fidelity.com

Vanguard
www.vanguard.com

Janus
www.janus.com

PBHG
www.pbhgfunds.com

Firsthand Funds
www.firsthandfunds.com

Blackrock
www.blackrock.com/funds

Firstar Funds
www.porticofunds.com

American Century
www.americancentury.com

Profunds
www.profunds.com

Northern Funds
www.northernfunds.com

Legg Mason Funds
www.leggmasonfunds.com

Home State Mutual Funds
www.homestatefunds.com

Turner Funds
www.turner-invest.com

Kopp Funds
www.koppfunds.com

Deutsche Funds/Deutsche Bank
www.deutsche-funds.com/

Mutual Fund Screening Tools

If you want to get really quantitative, special online tools can help you slice and dice the competition on mutual funds until you find the one that matches your criteria.

SmartMoney.com fund finder
www.smartmoney.com/si/tools/fundscreen/

FundAdvice.com
www.fundadvice.com

No Load Fundx
www.fundx.com

Investment Discovery
www.investmentdiscovery.com

Mutual Fund Investor's Center
www.mfea.com

Personal Fund
www.personalfund.com

Forbes Magazine
Forbes.com/funds

Bond Brokers

If you're really interested in fixed income assets, you may want to check out the following bond dealers in addition to buying bonds within your regular e-trading account.

BondAgent.com
www.taxfreebond.com

Lebenthal & Co.
www.lebenthal.com

MUNI Direct
www.munidirect.com

Carty & Co.
www.cartyco.com

Bernardi Securities
www.bernardisecurities.com

Far West
www.farwestservices.com

eBondTrade
www.ebondtrade.com

Online Sales and Auctions of Government Bonds

U.S. Treasury Department's Savings Bond Connection
www.publicdebt.treas.gov/ols/olshome.htm

Bond General Information Sites

You need not be utterly baffled by the variety of yields offered and the wealth of bond issuers. The following sites will give you the lowdown on fixed-income securities.

Bondsonline
www.bondsonline.com

Bondtrac
www.bondtrac.com

BradyNet
www.bradynet.com

Bureau of the Public Debt
www.publicdebt.treas.gov

E-Muni
www.emuni.com

Fixed Income Market
www.fixed-income-market.com

Investing in Bonds
www.investinginbonds.com

Moody's Investors Services
www.moodys.com

BondNet
www.bondnet.com

TradeWeb
www.tradeweb.com

Mutual Fund General Information Sites

Good mutual fund sites will give you a rundown and evaluation of how individual funds are performing and how they compare to other funds.

Brill's Mutual Funds Interactive
www.brill.com

Money Flow
www.moneyflow.com

Select Timing Service
www.dollarlink.com

Fabian Investment Resources
www.fabian.com

Find a Fund
www.findafund.com

FundAlarm
www.fundalarm.com

FundDiscovery
www.funddiscovery.com

ICI Mutual Fund Connection
www.ici.org

Index Funds Online
www.indexfundsonline.com

InfoFund
www.infofund.com

The Internet Closed-End Fund Investor
www.icefi.com

The Mutual Funds Investor's Center
www.mfea.com

Mutual Funds Magazine
www.mfmag.com

Mutual Funds Central
www.fundz.com

Mutual Funds Net
www.mutualfundsnet.com

Professional Mutual Fund Rating Services

Institutions such as Morningstar are well-known objective sources of fund performance data. Look to them to get a sense of which funds are in the lead.

Morningstar.com
www.morningstar.com

Lipper Analytical
www.lipperweb.com

Micropal
www.micropal.com

Fundalarm
www.fundalarm.com

Netstockdirect
Information about dividend reinvestment plans.
www.netstockdirect.com

Bond Rating Services

Bond rating services can tell you about the creditworthiness of the institutions issuing a particular bond.

Moody's
www.moodys.com

Standard & Poor's Ratings Services
www.standardandpoors.com/ratings/index.htm

Fitch IBCA
www.fitchibca.com

Mutual Fund Calculators

Forbes.com fund expense calculator
www.forbes.com/tool/toolbox/calc/fundcalc.asp

MoneyAdvisor
www.moneyadvisor.com

SEC mutual fund calculator
www.sec.gov/mfcc/mfcc-int.htm

Bond Calculators

Federal Reserve Bank savings bond calculator
http://app.ny.frb.org/sbr/

SmartMoney.com bond calculator
www.smartmoney.com/si/tools/onebond/
index.cfm?story=bondcalc

CompoundIt! from Bonds-Online.com
Note: this calculator must be downloaded to your hard drive.
www.bonds-online.com/democalc.htm

T-Bond fixed income calculator
Note: this calculator must be downloaded to your hard drive.
www.mkts.com/apps/tbondns.htm

Chapter 16: Day Trading Online

Online Materials Concerning Day Trading

Pristine Day Trader
A general interest super-site that features a question & answer
session on day trading topics.
www.pristine.com/

About.com's Guide to Day Trading
An enthusiast's page of tips.
http://daytrading.about.com/finance/daytrading/mbody.htm

FairMark's Tax Guide for Traders
A special guide to aspects of active trading that require special
tax considerations.
www.fairmark.com/traders/index.htm

SmartMoney's Taxes on Day Trading
A useful primer on special tax considerations related to day trading.
www.smartmoney.com/ac/tax/index.cfm?story=daytrading

CNNfn's Morning Call
Start the day with an overview of the market indices' behavior.
http://cnnfn.com/markets/morning_call/

Trading Day.com
A general list of links.
www.tradingday.com/

Day Traders Stock Picks
An amateur stock-picking newsletter.
www.daytraderpicks.com/

Day Trading Stocks.com
Notable for its collection of charts, chats, and stock quotes.
www.daytradingstocks.com/

Day Trading Firms

There are hundreds of day trading firms, and new ones are popping up all the time. What follows is an unscientific sampling of some of the more well-known firms.

Active Traders Network
www.activetraders.net

All-Tech Direct
www.attain.com

Avid Trading Company
www.avidtrader.com

The Daily Trader
www.dailytrader.com

Day Investor
www.dayinvestor.com

Daypicks
www.daypicks.com

Daytrader's Bulletin
www.daytradersbulletin.com

Daytraders On-Line
www.daytraders.com

Daytrader Toad
www.daytradertoad.com/index.html

Day Trading International
www.daytradingintl.com

Daytradingstocks.com
www.daytradingstocks.com

Dynamic Daytrader
www.dynamicdaytrader.com

Elite Trader
www.elitetrader.com

The Hard Right Edge
www.hardrightedge.com

Just in Time
Materials for learning about macro-level trends in market
direction and timing.
www.markettimer.com

Low Risk
www.lowrisk.com

Momentum Investing
www.momentuminvesting.com

Momentum Trader
www.mtrader.com

MoneyWolff
www.moneywolff.com

Mytrack.com
www.mytrack.com

Online Daytraders
www.onlinedaytraders.com

PC Trader
www.pctrader.com

Pristine Day Trader
www.pristine.com

The Rookie Day Trader
www.rookiedaytrader.com

SyeNet Investors Supersite
www.dtrades.com

Terra Nova Trading
www.terranovatrading.com

TradeHard
www.tradehard.com

Tradescape.com
www.tradescape.com

Tradingschool.com
www.tradingschool.com

Trading Systems Network
www.tradingsystems.net

Trading Tactics
www.tradingtactics.com

The Underground Trader
www.undergroundtrader.com

Day Trading Software

Just as there are dozens of brokers, there are dozens of different
software programs.

CyberTrader by CyberCorp
www.cybercorp.com/cybertrader

Tradecast
www.tradecast.com

e-Signal from Data Broadcasting Corp.
www.esignal.com

InterQuote.com
www.interquote.com

Hour 17: After-Hours Trading and Electronic Communications Networks

News and Information About After-Hours Trading

Invest-FAQ.com
A primer on the basics of after-hours trading.
http://invest-faq.com/articles/trade-after-hours.html

Stockmaster.com
Stockmaster's guide to where and how to trade after-hours.
http://invest-faq.com/sm/trade-after-hours.html

MSN MoneyCentral
Stock trading strategies for after-hours.
http://moneycentral.msn.com/articles/invest/strat/4760.asp

Nasdaq Trader
The Nasdaq offers a wrap-up of activity in after-hours sessions.
Go to *www.nasdaqtrader.com*, click the menu option for Trading
Data, and then click the option for Extended Hours Trading.

Bloomberg
The financial information channel offers daily wrap-up news
reports on developments in after-hours trading.
www.bloomberg.com/bbn/afterhours.html

ECNs

Island ECN
Island is one of the latest Electronic Communications Networks,
virtual market places that are increasing the number of places
to trade.
www.island.com

Instinet
Founded in 1969, Instinet is the prototype for the after-hours
electronic market.
www.instinet.com

REDIBook ECN
A joint venture of Schwab, Donaldson Lufkin, and Fidelity
Investments, Inc.
www.redibookecn.com

Archipelago
"Arca," as it's called, is backed by E*Trade, Goldman Sachs,
Instinet, Merrill Lynch, and others, and offers pricing from
several ECNs.
www.tradearca.com

NexTrade
Claims to be the first ECN to offer 24-hour trading, with the
option of placing limit orders for Nasdaq stocks around the
clock.
www.nextrade1.com

Attain
Attain is an order-matching system developed by the brokerage
firm All-Tech Direct.
www.attain.com

MarketXT
MarketXT, recently acquired by day trading firm Tradescape,
also allows access to its system to clients of Morgan Stanley,
Salomon Brothers, and MyDiscountBroker.com.
www.marketxt.com

STRIKE ECN
Strike is backed by a consortium consisting of major banks, such as Bank of America and Hambrecht & Quist, as well as technology companies such as Sun Microsystems.
www.strk.com

Bloomberg Tradebook
The online financial information network has teamed with CLSA Global Emerging Markets, an order settlements firm, to provide an ECN with access to 65 markets around the clock.
www.bloomberg.com/products/trdbk.html

GLOSSARY

Ask price   The price at which a securities owner offers to sell the security in the market.

Basis   The total cost to an investor, for tax purposes, of an investment. Basis on securities purchases, for example, will likely include not just the cost of the security itself, but also any fees and commissions paid to a broker.

Bid price   The price offered for a security in the market.

Bond   A form of debt financing, represented by an institution's obligation to repay a bondholder upon *maturity*. Also thought of as a fixed-income investment to distinguish it from other investments with variable *return*, such as *dividends* from shares of *stock*.

Call   An option that gives its owner the right to buy a security at a certain price up to a fixed date in time, in contrast to a *put*. When buying an options contract, a speculator is said to buy either a put or a call.

Capital gains   Appreciation of an investment in a security, over and above the original cost to the investor of owning the security. See *short-term gains, long-term gains,* and *realized gain (or loss)*.

Clearance   The process by which funds and title to securities are transferred between purchasing and selling parties in the sale of a security. Also referred to as the settlement process of buy and sell orders.

Coupon   The annual or semi-annual interest paid on a bond as a percentage of the face or par value at which the bond was issued. When the rate of interest is discussed for a given bond, sometimes the term *coupon rate* is used. Unless bonds are purchased at face value, the coupon will be different from the actual *yield* earned on the bond.

Current yield   The amount of return received on an investment— usually a fixed-income investment, such as a *bond*—for each year in the form of interest payments.

Derivative   A security whose value is derived from the change in value of some underlying security.

Distribution   Regular payouts made to mutual fund shareholders when the fund's investments are cashed in.

Dividend   A regular annual payment to holders of *stock*, often referred to as a type of income. Does not apply to all stocks. Dividends paid tend be small amounts, on the order of a few pennies to a few dollars per share per year. A form of variable income, to distinguish it from fixed-income securities such as *bonds*.

Dollar cost averaging   A method of achieving portfolio diversification by placing money into the same security on a regular basis over time so as to "average out" the highs and lows in the price of the security.

Exercise date   The date on which an options contract can be acted on. In some options, the exercise date means the only date the option can be executed. In some cases, it means the last day on which the option can be executed.

Good 'til canceled   A distinction in securities orders, meaning a buy or sell order that remains open in the trader's portfolio until either the order is filled or the investor requests cancellation of the order.

Hedging   The process of using one investment to limit the risk on another investment.

In-the-money   A term in *options* pricing meaning that the option's strike price would yield a profit in the current market for the underlying security. For a *put* option to sell a security, the strike price is higher than the current price in the market; for a *call* option, the strike price is below the current market price. Contrast to *out-of-the-money*.

Initial Public Offering (IPO)   The first time that stock in a company is offered for sale to the public, in contrast to an ordinary *public offering*, sometimes referred to as a follow-on offering or a "secondary" if it is the second time that shares are being offered to the public by the same company.

Investment interest   Interest paid on margin debt resulting from purchases of securities on margin.

Issue Designation of a bond's origin, telling which entity (company, municipal government, and so on) has issued the bond.

Leverage The ability to invest less money for an equal or greater return.

Limit order An order to purchase or sell a security up to but not beyond a certain price limit (in the case of a purchase) or down to but not below a certain price limit (in the case of a sale).

Liquidity The ability for investors to cash out of their investments. A market for stocks ensures there will be enough potential buyers or sellers to guarantee liquidity.

Long-term gains Capital gains earned on stocks held for a year or more, which are taxed at the low 20% tax rate. Contrast to *short-term gains*.

Maintenance requirement The amount of securities owned and cash, meaning equity, that you must maintain in your account as a percentage of the securities both owned and held on margin (or borrowed, as is the term in the case of securities sold short) in order to keep your margin account up to date.

Margin call A request by your broker to deposit funds to cover your account in the event that the amount in stocks and cash that you actually own, referred to as your equity, has dropped below a certain allowable percentage of your total holdings, both borrowed and owned, known as the *maintenance requirement*.

Marginable Term used to describe a security that can be borrowed against, as in a margin loan, or that can be purchased on margin. Individual securities will be designated by a broker as being marginable or non-marginable.

Market maker An individual or (more commonly) an institution that provides *liquidity* for securities by offering to meet any buy or sell order, thereby assuring the smooth operation of the market—effectively making a market.

Market order An order to buy or sell securities at the best price offered in the market at the time the order is executed. Contrast to *limit order* and *stop order.*

Maturity In bond parlance, the time at which the principal invested in a bond must be repaid to the bond holder.

Nasdaq Level II data   The display of data about which *market makers* are offering what prices for a security, and for how many shares, at any given moment in time. Traders use Level II data to gauge the interest in a stock among major brokerages.

Net Asset Value (NAV)   The value of a share of a mutual fund, derived by taking the total worth of a fund's investments and dividing it by the number of fund shares outstanding. The increase in NAV is a common measure of fund performance.

Odd lot   An order to trade less than 100 shares, or some multiple thereof, as contrasted to *round lot*.

Offer price   The price at which shares of stock are offered to the public in an *initial public offering*.

Options   A form of *derivative* that allows a speculator to purchase the option to buy or sell a security at a specified price at some time in the future. The term "option" is apt because the owner of the option has the option to execute the contract on the date of the option, or to let the contract expire worthless.

Out-of-the-money   Options whose strike price would yield no profit at the current market price of the underlying security.

Par value   The price at which a bond is originally issued. The term is synonymous with "face value," and you may see both terms in current usage.

Price-to-earnings ratio (P/E)   A measure of how expensive a stock is, expressed as the current price per share of a stock divided by the earnings per share of the company that stock represents. A common means of *valuation*. P/E can be an important indicator of whether a stock is expensive relative to other stocks or relative to the stock's own trading history.

Principal   The amount of any investment that is initially put forward by the investor. With *stock*, principal is the purchase price of a single share of stock or the total amount paid for multiple shares. In the case of bonds, principal is the initial investment in a bond that is to be repaid at the time the bond reaches *maturity*.

Prospectus   A formal report listing the amount of shares of stock or mutual fund, or the number of individual bonds, offered for sale and at what price. A stock prospectus may include such information as a company's historical revenue and earnings, a description of its business and market, its management team, and a listing of the major shareholders in the company and their percentage holdings of the company's outstanding stock.

Public offering   The first time that shares of a company's common stock are sold to the public. Secondary or other follow-on offerings of stock may be made later to raise additional capital.

Put   An options contract that gives its owner a right to sell a security at some point in the future at the specified price, in contrast to a *call*. When buying an options contract, a speculator is said to buy either a put or a call.

Realized gain (or loss)   Money made or lost on an actual sale of assets, defined as the profit (or loss) over and above the original cost of the investment as expressed in the *principal* or the *basis*.

Redemption   Cashing out of mutual fund or bond holdings, either in the form of the return of *principal* to the bondholder by the bond issuer in advance of the formal *maturity* date on the bond, or the cashing in of mutual fund shares by an investor.

Return   The profit from an investment over and above the *principal* invested.

Round lot   An order for 100 shares or some multiple thereof, as contrasted to *odd lot*.

Same day   A direction that tells a broker that an order to buy or sell securities should be canceled if it cannot be filled within the trading day on which the order is placed.

Selling short   The process of borrowing shares to sell, and subsequently buying those shares to reimburse the lender.

Short-term gains   Gains on stocks held for less than a year, and therefore taxable at the normal income tax rate.

Speculation   Purchasing a security solely with an eye to the security's appreciation in price, as opposed to investing, where the investor expects the asset itself to increase in value.

Spread   The difference between the *bid* and *ask* price of a security in the market.

Stock   A receipt of ownership in a company, often termed equity to distinguish it from debt investments, such as *bonds*.

Stop order   An order to initiate a *market order* to sell a security at the current market price once a lower price threshold is breached, or to purchase a security at the market price once an upper price threshold is breached.

Strike price   The price at which shares of a security covered in an options contract can be bought or sold. The strike price is usually different from the going price of the security in the market at the time at which the contract is sold.

Technical analysis   The use of data about the change in price of a security over time as the sole criterion when trading in that security.

Time value   A measure of risk applied to the duration between the *exercise date* of an options contract and the date on which the contract is purchased. The time value is a factor considered in assigning a price to an options contract.

Underwriter   Someone or some institution, usually an investment bank, that helps organize the sale to the public of new shares of debt or equity (that is, *bonds* or *stock*) in an *initial public offering* or a follow-on or secondary offering.

Valuation   The process of assigning a value to a security based on certain key metrics (or ratios), such as the *price-to-earnings ratio*, or *P/E*.

Venture capital   Private capital invested by experienced money managers known as venture capitalists, for the purpose of funding young companies, as opposed to public investment, which is obtained through the sale of stock in public capital markets through an *initial public offering* or other public offerings.

Volatile   A quality of a stock that is likely to experience substantial instability in price over time or erratic changes in price.

Wealth builder   A class of investor with limited or no savings who is primarily concerned with building savings through investment.

Wealth preserver   A class of investor who has already built a substantial amount of savings and who is focused mostly on protecting that wealth from depreciating over time. Contrast to *wealth builder*.

Yield   The return on a bond expressed as a percentage of the actual price paid for the bond. The yield will be different from the *coupon* of the bond if the bond is purchased at a price that is different from the *par value* of the bond. In addition to simple yield, there is also *yield to maturity*.

Yield to maturity   The interest rate earned on a bond as a percentage of the price paid for the bond, assuming all dividends are reinvested at the same interest rate, and assuming that the bond is held until maturity.

INDEX

Symbols

401K plans, 161

A

abuses, stock trading, 8
accepting
    orders, 123
    payments, 193
access to after-hours trading
    Archipelago, 337
    brokerage accounts, 341
    ECNs, 339-340
    Instinet, 334
    Island, 336
    Nasdaq, 344
    REDIBook, 336
accounts
    balances, 101, 105, 227
    brokerage, 94
    cash, 96, 102, 137-138, 140-141, 143
    for children, 163
    closing, 165-166, 168
    controlling, 19
    equity, 220
    funding, 99-101
    ID names, 101
        choosing, 103-104
        individual, 102
    joint, 102
    margin, 96, 102, 187, 227
    money, 140-143
    passwords, 101
    records, 109, 194-195
    signing agreements, 106
    statements, 10
    terminating, 192-194
    transferring, 192-194
accredited investors, 205
accuracy of online information, 192
active investors, 29
activity, volatile, 182
addictions, e-trading, 22
advisability, trades, 21
after-hours trading, 12, 330
    brokerage accounts, 341
    ECNs, 331, 335, 339-340, 343

    fees, 341-342
    time zones, 332
aggressive growth funds, 275, 280
aggressive investors, 28-29
agreements, legal options, 254
allocating assets, 161, 163
Amazon.com Web site, 184
America Online (AOL), 53
AMEX (American Stock Exchange), 11, 94
analyst ratings, stocks, 79
analyzing portfolios, 148-151, 155
annual reports, viewing, 82
anonymity, online postings, 192
AOL (America Online), 53
applications
    approved, 99, 108-109
    completing online, 102-107, 109
    denied, 99-100
    mailing, 107
    online brokers, 99-101
    options, 254
    required information, 100
    submitting, 99-100
appreciation, stocks, 138
Archipelago, 335-337
ask price (stock), 95
assessment, financial, 30
assets, 137, 161-163, 165-166, 168
assigning
    options contracts, 267-268
    passwords, 107
    user names, 107
attitudes, get-rich-quick, 192
auctions, 212-214
availability of Web sites, 177
avoiding
    fraud, 187, 192
    taxes, 160

B

balances
    accounts, 227
    cash, 105
    minimum, 101
balancing profit with risks, 294

Q-R

Tell Us What You Think!

As the reader of this book, *you* are our most important critic and commentator. We value your opinion and want to know what we're doing right, what we could do better, what areas you'd like to see us publish in, and any other words of wisdom you're willing to pass our way.

You can fax, email, or write me directly to let me know what you did or didn't like about this book—as well as what we can do to make our books stronger.

Please note that I cannot help you with technical problems related to the topic of this book, and that due to the high volume of mail I receive, I might not be able to reply to every message.

When you write, please be sure to include this book's title and author as well as your name and phone or fax number. I will carefully review your comments and share them with the author and editors who worked on the book.

> Fax: 317-581-4770
>
> Email: *internet_sams@mcp.com*
>
> Mail: Mark Taber
>   Associate Publisher
>   Sams Publishing
>   201 West 103rd Street
>   Indianapolis, IN 46290 US

SAMS
Teach Yourself
Today

Sams Teach Yourself
e-Personal Finance Today

Managing your money and investments online

Ken and Daria Dolan
ISBN: 0-672-31879-2
$17.99 US/$26.95 CAN

Other Sams Teach Yourself Today Titles

e-Real Estate
Jack Segner
ISBN: 0-672-31815-6
$17.99 US/$26.95 CAN

e-Bargains
Preston Gralla
ISBN: 0-672-31906-3
$17.99 US/$26.95 CAN

e-Baseball
*Bob Temple and
Rob Neyer*
ISBN: 0-672-31913-6
$17.99 US/$26.95 CAN

e-Banking
*Mary Dixon and
Brian Nixon*
ISBN: 0-672-31882-2
$17.99 US/$26.95 CAN

e-Job Hunting
*Eric Schlesinger and
Susan Musich*
ISBN: 0-672-31817-2
$17.99 US/$26.95 CAN

e-Parenting
*Evelyn and Karin
Petersen*
ISBN: 0-672-31818-0
$17.99 US/$26.95 CAN

All prices are subject to change.

SAMS

www.samspublishing.com